Universal Health Coverage for Inclusive and Sustainable Development

A WORLD BANK STUDY

Universal Health Coverage for Inclusive and Sustainable Development

Lessons from Japan

Naoki Ikegami, Editor

WORLD BANK GROUP

ISBN (paper): 978-1-4648-0408-3
ISBN (electronic): 978-1-4648-0409-0
DOI: 10.1596/978-1-4648-0408-3

Cover design: Debra Naylor, Naylor Design, Inc.

Library of Congress Cataloging-in-Publication Data has been requested.

Contents

Boxes

Figures

Tables

Foreword

Following the publication of the 2010 World Health Report, *Health Systems Financing: The Path to Universal Coverage*, there has been a growing interest and demand among low- and middle-income countries for a systematic assessment of global experiences with universal health coverage (UHC) and for technical advice and investment support in designing and implementing UHC policies and programs.

In 2011, Japan celebrated the 50th anniversary of its own achievement of UHC. On this occasion, the government of Japan and the World Bank conceived the idea of undertaking a multicountry study to respond to this growing demand by sharing rich and varied country experiences from countries at different stages of adopting and implementing UHC strategies, including Japan itself. This led to the formation of a joint Japan–World Bank research team under the Japan–World Bank Partnership Program for Universal Health Coverage. The program was set up as a two-year multicountry study to help fill the gap in knowledge about the policy decisions and implementation processes that countries undertake when they adopt UHC goals.

This report brings together 10 in-depth studies on different aspects of Japan's UHC experience, using a common framework for analysis focused on the political economy of UHC reform, and the policies and strategies for addressing challenges in health financing and human resources for health. Japan's commitment to UHC played a key role in the country's economic recovery after World War II, and helped ensure that the benefits of economic growth were shared equitably across the population.

We extend our appreciation to the government of Japan for providing financial resources to conduct these country studies. We also thank the governments of 10 other countries that took part in the study for their willingness to share their data and experiences, namely Bangladesh, Brazil, Ethiopia, France, Ghana, Indonesia, Peru, Thailand, Turkey, and Vietnam. The initial findings from all 11 countries' studies were presented at the Global Conference on Universal Health Coverage for Inclusive and Sustainable Growth, held in Tokyo on December 5–6, 2013. At the conference, Japan's Deputy Prime Minister Taro Aso and World Bank President Jim Yong Kim jointly made the case for UHC as one of the essential goals to which countries should aspire, for inclusive and sustainable development. All the studies are summarized in a companion publication; Akiko Maeda,

Edson Araujo, Cheryl Cashin, Joseph Harris, Naoki Ikegami, and Michael R. Reich, *Universal Health Coverage for Inclusive and Sustainable Development: A Synthesis of 11 Country Case Studies* (Washington, DC: World Bank, 2014).

The goals of UHC are to ensure that all people can access quality health services, to safeguard all people from public health risks, and to protect all people from impoverishment due to illness (whether from out-of-pocket payments or loss of income when a household member falls sick). Although the path to UHC is specific to each country, we believe that the topics covered in this book on different aspects of Japan's experience in achieving and maintaining UHC will provide useful insights for other countries on the path to UHC.

Keizo Takemi   Timothy Grant Evans
Member of the House of Councilors   *Senior Director for Health,*
National Diet of Japan   *Nutrition and Population*
                                                                The World Bank

Acknowledgments

This study was supported through the PHRD Grant (Japan) as a joint partnership program between the government of Japan and the World Bank Group. The program was steered by the Program Coordination Committee, co-chaired by Keizo Takemi, Member of the House of Councilors of the National Diet of Japan, and Timothy Grant Evans, Director of Health, Nutrition and Population Network of the World Bank Group.

The preparation of the book was undertaken by a team led by Naoki Ikegami, Department of Health Policy and Management, Keio University School of Medicine. The authors of each chapter are acknowledged below.

Overview: *Naoki Ikegami and Akiko Maeda*
Chapter 1:   The Political-Historical Context of Japanese Health Care
              John Creighton Campbell, Naoki Ikegami, and Yusuke Tsugawa
Chapter 2:   Macroeconomic Context and Challenges for Maintaining Universal Health Coverage in Japan
              Takashi Oshio, Naoko Miake, and Naoki Ikegami
Chapter 3:   Fiscal Disparities among Social Health Insurance Programs in Japan
              Reo Takaku, Shunichiro Bessho, Shuzo Nishimura, and Naoki Ikegami
Chapter 4:   Japan's Long-Term Care Insurance Program as a Model for Middle-Income Nations
              John Creighton Campbell
Chapter 5:   Controlling Health Expenditures by Revisions to the Fee Schedule in Japan
              Naoki Ikegami
Chapter 6:   The Political Economy of the Fee Schedule in Japan
              John Creighton Campbell and Yasuo Takagi
Chapter 7:   Factors Determining the Allocation of Physicians in Japan
              Naoki Ikegami
Chapter 8:   Licensed Practical Nurses: One Option for Expanding the Nursing Workforce in Japan
              Naoki Ikegami and James Buchan
Chapter 9:   National Hospital Reform in Japan: Results and Challenges
              Yohei Tagawa, Yusuke Tsugawa, and Naoki Ikegami
Chapter 10:   Improving Population Health through Public Health Centers in Japan
              Yusuke Tsugawa, Naoki Ikegami, Naoko Miake, and Michael R. Reich

The authors benefited greatly from the valuable comments received from the following peer reviewers: Mukesh Chawla, Sameh El-Saharty, Gerard La Forgia, John Langenbrunner, Christophe Lemiere, Philip O'Keefe, Tomoko Ono, Maryse Pierre-Louis, Aparnaa Somanathan, and Ajay Tandon.

The authors also thank Ms. Tomoko Suzuki and Kana Yoshioka at the Japan Center for International Exchange for their support in managing and coordinating all the research activities in Japan. Jonathan Aspin edited the English version of the book, and Daniela Hoshino assisted in preparing the documents for publication.

Abbreviations

BB	Budget Bureau
CDC	Centers for Disease Control and Prevention
CEO	chief executive officer
CHI	Citizens' Health Insurance
CT	computed tomography
CV	coefficient of variation
DPC	Diagnosis Procedure Combination
DPJ	Democratic Party of Japan
ENT	ear, nose, and throat
FFS	fee-for-service
GDP	gross domestic product
GHQ	General Headquarters of the Allied Forces
HIB	Health Insurance Bureau
HRH	human resources for health
IAA	Independent Administrative Agency
IPV	inactivated polio vaccine
JMA	Japan Medical Association
JNA	Japanese Nursing Association
LDP	Liberal Democratic Party
LPN	Licensed Practical Nurses
LTCI	Long-Term Care Insurance
MEXT	Ministry of Education, Culture, Science and Technology
MHLW	Ministry of Health, Labour and Welfare
MHW	Ministry of Health and Welfare
MIC	Ministry of Internal Affairs and Communication
MMR	measles-mumps-rubella
MOF	Ministry of Finance
MRI	Magnetic resonance imaging
NHIA	National Health Insurance Association

NHO	National Hospital Organization
NME	national medical expenditures
OECD	Organisation for Economic Co-operation and Development
OOP	out-of-pocket
OPV	oral polio vaccine
PDPS	per diem payment system
PET	Positron emission tomography
PHN	public health nurses
PPP	purchasing power parity
PUBHCs	public health centers
RN	Registered Nurse
SHI	social health insurance
SMHI	Society-Managed Health Insurance
THE	total health expenditures
UHC	universal health coverage

Overview

Naoki Ikegami and Akiko Maeda

This chapter provides an overview of Japan's health system and summarizes the key lessons from the 10 studies that describe the various aspects of Japan's experience in achieving and maintaining universal health coverage (UHC).

Japan is a high-income country with excellent health indexes, relatively low proportions of health expenditures to gross domestic product (GDP) and out-of-pocket (OOP) payments to total health expenditures (THE) (table I.1). The economy has been stagnant for the past 20 years, however. The share of the population 65 and over is 25 percent (Ministry of Internal Affairs and Communication—MIC 2013), the highest in the world.

Overview of Current Status

Legal and Statutory Basis

The Constitution states that all people should be entitled to a "minimum level of healthy and cultural life." The Citizens' Health Insurance (CHI) Law, which serves as the backbone of the country's social health insurance (SHI) system, stipulates that all those not enrolled in employment-based programs, or in programs for elders 75 and over, or are on public assistance, must enroll in the CHI.

What Is the Current Status of Coverage along the Key Dimensions of UHC?

Population. The entire population is entitled to access health services by being either enrolled in an SHI program or on public assistance.

Services. The statutory services are the same for all and are listed in the fee schedule of the Ministry of Health, Labour, and Welfare (MHLW). The services that are not listed in the fee schedule, but that hospitals are allowed to deliver, are restricted to hospital rooms with better amenities (constituting 19 percent of the total number of beds) and specific advanced treatments, accounting for 0.03 percent of the MHLW's national medical expenditures. The latter are listed once the efficacy and safety of the procedure have been proven. There are no differences in services by population groups, but people living in remote areas may face geographic barriers in accessing services. Preventive health services are not part of the statutory benefits but are independently financed by municipal governments (vaccines), or by the SHI programs (screening).

Table I.1 Data Overview of Japan

Population (2012)	127.6 million *
GDP (2012)	US$5.96 trillion *
Gross national income per capita in purchasing power parity (PPP) (2012)	US$47,870 *
THE as % of GDP (2010)	9.6% **
THE per capita (in current exchange rate dollars) (2010)	US$3,213 **
Public expenditure ratio of THE (2010)	82.1% **
OOP as % of THE (2010)	14.4% **
Life expectancy at birth (2011)	82.7 years for total population **
Hospital beds per capita (2011)	13.4 hospital beds per 1,000 population (of which 8.0 acute care hospital beds) **

Source: * World Development Indicators (country data for Japan), World Bank 2013.
** OECD Health Data 2013.
Note: GDP = gross domestic product; OOP = out-of-pocket; THE = total health expenditures.

Financial protection. The copayment rate is set at 30 percent, except for pre-school children six or under who pay 20 percent, and for 90 percent of the elders (70 and over) who pay 10 percent. For the 10 percent of elders having incomes higher than the average worker, the copayment rate is 30 percent, although catastrophic coverage cuts the copayment rate to 1 percent when the monthly copayment totals exceed the ceiling set by income levels. Those on dialysis, or being treated for hemophilia and other designated diseases, have their copayment substantially reduced. Charging patients above the prices set by the fee schedule (balanced billing) is strictly prohibited. Extra billing for services not listed in the fee schedule together is also tightly regulated: it is restricted to extra charge rooms, new technologies registered for evaluation of their efficacy and safety, and so forth. In all other cases, extra billing cannot be combined with services covered under fee schedule, and therefore patients must pay for all these services. Patients may give "gifts" to physicians but this is generally restricted to inpatients in private rooms of big city hospitals. Physicians in public hospitals, as civil servants, are prohibited by law from accepting such gifts.

How Is Governance Structured?

Goal setting and payment. The MHLW is responsible for setting policy goals, listing the statutory services, and defining payment in the fee schedule. The fee schedule is nationally uniform, and applied to all SHI programs and virtually all providers. It sets not only the price of each service, drug, or medical device but also the conditions under which providers are allowed to bill, such as patient's diagnosis (for example, off-label prescribing is prohibited) or facility standards (the facility must, for instance, employ the prescribed number of therapists to bill for rehabilitation therapy). Payment is, basically, fee for service.

The policy goals are set by deliberative councils within the MHLW. Among these, the Central Social Insurance Medical Council is the most powerful because its role is to translate goals into payment incentives and disincentives for providers in the fee schedule. This council comprises members from providers (the Japan Medical Association [JMA], hospital associations, and other provider organizations), from payers (SHI programs, employer organizations, labor unions, and local governments), and from academia and others to represent public interests. All council meetings are open to the public, and their minutes are publicly shared.

Financing. The Japanese government formally uses the national medical expenditures (NME) figures for making policy decisions. The NME exclude over-the-counter drugs, extra charges for hospital rooms, and other private OOP expenditures that are not linked to the social health insurance programs (copayments). Therefore, the NME differ from THE as calculated by the Organisation for Economic Co-operation and Development (OECD) and are generally about 20 percent less than THE. Of the NME, 49 percent comes from premium contributions, 25 percent from national government, 12 percent from local governments, and 14 percent from patients (in 2009). There is no defined share of national government expenditures earmarked for UHC, but the ratio has been about 9 percent over the last decade.

Apart from the public assistance program, there are no targeted programs for the poor or for the informal sector. Instead, the government provides subsidies to programs that enroll those on relatively low income and forces programs to contribute to financing the health care costs of elders. The SHI programs are either employment based or residence based, with all dependents (regardless of age) covered by the program of the household head.

The more than 3,000 programs can be grouped into four. The first group consists of programs for those employed in large companies and public sector organizations and receives no subsidy from general tax revenue. The second is the quasi-government National Health Insurance Association for those employed in small to medium companies, which receives 16.4 percent of benefit expenditures as subsidies. The third comprises the residence-based health insurance (CHI) managed by municipalities for those not covered by the other programs, such as the self-employed, the irregularly employed, and pensioners below 75, and gets 50 percent in subsidies. The fourth is composed of the programs for those 75 and over organized at prefectural level, which take in 50 percent as subsidies plus 40 percent as contributions from programs in the other three groups. Within each program, contribution rates (the share of income levied as premiums) are the same up to an income ceiling (¥14 million in employment-based programs and ¥7 million in residence-based programs) (figure I.1).

Service delivery. In principle, everyone can access virtually all providers without referral. There is no clear differentiation in primary, secondary, and tertiary levels of care, or in the function of the public and private sectors. The private

Figure I.1 Subsidies and Cross-Subsidization among Social Insurance Programs

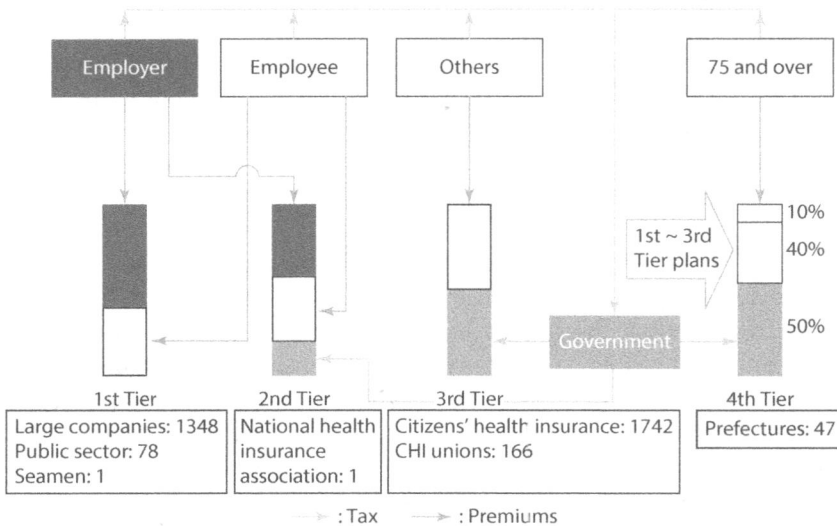

Source: Ikegami et al. (2011), updated.

sector dominates, accounting for 82 percent of hospitals and 72 percent of hospital beds (in 2010). At primary care level, virtually all clinics are solo practices owned by physicians, although 41 percent proclaim specialties other than internal medicine or pediatrics, such as ENT (ear, nose, and throat) or ophthalmology, as their main specialty (again in 2010). Public hospitals tend to have a larger share in tertiary care because they can obtain subsidies for their recurrent and capital costs. However, these subsidies and the rigid management by local governments have led to inefficiencies. The successful transfer of the national hospitals from direct control by the MHLW to an independent nonprofit organization has shown that public hospitals can be run at a profit without charging patients more OOP payments (see chapter 9).

Current Status of Health Financing

How Sustainable Is the Current Coverage?

Fiscal space. Fiscal space has diminished because of the economic stagnation since 1991 and the resulting decline in government revenue. This decline has had serious consequences for the SHI system because one-quarter of the NME is financed from the national government's general budget in the form of the subsidies to the SHI programs in the second to fourth groups just described. The imbalance between government revenue and expenditure has been financed by debt, which currently amounts to more than twice GDP (see chapter 2). Although the consumer tax rate has increased from 5 percent to 8 percent in April 2014 and is scheduled to increase again to 10 percent in October 2015, this will not be enough to restore the primary balance (current government spending less current income from taxes, excluding interest payments on government debt). Moreover, the share of the NME financed by the general budget is likely to increase with population aging and the changes in employment patterns, resulting in more people being enrolled in the tax-subsidized SHI programs (see chapter 3).

Cost management and value for money. Costs have been managed by revisions every two years to the fee schedule. The revision process starts with the Ministers of Finance, and of Health, Labor, and Welfare, alongside top bureaucrats, deciding on the "global" (or overall) revision rate. Next, the extent to which drug prices is reduced is determined, primarily on the MHLW's survey of the market price and volume of each product. Prices tend to be lower than in the fee schedule because of competition to sell products. Last, item-by-item revisions are made following the deliberations made in the Central Social Insurance Medical Council. The MHLW negotiates with professional organizations on the price revisions and conditions for billing. Adherence to these conditions is monitored by claims reviews and on-site audits, which have mitigated cost escalations because of non-price factors (see chapters 5 and 6).

The item-by-item revisions are fine-tuned. For example in the 2002 revision, the global rate was reduced by 2 percent, but the price of taking a magnetic resonance image was reduced by 30 percent because the number of examinations had increased "inappropriately." In the 2008 revision by contrast, prices in emergency care and obstetrics were increased because the government had to respond to media reports of insufficient resources in these areas.

Case mix–based payment for acute inpatient care was introduced in 2003 and has expanded to cover half of all acute beds, although there is no evidence if it has contributed to containing health care expenditures.

Most measurements of quality of care in Japan has focused on structural aspects, such as setting higher per diem rates for inpatient care if the hospital meets the prescribed nurse staffing levels or setting the number of therapists as a condition for billing rehabilitation therapy. One study at least has shown that the outcome of surgical treatments appears to be at the same level or better than in the United States (Hashimoto et al. 2011).

How Equitable Is Coverage?

Solidarity and redistribution. Premium contributions in each SHI program are based on the ability to pay and are mainly set as a proportion of income for all those enrolled. To mitigate differences in income and demographic structure of enrollees, the national government provides subsidies to programs that enroll those on relatively low income. In addition, programs must contribute to financing the health care expenditures of elders. This system of redistribution has mitigated differences in incomes and in the composition of elders 65 and over among the SHI programs. However, premium contributions as a proportion of income still vary more than threefold among the SHI programs, mainly reflecting differences in incomes rather than in health expenditures.

Targeting for priority population groups. Special groups of patients, including those on dialysis and those with hemophilia or other designated diseases, have their copayments greatly reduced. The CHI or the municipalities where health care resources were inadequate established their own clinics and hospitals. The most sustained financial support to provide services for "areas without a physician," defined as areas with 50 or more inhabitants living within a radius of 4 kilometers which have difficulty in accessing a health care facility, came as part of the subsidies for remote areas from the national government to the prefectures (see chapter 7).

Current Status and Policies for Human Resources for Health

The current physician density of 2.2 per 1,000 (table I.2) is below the OECD average, but this ratio will increase both because the number of medical school entrants increased by 20 percent in 2007–12 and because of the projected decrease in population. The number of nurses is about the OECD average but that of midwives is below, indicating that their function is being served by physicians and nurses.

Using the 47 prefectures with populations of 0.7 million–13 million as the basic unit for comparison, the ratio between highest and lowest in physician density was 2.00 in 2010, declining from 2.24 in 1990. Prefectures with higher

Table I.2 Current Status of Human Resources for Health

| | Current number per 1,000 population (2010)* | Entry | | | | Exit | |
		Qualifications	Government determines the number of new entrants	Number of entrants per year (2012)		Number of years of education	Number of newly licensed per year
Physicians (specialists, primary care)	2.2	High school graduate	Yes	9,075		6 years	8,611
Nurses	10.1	Registered nurse (RN): Senior high school graduate or licensed practical nurse (LPN) LPN: Junior high school graduate	No	RN: 49,479 LPN: 11,867		RN: 3 years + or LPN + 2 years LPN: 2 years	RN: 50,232 (2013) LPN: 10,350
Midwives	0.22	RN	No	2,000		1 year	2,026
Community health workers[a]	n.a.	n.a.	n.a.	n.a.		n.a.	n.a.

Source: MHLW 2012 and 2013a; * OECD Health Data 2013.
Note: n.a. = not applicable.
a. Japan has virtually no community health workers.

numbers were not restricted to the major metropolitan centers such as Kyoto and Tokyo, but tended to be in the west. For nurses, the difference between the highest and lowest prefecture was 2.10 (for RNs 2.36) in 2010. More so than for physicians, the per capita number tended to be greater in the west, reflecting the distribution of hospital beds. For midwives, the difference is 2.00 with no consistent pattern in distribution.

The government has regulated the number enrolling in medical schools and has imposed strict conditions on opening new schools. No new medical school has opened since 1981, but the total number allowed entry has fluctuated according to policy. The development of formal postgraduate education has been retarded, nor is there a clear distinction between generalists and specialists, while physicians and hospitals can proclaim any subspecialty service at their discretion. Very few specialist organizations have a formal recertification process or a designated quota of training positions.

To reduce geographic disparities in the distribution of physicians, prefectural governments pay for the tuition and living expenses for the two to three entrants to the special medical school whose graduates are obligated to work in remote areas and award scholarships to a few entrants in their contracted medical school under similar conditions (see chapter 7).

The pay scale for health workers tends to be seniority based, and especially so in public hospitals. Among physicians, there is usually no difference by specialty, although some hospitals link their performance to remuneration (see chapter 9). Professional recognition may be the primary motivating factor in Japan's unique system of hiring physicians. Traditionally, newly licensed physicians would join a university clinical department to receive their training. After completion, they would then spend their entire professional lives practicing within the closed network of its affiliated hospitals. They can opt out by opening their own clinic but then they would no longer have access to hospital facilities. However, their income would tend to be higher than hospital-based physicians' because the fee schedule favors services provided in primary care clinics.

Becoming an LPN provides relatively easy entry as it requires only two years' training after graduating from junior high school. They can then become an RN after taking a two-year course. Some private hospitals hire unlicensed care workers, and then support their tuition to become an LPN and subsequently an RN. However, the proportion of LPNs declined from 46 percent of all licensed nurses in 1990 to 28 percent in 2010 (see chapter 8).

The fee schedule has played a major role in allocating health workers by paying the same fee for the same service, regardless of the local cost of living, and by setting fees for primary care services higher than specialist services. The former has allowed hospitals in rural areas to pay higher wages to their physicians than those in big cities from the savings made by paying their nonphysician staff lower wages. Physicians are willing to work at lower wages in large city hospitals because they prefer practicing in well-equipped hospitals and living in big cities, while nurses tend to be more home district bound and more willing to work at wages reflecting the local level (see chapter 7). On the latter, the dominant role that the JMA has played in revising the fee schedule has contributed to fees in primary care settings being higher than in specialist services.

Sequencing of Reforms

How and Why Were the Relevant UHC Reforms Put into Effect?

SHI was first implemented as employment-based programs for manual laborers in 1927 to mitigate labor unrest and to make workers more productive. Another start was made in 1938, when residence-based programs (CHI) were legislated for farmers and self-employed workers. Municipalities were encouraged to establish CHI programs and, once 80 percent of their residents were enrolled, it was made mandatory for all (except for those enrolled in employment-based programs). The population covered by these programs increased from just 3 percent in 1927 to virtually everyone by the end of the war in 1945, at least on paper. The primary force for this expansion was to build up a "warfare" state of "healthy people and healthy soldiers."

After World War II, UHC became a tangible goal for establishing a welfare state that had wide popular support. Both government and opposition parties supported UHC when democracy was restored and the economy started to recover. An important step was the decision to increase subsidies to municipalities for establishing and maintaining CHI programs in 1952. UHC was achieved in 1961 when the last municipalities established CHI and enrollment became compulsory for all those not covered by employment-based programs (see the chapter 1). Since then, there has been a long-term political commitment to UHC.

The government set the fee schedule for the services covered by the national program for employees of small and medium (second-group) companies when SHI was implemented. This fee schedule was expanded to all employment-based programs in 1943, as part of the war effort to unify and consolidate resources. It was extended to CHI programs in 1959 so that CHI enrollees could access virtually all providers. By doing so, benefits were harmonized across programs, allowing the Ministry of Health & Welfare to effectively control the delivery of health care through revisions to the fee schedule. Thus, equity in services available was achieved before equity in population coverage in 1961. Financial protection for all was achieved in 1973 when catastrophic coverage became available in all SHI programs. That year, economic growth was at its peak and the government faced strong opposition from progressive parties. Before then, employees did not have to pay a copayment, but all others had to pay 30–50 percent, with no caps.

Following the decline in economic growth, the copayment rate was raised for those who had been previously favored, that is, for employees from zero in 1983 to the current 30 percent in 2003. Thus, equity in copayment was achieved last. Costs have been contained by making small increases or decreases in the fee schedule's global revision rate.

These measures, with the contributions to finance elders' health care, have helped keep UHC sustainable. However, a more than threefold difference remains in the share of premium income contribution. These disparities, and the subsidies provided from the government's general budget and the contributions made by the programs to pay for elders' health care to mitigate them, pose a threat to UHC's sustainability. A reform to merge CHI programs at prefectural level was proposed by the government's Social Security Reform Council in 2013, but there has been no mention of merging residence-based programs with employment-based programs.

Actors

In his 1956 administrative policy speech, Prime Minister Ichiro Hatoyama of the ruling conservative Liberal Democratic Party announced that plans should be made for UHC. UHC had the greatest support from the municipal governments that were eager to establish and consolidate their CHI programs. Management and labor also supported UHC. After postwar reconstruction and alleviation of poverty, UHC appeared to be the next natural goal. Rapid economic growth provided funding for subsidies to municipalities.

At that time, the JMA thought that UHC was premature, and feared infringements on its professional autonomy by fee schedule regulations. However, private practitioners—the dominant majority at that time—were bought off with concessions allowing them more autonomy in prescribing and dispensing pharmaceuticals and with tax concessions on their income. They were also concerned about the increase of physicians after demobilization, those returning from former colonies, and increased medical school enrollment during the war years. Hospitals did not have much power, being divided between the more prestigious public sector and the numerically larger private sector.

Sustained high economic growth and the election of progressive prefectural governors in the late 1960s pressured the government to lower copayment rates in 1973. Since then, as economic growth faltered, the government and business leaders have generally pursued a cost-containment policy, while the JMA has become a major supporter of UHC, opposing copayment increases.

Key Lessons from Japan

Political Economy and Policy Process of UHC

After the country recovered from World War II, nearly all political groups shared a political commitment to UHC. Despite having multiple SHI programs covering different population categories, benefits, and copayment rates were harmonized across the different programs by establishing a system of subsidies and redistribution to improve equity in the conditions of access to health care. However, fiscal disparities among SHI programs have risen, highlighting the risk of maintaining multiple health programs requiring complex redistribution systems to maintain equity. Still, on the payment side, the institutionalized process of negotiating resource allocation and benefits among all key stakeholders through a single payment system—the fee schedule—has been relatively successful in containing costs despite what is basically a fee-for-service form of payment.

Universal Health Coverage for Inclusive and Sustainable Development
http://dx.doi.org/10.1596/978-1-4648-0408-3

Health Financing Strategy for UHC

SHI coverage to farmers, informal and self-employed workers, and the unemployed was made possible by making it mandatory for all municipalities to establish CHI programs and by requiring all those not covered by employment-based programs to enroll in the CHI. Health care expenditures are managed through the fee schedule, which not only controls prices but also sets detailed conditions of payments, such as nurse staffing levels, diagnosis criteria for procedures, and so forth. Adherence to these conditions is regularly audited, which has mitigated inappropriate use of services. The payment system also prohibits balanced billing by the providers and strictly restricts extra billing.

The system has not kept pace with shrinking fiscal space, however, because of rapid aging and a slowing economy. There is now debate on the need for structural reforms in the social security system, including health insurance. Public health programs are funded through the general budget and are not part of the benefit package funded by SHI. This division may have secured more funding in the past, but has placed obstacles in integrating prevention with treatment.

Health Services and Human Resources for Health Strategy for UHC

Although 80 percent of hospitals and nearly all clinics are private, they are all integrated with the harmonized and streamlined delivery system because almost all their revenue is derived from services regulated by the fee schedule. Public hospitals have additional sources in the form of subsidies from the national and local governments' general budget. Under pressure to reform, national hospitals were transferred to an independent nonprofit agency in 2004, which has improved managerial accountability and efficiency. Geographic disparities in the distribution of physicians remains an issue, but innovative approaches include prefectural governments paying for the tuition and living expenses for the two or three entrants to the special medical school whose graduates are obligated to work in remote areas and awarding scholarships to a few entrants in their contracted medical school under similar conditions.

The fee schedule has also mitigated the concentration of physicians as specialists and in large urban hospitals by balancing monetary and nonmonetary rewards. Higher fees are set for primary care services, which has the effect of counterbalancing the concentration of resources in hospital settings. The same fees are paid for the same services throughout the country: one of the effects of the payment system is that rural hospitals have been able to offer higher salaries for doctors than those in urban areas to attract and retain them—possible because they can offset the higher cost of physicians by offering lower salaries to nurses and other staff, who are generally local and willing to work at these lower salaries. To meet the rising demand for care, Japan introduced lower entry and education requirements for Licensed Practical Nurses (LPNs), which helped to address the need for workforce growth during the rapid expansion of health coverage in the 1960s. The proportion of LPNs has since declined, as the number of Registered Nurses has increased much more.

Case Studies on Japan

The book presents 10 case studies that provide insights Japan's experience in achieving and maintaining UHC. These studies fall broadly under the topics related to political economy, health financing, and human resources for health, consistent with the conceptual framework adopted for all the studies conducted under the Japan-World Bank Program on Universal Health Coverage.

These topics were chosen because they are key to understanding health policy decisions in Japan and because they also might offer lessons—both positive and negative—for other countries interested in gaining insights on the implementation challenges and opportunities faced by policy makers in Japan.

A brief description of the chapters is provided below to guide the readers on the overall structure and content of the report.

1. *The Political–Historical Context of Japanese Health Care*: Japan's health care system evolved gradually. New needs from industrialization, plus fear of socialism, led to social health insurance (1927). Wartime exigencies brought expansion, then a national drive to catch up with the West alongside partisan competition led to universal coverage (1961). Threats from progressive political parties in a context of rapid economic growth led to its further expansion (1973). Subsequent economic stagnation has led to some retrenchment.

2. *Macroeconomic Context and Challenges for Maintaining Universal Health Coverage in Japan*: Strong economic growth after the recovery from World War II's devastation through 1973 provided the fiscal space to expand benefit levels of UHC to all. Since then, however, as economic growth has stuttered aging has picked up pace, contributing to huge fiscal deficits and to shifting the redistributive effect from intra- to intergenerational transfers. Since these trends appear to be inevitable as a country matures, UHC programs should be designed with this future in mind.

3. *Fiscal Disparities among Social Health Insurance Programs in Japan*: Japan has over 3,000 SHI programs, each differing in their age and income distributions among enrollees. Although fiscal disparities have been mitigated by subsidies from taxes and transfers across programs to pay for elders' health care, the fiscal basis of residence-based CHI programs has been eroding, and the disparities in their premium rates (the share of income levied as premiums) among SHI programs have increased.

4. *Japan's Long-Term Care Insurance Program as a Model for Middle-Income Nations*: Faced with a rapidly aging society, Japan implemented long-term care insurance as the fourth pillar of SHI in 2000. New premiums procured additional sources of revenue, and formal services have expanded. If middle-income countries could establish systematic long-term care programs at an earlier stage, they might be able to mitigate two constraints facing Japan: excessive institutionalization and the burden on the health care system.

5. *Controlling Health Expenditures by Revisions to the Fee Schedule in Japan*: Japan's health expenditures are relatively low for a high-income country with

generally excellent health indicators. One of the main reasons is the system of revising the fee schedule every two years. The two-step approach of setting a global revision rate, then fine-tuning item-by-item revisions and setting conditions of billing, provides a unique model for containing costs with fee-for-service payments.

6. *Political Economy of the Fee Schedule in Japan*: A structured process of negotiation has gradually arisen to accommodate and reflect changes in government policy. Central are negotiations between, on the one hand, the Ministry of Finance and the MHLW (seeking to hold down spending) and, on the other, medical providers led by the JMA and backed by the majority political party (seeking higher fees). This has led to a usually predictable and incremental process, but it has also allowed the political leadership to take a direct role. This process may provide a useful model to some other countries.

7. *Factors Determining the Allocation of Physicians in Japan*: The Japanese experience suggests that physicians can be better allocated to primary care and to rural areas than otherwise by the following: providing dual entry levels and offering multiple career paths for physicians; limiting the development of high-tech hospitals; extending the power of university clinical department chiefs to physicians in affiliated hospitals; and balancing monetary and nonmonetary rewards.

8. *Licensed Practical Nurses—An Option for addressing Health Workforce expansion in Japan:* The Licensed Practical Nurses (LPNs), who require only a two-year course and then passing a prefectural-level examination, are a way to tap into a broader pool of less well qualified applicants, with faster turnaround in producing graduates, and with scope for some to then step up to RN level. Since 1978, however, their proportion has declined, as the number of first-level Registered Nurses have increased at a faster rate.

9. *National Hospital Reform in Japan: Results and Challenges:* In response to the inefficiencies and high budget subsidies required to run government-managed hospitals, Japan reorganized its national hospitals into an independent agency. This gave stronger authority to, and demanded greater accountability from, the hospital directors, such as hiring more nurses that led to more revenue. All these measures improved hospital efficiency.

10. *Improving Population Health through Public Health Centers in Japan*: Effective public health interventions to reduce the prevalence of major preventable diseases, such as tuberculosis and stroke, were important for improving population health after World War II, and public health centers played a key role in these achievements. Such government-provided preventive services were crucial for progressing toward UHC by complementing the personal medical services covered under health insurance programs.

Universal Health Coverage for Inclusive and Sustainable Development
http://dx.doi.org/10.1596/978-1-4648-0408-3

Bibliography

Hashimoto, H., N. Ikegami, K. Shibuya, N. Izumida, H. Noguchi, H. Yasunaga, H. Miyata, J. M. Acuin, and M. R. Reich. 2011. "Cost Containment and Quality of Care in Japan: Is There a Trade-Off?" *Lancet* 378 (9797): 1174–82.

Ikegami, N., B. K. Yoo, H. Hashimoto, M. Matsumoto, H. Ogata, A. Babazono, R. Watanabe, K. Shibuya, B.-M. Yang, M. R. Reich, and Y. Kobayashi. 2011. "Japanese Universal Health Coverage: Evolution, Achievements, and Challenges." *Lancet* 378 (9797): 1106–15.

MHLW (Ministry of Health, Labour and Welfare). 2012. "2011 Survey on Nursing School Entrants and Graduates." http://www.e-stat.go.jp/SG1/estat/NewList.do?tid=000001022606 (accessed October 2013).

———. 2013a. "2012 Results of Nursing School Examination." http://www.mhlw.go.jp/kouseiroudoushou/shikaku_shiken/hokenshi/about_tsuika.html (accessed October 2013).

———. 2013b. "National Medical Expenditures 2012." http://www.mhlw.go.jp/toukei/list/37-21.html (accessed October 2013).

MIC (Ministry of Internal Affairs and Communication). 2013. "Basic Resident Registration." http://www.stat.go.jp/data/idou/ (accessed November 2013).

OECD (Organisation for Economic Co-operation and Development). "OECD Health Data 2013." http://www.oecd.org/health/health-systems/oecdhealthdata.htm (accessed October 2013).

World Bank. 2013. "World Development Indicators 2013." http://data.worldbank.org/country/japan (accessed October 2013).

CHAPTER 1

The Political-Historical Context of Japanese Health Care

John Creighton Campbell, Naoki Ikegami, and Yusuke Tsugawa

Abstract

Japan's health care system evolved gradually. New needs from industrialization plus fear of socialism accounted for the earliest health insurance programs, wartime exigencies brought expansion, and a national drive to catch up with the West combined with political party competition led to universal coverage. Because Japan had achieved universal health coverage before its transition to a high-income country, an egalitarian pattern was well established, and it was reinforced by the political effects of rapid growth. When public finances turned sour due to lower growth, higher copayments and premiums passed some of the burden to households and companies while the fee schedule system continued to hold down total expenditure and the health care system retained its egalitarian characteristics.

Context and Objectives

The long-term evolution of the Japanese health care system is hardly unique. Its pre–World War II origins, wartime and postwar development, achievement of universality, drive for equality, growing concern about costs, and then reaction to that concern parallel what happened in many European countries. The prime driver of health care and other welfare state policies in all nations was industrialization, and the secondary driver was progress in other countries. Most of the important Japanese events occurred at the same level of economic development as elsewhere, and most were influenced by policies abroad (Kasza 2006).

Having said that, it is equally true that each initiative, expansion, or other policy change was the product of the politics of the time. Politics, in the broad sense, includes changing national goals such as the pursuit of both growth and equality, catching up with the West, and minimizing public spending. In another sense, it also includes the objectives and the relative power of contending political actors: prime ministers, bureaucratic organizations, political parties, interest groups of various kinds, and, in a sense, even public opinion. Box 1.1 highlights some key features.

Box 1.1 Key Features of Japan's Political System

- Under the 1947 Constitution, Japan is a parliamentary system. Its parliament (the Diet) has two houses elected at different times with different rules.
- The formal powers of the prime minister and cabinet ministers are wide, but in practice Japanese leaders have followed more of a consensus style of governing than strong individual leadership.
- The bureaucracy, or more accurately the various ministries and agencies, are quite powerful. In health policy the Ministry of Finance with its power of the purse and the Ministry of Health, Labour, and Welfare (Ministry of Health and Welfare until 2001) are the key actors.
- The "1955 system," which lasted until 1993 and in some respects until 2009, refers to continual rule by the conservative Liberal Democratic Party (LDP). Compared with most parliamentary systems, rank-and-file LDP Diet members have been active and influential in policy making.
- Pressure groups aligned with the LDP, particularly big business on the one hand and rural interests on the other, are the most influential, but opposition from other groups and social movements, as well as public opinion, has often been important.

This chapter chronicles the key turning points in Japanese health care policy over the years, but with little attention to the policies themselves as these are recounted in other chapters. Rather, it focuses on the political situation at the time as partial explanations of what happened.

Origins of Health Care in Japan

Japan had a complicated history from the Meiji Restoration in 1868 to the prewar buildup in the 1930s. The new Constitution in 1890 brought a legislature, and political parties were competing for power from the 1910s, but these democratic developments were nearly irrelevant to the health policy domain in the early years, which was dominated by the state bureaucracy and industrial leaders.

A distinctive feature of Japan's health insurance system is that it consists of two structures: employment-based health insurance and residence-based health insurance (that is, Citizens' Health Insurance [CHI] plans). They developed along different paths and played complementary roles in expanding coverage to the entire population. With the former, the sequence of coverage for health care was similar to that in most other countries: government employees first, industrial workers second, and other groups more slowly. The latter structure (box 1.2) originated in grassroots residence-based health insurance programs, which were then expanded with the support of the government, and eventually became a mandatory health insurance system for the self-employed and nonemployed.

Box 1.2 CHI: Residence-Based Health Insurance

CHI (*Kokumin kenko hoken*) is a residence-based health insurance administered by municipalities. It is mandatory for all residents of the municipalities who do not have health insurance coverage through the other social health insurance programs.

Figure B1.1 Health Insurance Programs in Japan

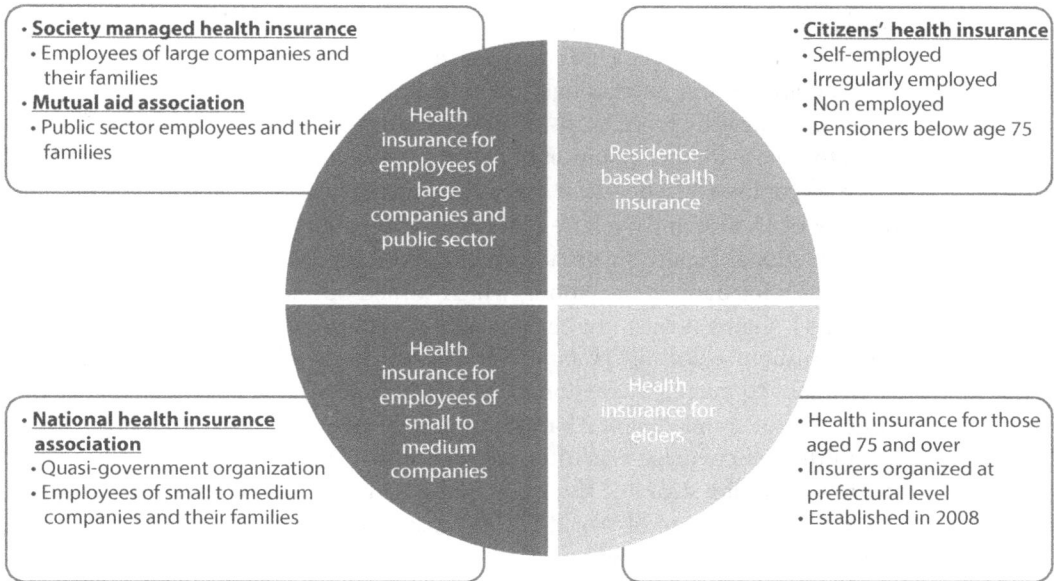

- **Society managed health insurance**
  - Employees of large companies and their families
- **Mutual aid association**
  - Public sector employees and their families

Health insurance for employees of large companies and public sector

Residence-based health insurance

- **Citizens' health insurance**
  - Self-employed
  - Irregularly employed
  - Non employed
  - Pensioners below age 75

Health insurance for employees of small to medium companies

Health insurance for elders

- **National health insurance association**
  - Quasi-government organization
  - Employees of small to medium companies and their families

- Health insurance for those aged 75 and over
- Insurers organized at prefectural level
- Established in 2008

Source: World Bank.

A prototype of the residence-based health insurance system is found in the historical record of *Jyorei*, which literally means "giving affordable compensation in a regular manner." It is documented that *Jyorei* first appeared in 1835 in Munakata District in Fukuoka Prefecture (although another one may have been operating in 1716).

Jyorei reflected the need of village populations to attract and retain doctors, as poor harvests and famine in the early 1800s had made it hard to keep doctors in rural villages. Local doctors therefore negotiated with village heads, and they agreed to establish *Jyorei*, in which villages collected prepayments from residents and ensured stable remuneration for doctors. The prepayments were set progressively based on the household's income: richer people paid more. These prepayments were separately earmarked as payments to doctors (rather than lumped together with general local tax revenues), which led to greater accountability and transparency.

Source: Ogawa et al. 2003.

The biggest event in the history of Japanese social health insurance was enactment of the Health Insurance Law of 1922. Bureaucrats and businessmen had similar motives: to keep workers healthy and ward off the appeal of socialism. A somewhat unusual feature in Japan was that employees of small firms were included. In 1933, the Ministry of the Interior carried out a survey of *Jyorei*, and the government found it a promising base from which to expand health insurance coverage for the self-employed and nonemployed populations nationally. Between 1934 and 1935, the government piloted 12 government-sponsored residence-based health insurance programs, in which it provided subsidies for the poor who could not afford the prepayments (Ogawa et al. 2003; Shimazaki 2011).

As policy became increasingly dominated by military priorities, in particular the need for healthy recruits, in 1936 Army Surgeon General Chikahiko Koizumi began to agitate for an expansion of public health care to cover the self-employed and nonemployed (who were overwhelmingly farmers). Accordingly, a new Ministry of Health and Welfare (MHW) was created in January 1938, followed by the National Health Insurance Law in April that year. It relied on voluntary local health insurance associations, which turned out not to be very popular.

In 1941, General Koizumi became MHW minister and first coined the slogan "health insurance for all" (*kokumin kaihoken*). Legislation in 1942 allowed the government to mandate creation of local health insurance associations. By 1944, 95 percent of municipalities had such associations, with over 50 million members (although coverage was often more nominal than real, given the dire situation in the closing stages of the war). Along with the insurance systems covering employees, by the end of World War II Japan had very nearly achieved universal health coverage, at least on paper.

After the war, social confusion and economic pain disrupted health care financing. Under the American-led Occupation, the MHW focused on rebuilding employee-based systems. Many local health insurance associations went out of business; they were once again voluntary (though with a national subsidy), and they came back slowly. The framework for universal coverage—separate systems for public employees, for workers in large firms and small firms, and for nonemployees—remained in place from the wartime years, but in 1956 some 30 percent of Japanese still had no coverage (Kondo and Shigeoka 2011).

Health Insurance for All

The political situation was confused after the end of the Occupation in 1952. Three conservative and two socialist parties (plus the Communist Party and other smaller groupings) contended for support until each side consolidated in 1955. Health care was a natural focus. As early as the 1952 general election, left-wing socialists had called for an expansion of health insurance and state-guaranteed medical care. On January 30, 1956, in his policy speech delivered to both houses of the Diet, Prime Minister Ichirou Hatoyama (1954–56) said:

… since it is considered that a central issue in social security is establishing medical security to deal with illness, [the government] intends to carry a plan forward with the goal of achieving comprehensive medical security that encompasses all citizens in the future.

Shortly thereafter, before the July, 1956 Upper House election, the newly merged LDP brought back the slogan "health insurance for all" in its election platform. Prime Minister Nobusuke Kishi (1957–60) was more specific in his first policy speech to the Diet in November, 1957:

In the shadow of economic prosperity, families have lost supports, and for the sake of those whose livelihoods have been threatened by unemployment, aging, and illness we have been working hard on effective policies. In particular we are making concrete plans for the health insurance system, the citizens' pension system, and the minimum wage system. I am devoting all my efforts to bringing about the prompt realization of a welfare state (*fukushi kokka*) that will meet the hopes of the people.[1]

As this makes clear, universal health coverage was a key component of a broader attack on problems of economic inequality that had emerged "in the shadow of economic prosperity." Although Kishi himself is best known for his strongly conservative views on national security, civil liberties, and the like, he also believed that a commitment to equality via welfare state programs was key to future LDP electoral success.[2]

Japan surely would have adopted universal coverage before long in any case, as had most advanced nations at equivalent levels of economic development. The MHW clearly had it in mind, as evidenced by reports of several advisory committees (Tsuchida 2011). But in the event it was the LDP that forced a new CHI Law in 1958; implementation started in 1959 and was completed in 1961. Rather than establishing a unified system, all the existing health insurance programs created before the war were continued. Since all employees were already covered, universality was achieved by making CHI for nonemployees mandatory and then making CHI mandatory for all municipalities. A unified system was impossible, particularly as the expansion had to be carried out so quickly, mainly because employers and employees did not want their relatively generous programs diluted.

A key point is that the new system provided the same access to health care as the existing programs for employees: enrollees were free to go to any physician or hospital they chose and could receive the same procedures and medications. Because the same fee schedule was applied, providers were paid the same, regardless of the insurance plan and so had no reason to discriminate. It is true that copayments were high in CHI, at 50 percent, but in fact dependents in employee health insurance also paid 50 percent (only employees themselves had free care).

Universal Health Coverage for Inclusive and Sustainable Development
http://dx.doi.org/10.1596/978-1-4648-0408-3

The key political conflict in establishing the national CHI system was between the MHW and the Japan Medical Association (JMA). The JMA was made up predominantly of private-practice physicians; it was and is a formidable political actor (as shown in some of the other chapters). That was particularly true after 1957 when Tarou Takemi, nephew-in-law of postwar Japan's preeminent politician Shigeru Yoshida, became president. In the eyes of the JMA, the MHW was intending to take advantage of universal health coverage to extend bureaucratic control of medical practice.[3]

Right before the new law went into effect, the JMA led a strike of private-practice physicians in the name of protecting clinical autonomy. The LDP leadership immediately intervened, and negotiated a settlement in which the JMA accepted the new system in exchange for the government loosening controls on prescribing and dispensing expensive drugs, allowing higher fees, and not incidentally giving private-practice physicians a tax exemption for a substantial part of their revenue. (Behind the scenes, it is likely that the JMA was not very opposed to universal health coverage, as it was set to increase demand for medical services at a time when physicians were worried about oversupply, following the war-time doubling of medical school enrollment and the return of physicians from former colonies.)

Drive for Equality and Expansion

Japan was torn by controversy in 1960, including big demonstrations over revisions to the Security Treaty with the United States.[4] Partly as a result, the LDP easily won a general election late that year. Hayato Ikeda, a former economic bureaucrat, took over as prime minister(1960–64). His strategy was to avoid divisive left–right issues and focus on economic growth, which everyone could support. The country enjoyed rapid economic growth in the 1960s, driven by the Income-Doubling Plan, designed by the economist Osamu Shimomura and introduced by Prime Minister Ikeda in 1960. The plan aimed to double per capita national income in 10 years by achieving annual gross domestic product (GDP) growth of 11 percent. In fact, real per capita national income doubled between 1960 and 1967, making it easier for Japanese citizens to pay the premium to contribute to the social health insurance system and for the government to allocate more budget to health.

The celebrated Income-Doubling Plan relied on rapid expansion of industry in the modern sector. LDP leaders pointed out to Prime Minister Ikeda that urban, educated modern-sector workers were a natural constituency for the opposition, while the LDP relied heavily on the traditional sector of farmers, small-scale manufacturing, retail shops, construction companies, and the like in rural areas. They insisted that a balanced growth strategy was necessary. Ever since, as part of what is sometimes called the Japanese-style welfare state, the traditional sector has disproportionally been supported by budget subsidies, public works spending, and various forms of protectionism.

In the 1960s, with an average annual growth rate of over 10 percent, the economy tripled, with much of the growth benefiting households. There was a remarkable degree of income equality across urban and rural areas and among households. However, rising prosperity also highlighted inequalities and groups that had barely benefited at all, including older people and victims of industrial pollution. Trading on such discontents, progressive politicians started winning more elections, both for national and local legislative seats but especially as governors and mayors at prefectural and municipal levels. Indeed, around the end of the decade more than half the Japanese population had a progressive governor or mayor, or both.

The result was a surge of progressive initiatives at local level and then at national level as the ruling LDP responded to this threat. In the health care area, the gap in the amount of copayments at point of service (as said, initially zero for employees and 50 percent for dependents) was narrowed. In the early 1970s, a "catastrophic cap" on monthly health care expenditures was initiated, bringing financial protection into all health insurance programs. The most dramatic new policy was free health care for older people.

Old-age health care was a potent issue because the elderly were far likelier to be ill than middle-aged people but used medical care at only about the same rate. Their incomes were low, and although they were all covered by health insurance, they faced a 30–50 percent copayment, an issue highlighted by labor unions and other progressive activists in Tokyo, and picked up by Governor Ryoukichi Minobe, who had been elected with Socialist and Communist support in 1967 and was alert to issues to differentiate his policies from the LDP's.

In 1969, the Tokyo Assembly passed a bill to cover copayments from public funds for everyone 65 and over who passed a very lenient income test. The idea was immediately popular and was emulated in prefectures and cities all over Japan, even some with conservative chief executives. Although many had enacted less expensive variations, the localities soon found that costs were very high (local spending on older people doubled from 1971 to 1972), and they called for the national government to step in. Of course the progressive parties in the Diet were even more vociferous.

What about the bureaucrats? The Ministry of Finance was naturally appalled, as was the MHW—its officials knew that free medical care for the elderly would be very expensive, threatening other policies, and moreover a bonanza for the physicians who had long been at loggerheads with the ministry over control of health policy. In fact MHW officials and associated experts had been working on ideas for dealing with older people's medical problems for some time, but under great time pressure, its four bureaus with ties to the issue could not compromise on any particular program, and so the MHW failed to make a proposal of its own.

By default, the key decisions were left to the governing LDP, which was dominated by Kakuei Tanaka (prime minister 1972–74). In the heat of the moment, the LDP wound up adopting a far more expansive plan than the great majority of its legislators preferred. A bill passed in 1972 removed the copayment for almost everyone aged 70 and over. This enthusiasm was not only for older people: other copayments for nonemployees were decreased. Nor was it only health care: pension benefits were also increased sharply. Along with the political context of increased pressure from opposition parties, an important factor was that after the "economic miracle" of almost continuous rapid economic growth over 15 years, Japanese policy makers had the impression that the nation could afford almost anything—an illusion soon dispelled by the oil shock of late 1973.

Switch to Spending Restraint

The oil shock threw Japan into a sharp recession, followed by a return to much slower economic growth (3–5 percent a year rather than 8–10 percent).[5] The expansive policy changes of the early 1970s now looked rash, and social spending was an obvious target. Ironically, progressive chief executives of localities that suddenly faced severe budget troubles were among the first to call for a "reconsideration of welfare," and the Ministry of Finance strongly warned about "indiscriminate" spending that would cause great burdens in the future. However, efforts to constrain spending across the government were inhibited by a political barrier: the ruling LDP had lost so much ground to the progressive parties that its majority in the Diet was quite precarious (called *hakuchuu*, conservative–progressive balance). Cutting popular programs was the last thing politicians wanted to think about.

Rapid increase in spending on health care, which in the 1970s was growing at about the same rate as in the profligate United States system, was a problem that could not be long ignored. In large part, such spending was blamed on free medical care for the elderly. The issue was not so much the direct public subsidy to cover copayments, but rather that older people started going to the doctor, and especially checking into the hospital for protracted stays, much more than previously (often called "social admissions").[6] Most were enrolled in the CHI system for nonemployees, administered by local governments. Treasury spending on old-age health care soared from ¥218 billion in 1973 to ¥958 billion in 1980,[7] as it had to finance not only the amount equivalent to the older people's copayments but also the increases in subsidies to the CHI due to more usage.

Various reforms were proposed in the late 1970s, but none was enacted. What changed matters was a landslide electoral victory for the LDP in 1980. The LDP governments of Zenkou Suzuki (1980–82) and particularly Yasunari Nakasone (1982–87) led Japan into an era of austerity, much as had been happening overseas under Prime Minister Thatcher and President Reagan.

The intense top-down campaign was called "administrative reform," though the target was big government in general, not just the bureaucracy. The campaign had considerable success in constraining budgetary expenditure, and some success in cutting back on regulation and other government "interference" in the economy, including deregulation. As for health care reform, the campaign itself did not produce meaningful proposals, but severe across-the-board budget constraints put intense pressure on the MHW, where among its various policy areas only the medical sector offered any possibility of substantial savings.

The ministry thus came up with two major reforms in the early 1980s. One was a technical alteration in the biennial fee schedule revision process, the government's main tool for controlling growth in medical expenditures by altering the prices of procedures and products. By changing the formula for estimating providers' revenues due to "natural" increases, greater reductions in prices and thus lower growth in spending became possible.[8] The other was the Health Care for the Aged Law, drawn up by the ministry in late 1980. After a long legislative process including many amendments, it was enacted in August 1982 and implemented in 1983.

This law symbolically ended free medical care for the elderly by imposing a tiny copayment; more important, it revolutionized health care finance by cross-subsidizing the high cost of medical care for people 70 or more by transferring large portions of premium revenue from employee health insurance to the impoverished municipally run CHI system that covered the great majority of older people. Credit for this major reform—probably the biggest explicit policy change in health care since the passage of universal coverage in 1959—belongs to effective leadership by MHW officials under Hitoshi Yoshimura (chief of staff). Having said that, the new political mood of austerity was certainly a major stimulus.

Continued Attempts to Control Public Spending

The health policy agenda was dominated for many years by concerns about costs. Following the Health Care for the Aged Law, the MHW moved directly to deal with the social admissions problem by changing regulations for hospitals with high proportions of elderly inpatients, including moving from fee-for-service to inclusive payments. Moves to improve residence-based care for frail older people, later culminating in the Long-Term Care Insurance System enacted in 1997, were more strategic attempts to reduce expensive hospitalization.

The MHW also extended the logic of cross-subsidization to people aged 60–69. Another move was to introduce copayments for employees (not just their dependents) and then gradually raise the amounts for various categories of people, tailoring each step to minimize the inevitable political opposition from both LDP and opposition Diet members.

Through all these years, there were constant calls by pundits and politicians for a radical reform (*bappon kaikaku*) of the purportedly broken health care system. As with most critiques of Japanese institutions from the late 1970s, the diagnosis was that the hand of government was too heavy and the proposed remedies were market-oriented reforms—remarkably, often holding up the United States as a positive example.

It was not until the neoliberal regime of Jun'ichirou Koizumi (2001–06) that any of these attempts came close to fruition: lifting the ban on "extra billing"

Universal Health Coverage for Inclusive and Sustainable Development
http://dx.doi.org/10.1596/978-1-4648-0408-3

(*kongou shinryou*) would allow various advanced procedures and drugs to be paid out of pocket alongside regular insured treatments. With a companion proposal to allow new investor-owned hospitals, it meant a substantial inroad of free market ideas into Japan's highly regulated health care system. Critics saw this as a threat to egalitarian principles, and determined opposition from the JMA brought its defeat, except for some minor reforms. Prime Minister Koizumi had more success in constraining—and in one year even reversing—growth of medical expenditures.[9]

"Collapse of Medical Care"

After some 25 years of health policy dominated by austerity, culminating in Prime Minister Koizumi's severe constraints on spending, reaction set in. Growing complaints about financial distress including closure of hospitals or departments in rural areas, shortages of doctors, particularly in specializations like obstetrics and pediatrics, inadequate emergency room availability, and so forth brought a media chorus about the "collapse of medical care" (*iryou houkai*). In the seven years from 2000 to 2006, articles using the term had appeared in the *Asahi* newspaper only 10 times, but mentions grew to 157 in 2007–08 and 196 in 2009–10. The issue became a major campaign slogan for the Democratic Party of Japan in its landslide victory in the 2009 general election. It promised both to increase health care spending and to redirect resources from private-practice physicians to acute-care hospitals. The party honored these promises in its three years in power,[10] but the dismal economic situation plus continued resistance from the JMA prevented any major shifts. Media attention and public interest in health policy declined.

Still, important issues remain. For example, the National Council on Social Security System Reform (*Shakai Hoshou Seido Kaikaku Kokumin Kaigi*) was a blue-ribbon commission established in the Prime Minister's Office to see how revenues from the forthcoming consumption tax hike should be spent in the context of broad reforms. In its April 19, 2013, session, the council discussed a proposal to finance hospital care and other local needs directly from the new tax revenues, rather than relying only on fee schedule revisions to carry out important health policies.[11]

Insights

The lessons of Japan's experience with universal health coverage for developing nations lies mainly in specific programs and policies, which have been analyzed in other chapters. This chapter has been more about the political and historical contexts of how these policies came about, and such contexts are generally too particular to a given time and country to yield straightforward lessons. However, there are some implications of the process itself that may be helpful.

The sequence of policy change can be important, and Japan offers both a positive and negative example. The positive side is that the health care system was already relatively egalitarian before its major expansions in the 1960s and early 1970s. Similar to most countries, in Japan health insurance started with government employees and was then expanded to industrial workers; but in contrast to many other countries, health coverage in Japan was extended to workers in small firms at the same time as those in large firms. When universality was achieved with a new system for nonemployees, access to care was the same as in the employee system, and even the 50 percent copayment was the same as for employee dependents. This pattern of equality was thus in place before the big benefit expansions.

A negative lesson is that the Japanese government never tried hard to consolidate its health insurance programs, even when there might have been a window of opportunity in 1959. It continually took the path of least political resistance by layering on new and different programs for each group covered—small-firm employees, self- and nonemployees, poor people, and older people. The resulting anomalies and imbalances have continued to plague health policy making and have added to the system's complexity, making it hard to understand—let alone reform.

A key point more true in Japan than in many countries is that the government was always concerned with holding down spending, and realized that doing so required controls on provider behavior. The techniques evolved from direct controls to incentives through the price system, which were frequently adjusted (particularly in the early 1980s). An important facilitating condition was that the year-to-year politics of health policy making centered on the confrontation between the government and organized private-practice physicians. As pointed out in chapter 6, that confrontation gradually brought about a structure of negotiations that could accommodate shifting pressures on health policy without much real disruption.

Finally, a broader structural point. A crucial role throughout was played by highly skilled and relatively independent bureaus within the ministry in charge of health. Building and protecting such competency is a key to effective policy, including cost control. However, at least as important is a political leadership, focused on the well-being of citizens, that can intervene to improve (at the least maintain) the quality and quantity of medical services, particularly for groups not so well served. Inevitably the balance between managerial and political concerns will swing back and forth; a lesson from Japan is that even rather substantial swings can result in appropriate health policy.

Notes

1. Policy speech texts from Database Chronology for Twentieth and Twenty-first Century (1990–December, 2006) at http://www.ioc.u-tokyo.ac.jp/~worldjpn/index.html; translated by author.

2. See Otake (1996).

3. At the time, the MHW was following a policy of limiting medical services by enforcing strict protocols in dispensing expensive medications, in order to contain health

expenditures (called "restricted clinical practice" or *seigen shinryou*). Private-practice physicians earned a large proportion of their income from dispensing drugs at that time (Tsuchida 2011; also see Steslicke 1973).

4. This section is based mainly on Campbell (1990), chapters 4–5; see Calder (1988) for a parallel analysis.

5. For details, see Campbell (1990), chapters 7 and 9.

6. Doctors quickly responded to this opportunity by building many new "hospitals" that were really little more than nursing homes. Such social admissions aside, usage of actual medical care by older people did not increase disproportionally considering their much higher rate of illness (although of course anything that looked like overuse was deplored by conservatives).

7. Internal MHW documents cited in Campbell (1990), chapter 9.

8. See chapters 5 and 6.

9. See chapter 6. A decade later, the second cabinet of Abe Shinzou (he had been prime minister in 2006–07) proposed similar neoliberal health care reforms in connection with the Trans-Pacific Partnership free trade negotiations, but met similar opposition.

10. See chapter 6.

11. For a summary of the final report, see http://www.kantei.go.jp/foreign/971228 finalreport.html.

Bibliography

Calder, Kent E. 1988. *Crisis and Compensation: Public Policy and Political Stability in Japan, 1949–1986*. Princeton: Princeton University Press.

Campbell, John Creighton. 1990. *How Policies Change: The Japanese Government and the Aging Society*. Princeton: Princeton University Press.

Ikegami, Naoki. 2006. "Should Providers be Allowed to Extra Bill for Uncovered Services? Debate, Resolution, and Sequel in Japan". *Journal of Health Politics, Policy and Law* 31 (6): 1129–49.

Kasza, Gregory J. 2006. *One World of Welfare: Japan in Comparative Perspective*. Ithaca, NY: Cornell University Press.

Kondo, Ayako, and Hitoshi Shigeoka. 2011. "Effects of Universal Health Insurance on Health Care Utilization, Supply-side Responses and Mortality Rates: Evidence from Japan." http://www.columbia.edu/~hs2166/Kondo_Shigeoka_Oct4_2011.pdf.

Ogawa, Sumiko, Toshihiko Hasegawa, Guy Carrin, and Kei Kawabata. 2003. "Scaling up Community Health Insurance: Japan's Experience with the 19th Century *Jyorei* Scheme." *Health Policy and Planning* 18 (3): 270–78.

Otake, Hideo. 1996. *Sengo Nihon no Ideorogi Tairitsu (Ideological Confrontation in Postwar Japan)*. Tokyo: San'ichi Shobo.

Shimazaki, Kenji. 2011. *Nihon no Iryou: Seido to Seisaku (Japan's Medical Care: System and Policy)*. Tokyo: Tokyo Daigaku Shuppankai, 44–45.

Steslicke, William E. 1973. *Doctors in Politics: The Political Life of the Japan Medical Association*. New York: Praeger.

Tsuchida, Takeshi. 2011. "Kokumin Kaihoken 50nen no Kaiseki." *Kikan: Shakai Hoshou Kenkyuu* 47 (3): 244–56.

CHAPTER 2

Macroeconomic Context and Challenges for Maintaining Universal Health Coverage in Japan[1]

Takashi Oshio, Naoko Miake, and Naoki Ikegami

Abstract

Japan's annual average economic growth rate has slowed from 9.6 percent in 1955–70 to 1.0 percent in 1990–2011. During the latter period, government expenditures continued to increase while tax revenues declined. This took the ratio of general government gross debt to gross domestic product (GDP) to 230 percent by mid-2013. Widening income disparities among the working age population have also strained principles of equity in universal health coverage (UHC). Within social security, pensions have more weight than health care benefits. Aging has had major impacts on raising health expenditures for two reasons. First, extent and speed: the population 65 and over climbed from 5 percent in 1950 to 25 percent in 2013. Second, price inflation has been controlled by the government's fee schedule, increasing the weight of elders 65 and over in health spending from a quarter in 1977 to over a half in 2010. One implication is that UHC programs should be designed to adjust to slower economic growth as a country ages.

Objectives

The objectives of this chapter are to analyze the following: the effects of the decline in economic growth on fiscal space, which is needed to achieve and sustain UHC; widening income disparities (because greater disparities would make it harder to implement the equity principles of UHC); the redistribution function of social security and taxes; changes in funding sources; the impact of aging on fiscal space; and the prospects for improving that space.

This chapter uses published government data. "Health expenditures" are those of the national medical expenditures (*kokumin iryouhi*), as calculated by the Ministry of Health, Labour and Welfare (MHLW).[1]

Decline in Economic Growth and Its Impact on Fiscal Space

Real GDP growth has declined gradually from 9.6 percent a year during 1955–70 to 4.5 percent in 1970–90 and then to 1.0 percent in 1990–2011 (figure 2.1).

Per capita real compensation of employees has reflected these trends in real economic growth. It first increased sharply by 3.6 times from 1955 to 1975,[2] and then gradually slowed, followed by a decrease of 12.0 percent in 2012 from its peak in 1996 (figure 2.2). The delay between the deceleration in GDP growth and the decline in employee compensations is probably because employers needed time to cut labor costs by lowering wages. The fall in wage income led to reductions in government revenues from taxes. However, the share of revenues from social security premiums to GDP increased from 8.2 percent in 1990 to 12.5 percent in 2011 because contribution rates were raised to balance expenditures and revenues (figure 2.3). In contrast, the government was not faced with the same constraints in forming the general budget: the shortfall was met by debt financing.

The fiscal gap between government expenditures and revenue has continued to increase (figure 2.4) so that the debt-to-GDP ratio almost reached 230 percent by mid-2013. This was a record high, exceeding the war-time rate (figure 2.5). The debt has been financed by issuing special deficit-financing bonds since 1975.

Figure 2.1 Real GDP Growth

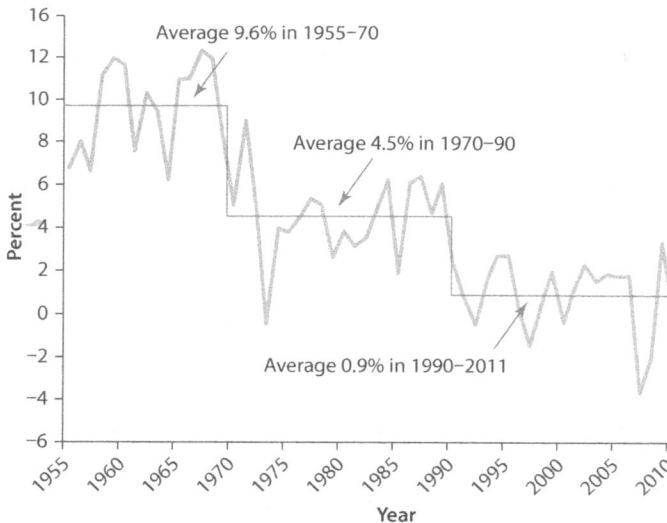

Source: Cabinet Office 2012.

Figure 2.2 Real Per Capita Employee Compensation

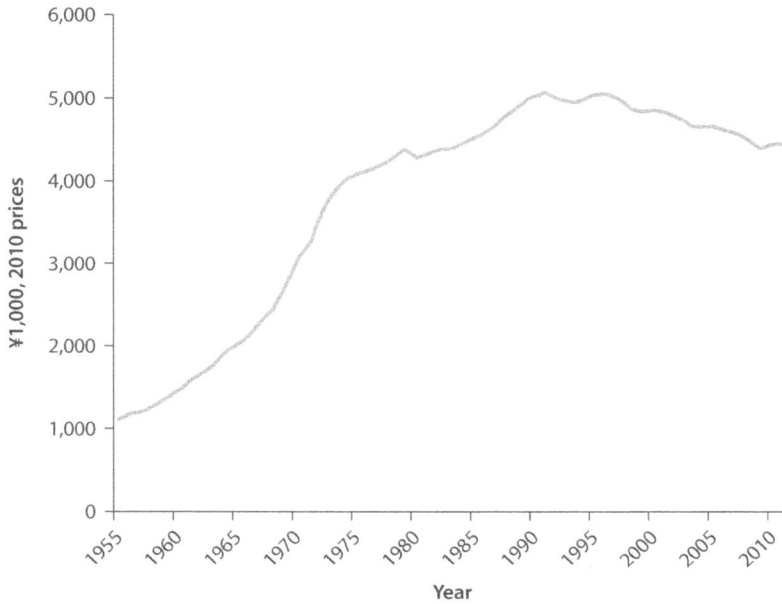

Source: Cabinet Office 2012.

Figure 2.3 Ratio of Social Security Contributions and Taxes per GDP

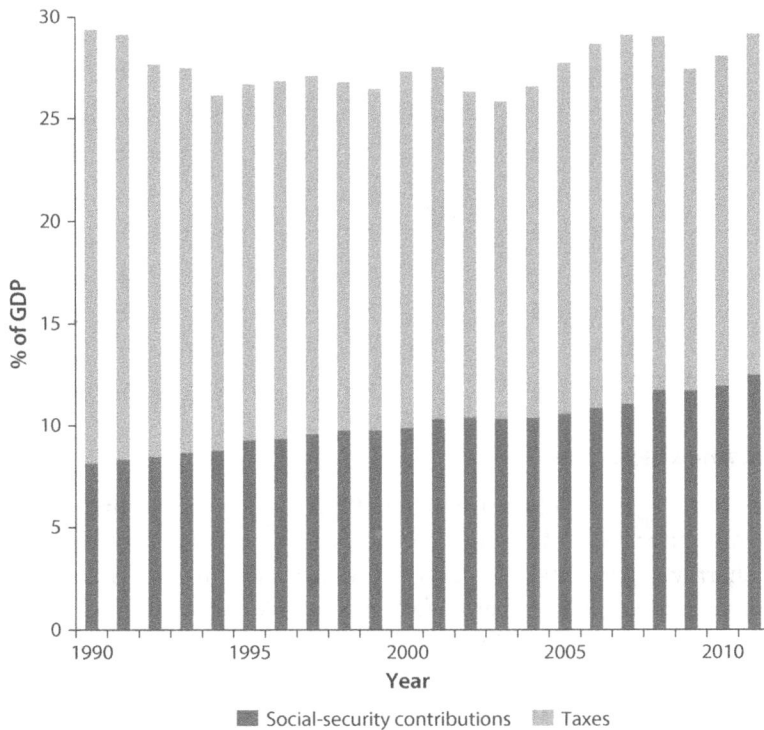

■ Social-security contributions   ■ Taxes

Source: Cabinet Office 2012.

Universal Health Coverage for Inclusive and Sustainable Development
http://dx.doi.org/10.1596/978-1-4648-0408-3

Figure 2.4 Trends in General Account Tax Revenues and Total Expenditures

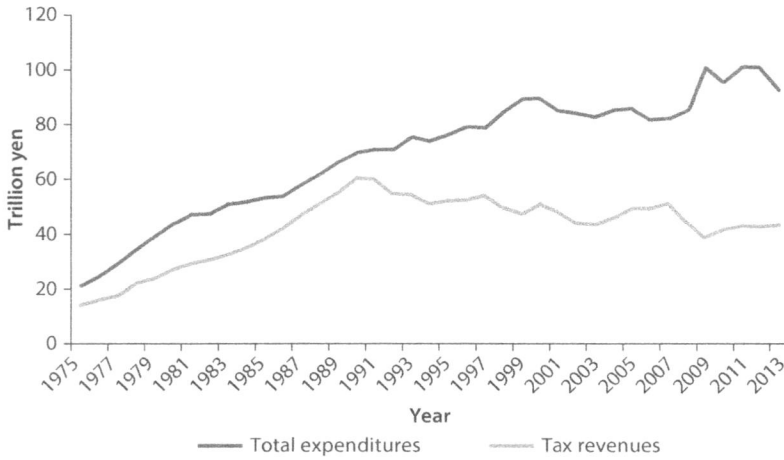

Source: MoF 2013; Cabinet Office 2012.

Figure 2.5 Ratio of General Government Gross Debt to GDP

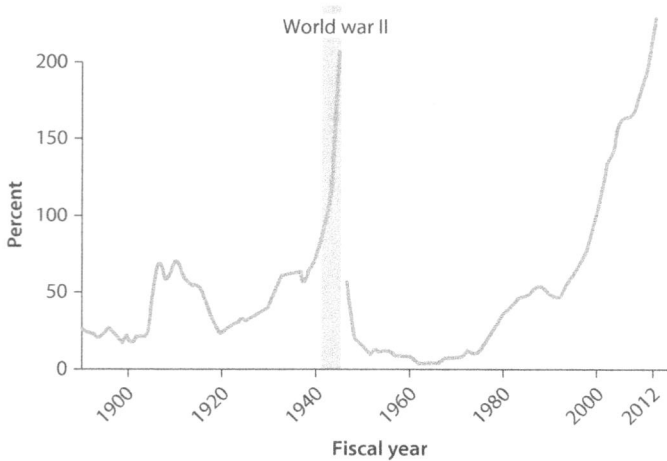

Source: MoF 2013.
Note: The shaded column highlights the war years, 1941–45.

Widening Income Disparities

Income distribution began to widen from the 1980s, before the decline of the third period set in after 1991. The Gini coefficients before taxes and transfers have climbed sharply (figure 2.6). However, more than half this increase can be attributed to demographic changes, particularly a rising proportion of elders, who tend to show a more unequal distribution than the young (Ohtake and Saito 1998; Oshio 2005). The decrease in average household size from 3.15 in 1984 to 2.34 in 2012 has also contributed to this increase (MIC 2013).[3]

Figure 2.6 Income Inequality and Other Factors Contributing to Income Redistribution

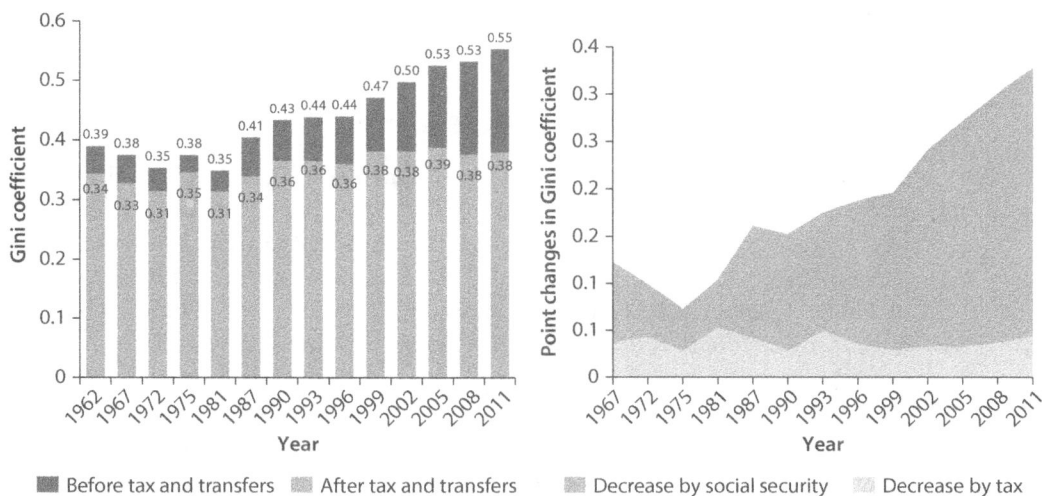

Before tax and transfers   After tax and transfers   Decrease by social security   Decrease by tax

Source: MHLW 2013a.
Note: Benefits in kind are included in transfers, and household size is not adjusted. Tax-financed government spending and the deduction of social security contributions from the income tax base are not considered; hence, the contribution to income redistribution from taxation tends to be underestimated.

Figure 2.7 Gini Coefficient by Age Group, 1984 and 2011

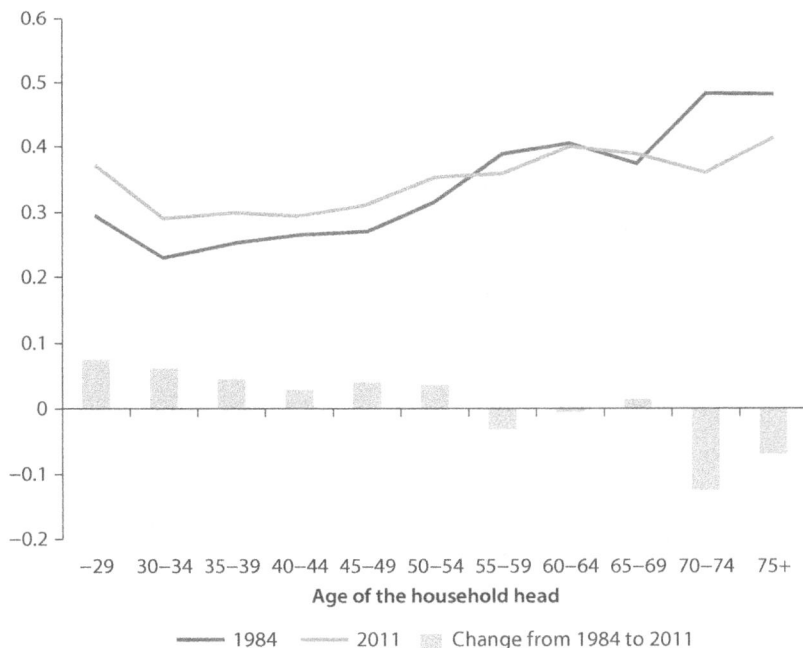

Age of the household head

——— 1984   ——— 2011   Change from 1984 to 2011

Source: MHLW 2013a.

To adjust for these factors, figure 2.7 compares the Gini coefficient by age groups between 1984 and 2008. The increase in the working age groups can be attributed not only to the stagnant growth in average incomes but also to the

Universal Health Coverage for Inclusive and Sustainable Development
http://dx.doi.org/10.1596/978-1-4648-0408-3

increase in the proportion of nonregular employees from 20.2 percent in 1990 to 35.2 percent in 2012 (Cabinet Office 2012). The mean monthly wages of nonregular employees were 62.0 percent those of regular employees in 2012.

Redistribution Effects of Taxes and Social Security

The redistribution effect of social security has been greater than that of taxes except for 1978 and 1981 (see figure 2.6). The relative weight of social security has increased from three times that of taxation in 1984 to seven times in 2008. Most of this increase can be attributed to more benefits for elders in the form of public pension, health care, and long-term care. Those aged below 60, however, saw no reduction in the Gini coefficient, and the relative poverty rate for households with children and single working adults is one of the highest among Organisation for Economic Co-operation and Development (OECD) member countries (OECD 2013). Even among elders, the redistribution effect is marginal because public pension benefits differ substantially: retired employees receive both flat-rate and wage-proportional benefits, while the self-employed receive only flat-rate benefits. This inequity has been exacerbated by the fact that most of the income from public pensions is excluded when calculating income tax and health insurance contributions.

Since there are no data that break down the effect of reducing the Gini coefficient by social security into health care benefits in kind and benefits in cash (pension and public assistance), we compared the amount of benefits received by income classes for 1967 (the earliest year available) and 2011 (figure 2.8). In 1967, health care benefits in kind were more than benefits in cash (pension and public assistance) for all income classes in 1967. Since social security made a greater contribution to income redistribution than taxes in that year, we can infer that health care benefits in kind had a substantial effect on income redistribution. However, in 2011, benefits in cash were greater across all income classes, reflecting the maturation of public pensions.[4] Note that social security contributions increase as income class rises.

Changes in Funding Sources

The proportion funded by taxes rose from 16 percent in 1954 to 34 percent in 1974, which was instrumental in lowering the proportion funded out of pocket from 38 percent to 13 percent (figure 2.9) (MHLW 2013b). Since then, however, the proportion of the latter has remained unchanged and taxes have come to replace financing by premiums. The proportion funded by insurance premiums reached its peak, 58 percent, in 1992 and thereafter declined to 49 percent in 2011 (figure 2.9). The initial jump to 54 percent in 1964 is probably due to the expansion of coverage, and the later increase, until its peak in 1992, to the introduction of transfer contributions from programs to pay for the health care expenditures of elders. The subsequent decline probably stems from the growing number of the elders who are enrolled in programs that have a greater proportion financed by taxes (see the chapter 3).

Universal Health Coverage for Inclusive and Sustainable Development
http://dx.doi.org/10.1596/978-1-4648-0408-3

Figure 2.8 Benefits and Social Security Contribution by Income Class, 1967 and 2011

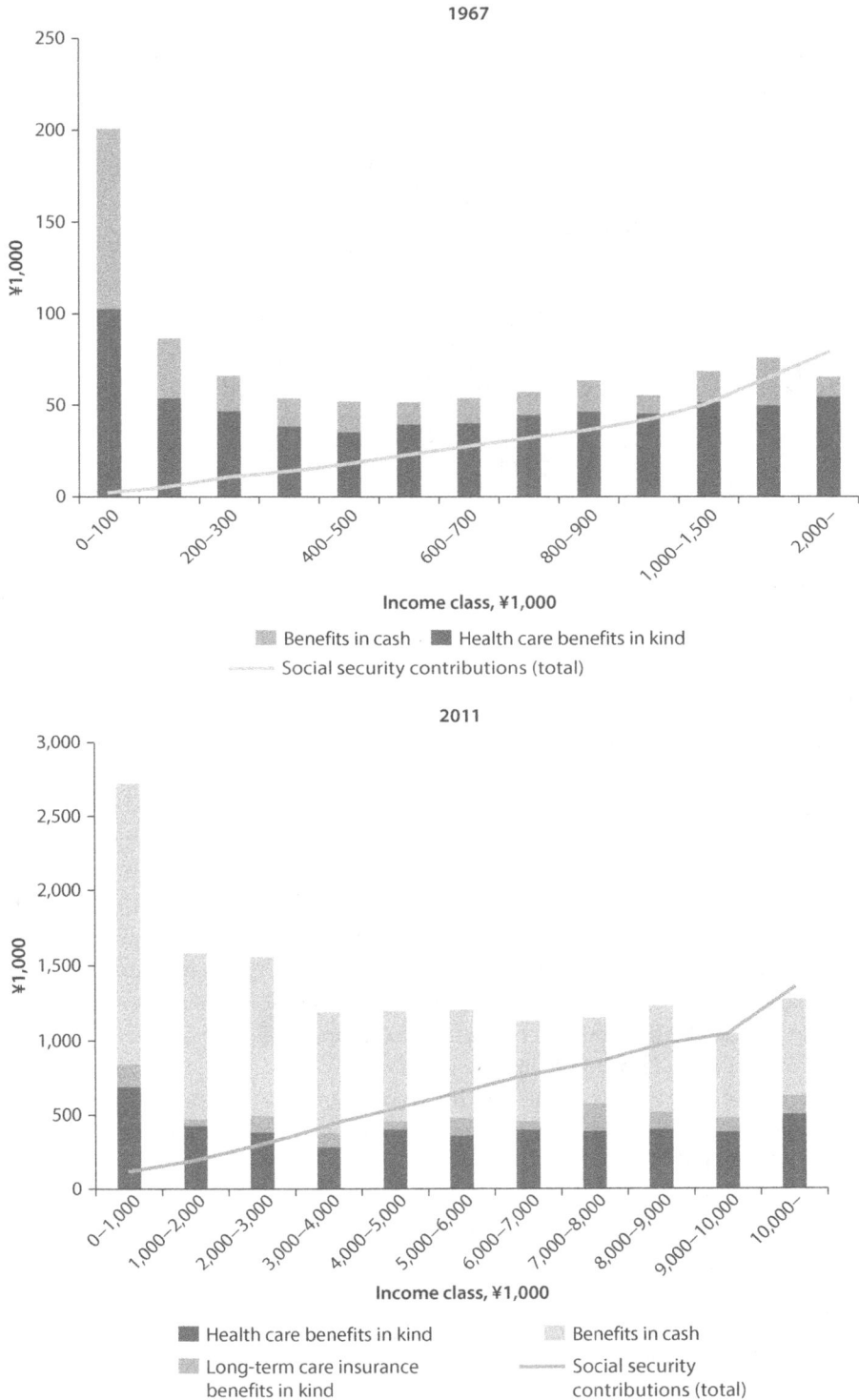

1967

¥1,000

Income class, ¥1,000

▨ Benefits in cash   ▪ Health care benefits in kind
— Social security contributions (total)

2011

¥1,000

Income class, ¥1,000

▪ Health care benefits in kind   ▨ Benefits in cash
▨ Long-term care insurance   — Social security
    benefits in kind   contributions (total)

Source: MHLW 2013a.

Universal Health Coverage for Inclusive and Sustainable Development
http://dx.doi.org/10.1596/978-1-4648-0408-3

Figure 2.9 Changes in Funding Sources of Health Expenditures, 1954–2011

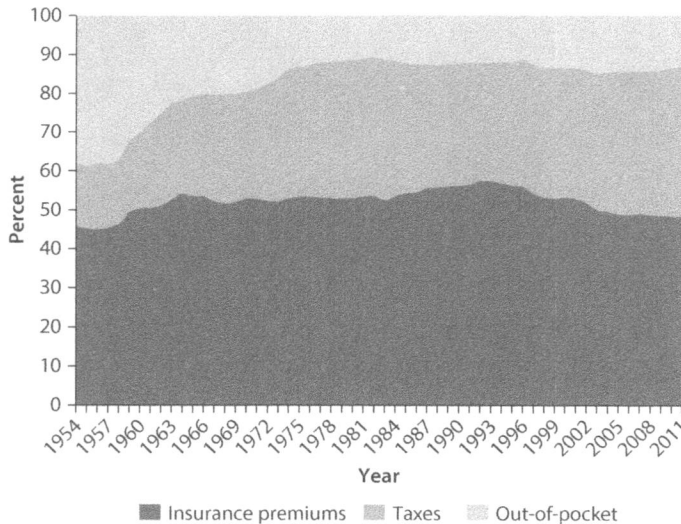

Source: MHLW 2013b.
Note: Out-of-pocket expenditures include compensation for environmental pollution, but the latter compose at most 1 percent of the total in some of the years.

Impact of Aging on Fiscal Space

Aging has a major effect on fiscal space, both revenue and expenditure. On the revenue side, elders tend to have lower income so that the amount they contribute is less. Moreover, since public pension income is applied lower rate for tax and health insurance contributions relative to wage income, this effect has been magnified. On the expenditure side, elders consume more health care. While some economists (Zweifel, Felder, and Meiers, 1999) believe that this increase could be explained by adjusting for time to death, this is not the case for Japan. As figure 2.10 shows, per capita health expenditures increase as the age group becomes older, but this trend is *less* so in 2010 than in 2001, despite the fact that, between these two years, the proportion of deaths occurring after 75 climbed from 58.4 percent to 69.1 percent. If increases in health expenditures were due to the postponement of end-of-life care to older age groups, the per capita amount for those 75 and above should have *increased* in 2010.[5]

One reason why aging has had a major impact on health expenditure in Japan is its speed and extent. The share of the population aged 65 and over has shot up to stand at 25 percent in 2013 (MIC 2013); Japan was the oldest country in the world in 2010 (United Nations 2010) (figure 2.11).

The other reason is that price inflation has been contained by the fee schedule of the MHLW, increasing the weight of elders in health expenditures.[6] When

Figure 2.10 Per Capita Health Expenditures, by Age Group, 2001 and 2010

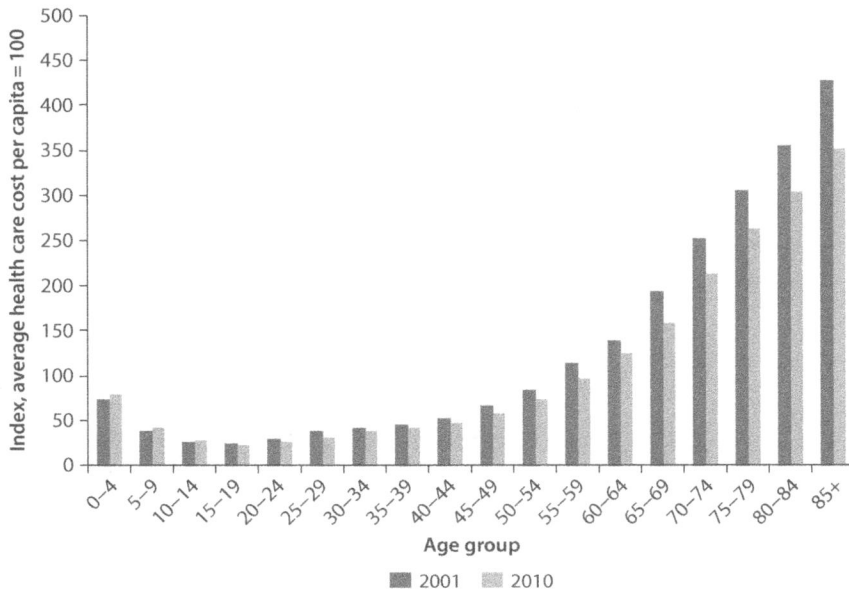

Source: MHLW 2011.

Figure 2.11 Percentage of Population Aged 65 Years Old and Over, 1950–2010

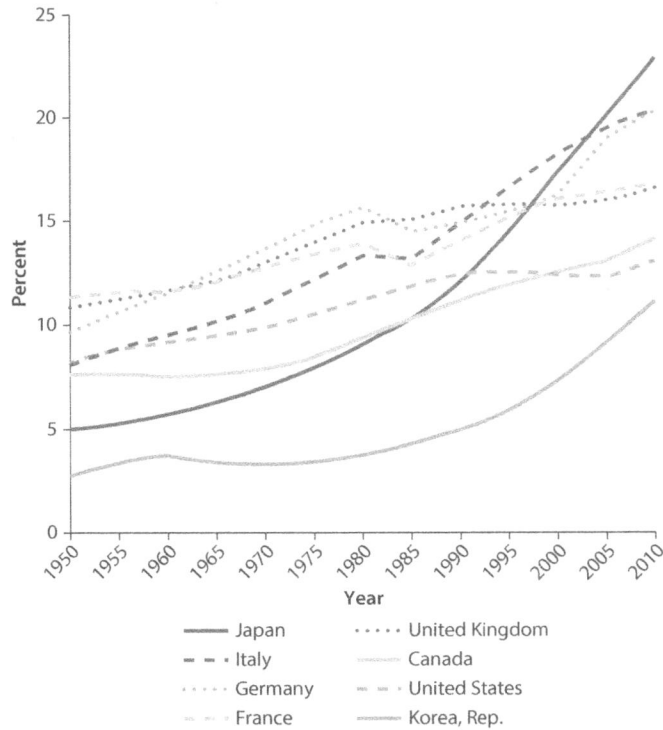

Source: United Nations, "World population prospects. The 2010 Revision" 2010 Population Census
(Statistics Bureau of Japan)

Universal Health Coverage for Inclusive and Sustainable Development
http://dx.doi.org/10.1596/978-1-4648-0408-3

health expenditure increases are decomposed into four factors (table 2.1), aging and the residual (mainly attributed to advances in technology) are the primary drivers (MIC 2011).

Elders' weight in health expenditures has risen much more than the underlying demographic change, from a quarter (27.1 percent) in 1977 to a half (55.4 percent) in 2010, compared with the population weight from 8.2 percent to 23.2 percent between the two years (figure 2.12). Since funding is on a pay-as-you-go

Table 2.1 Factors Increasing Health Expenditures, 2002–12

percent

	2002	2003	2004	2005	2006	2007	2008	2009	2010	2011	2012
Increase in health expenditures (A)	−0.5	1.9	1.8	3.2	0.0	3.0	2.0	3.4	3.9	3.1	1.7
Fee schedule revision (B)	−2.7	n.a.	−1.0	n.a.	−3.16	n.a.	−0.8	n.a.	0.2	n.a.	0.0
Population changes (C)	0.1	0.1	0.1	0.1	0.0	0.0	−0.1	−0.1	0.0	−0.2	−0.2
Aging effect (D)	1.7	1.6	1.5	1.8	1.3	1.5	1.3	1.4	1.6	1.3	1.4
Residual: Others (technological advancement, and so on) (A-B-C-D)	0.4	0.2	1.2	1.3	1.8	1.5	1.5	2.2	2.1	2.1	0.5

Source: MHLW 2013c.
Note: n.a. = not applicable.

Figure 2.12 Health Expenditures, by Age Group, 1977–2010

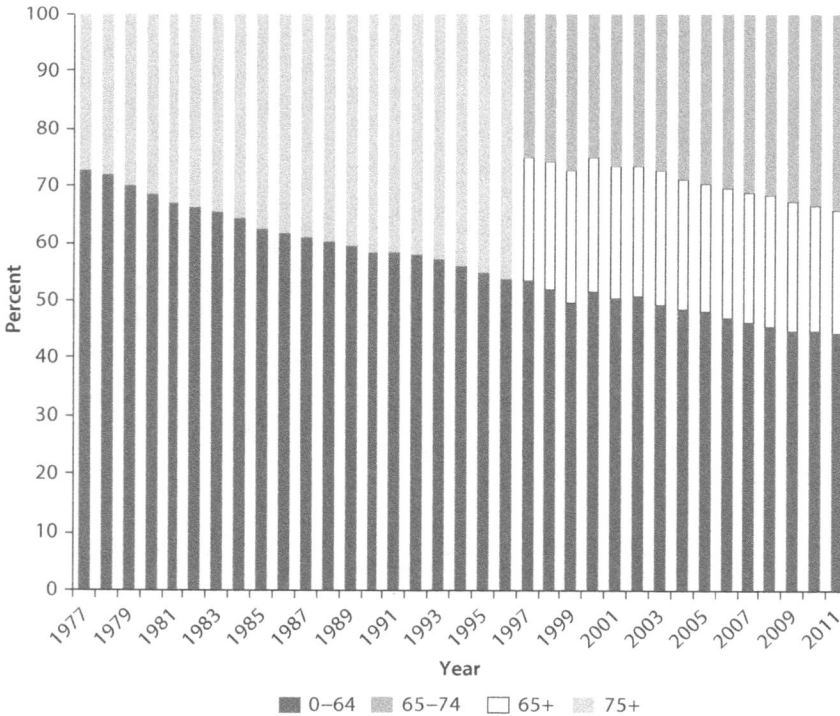

Source: MHLW 2013b.
Note: Age is that of the household head.

Figure 2.13 Health Insurance Premium Payments and Benefits, by Age Group, 2011

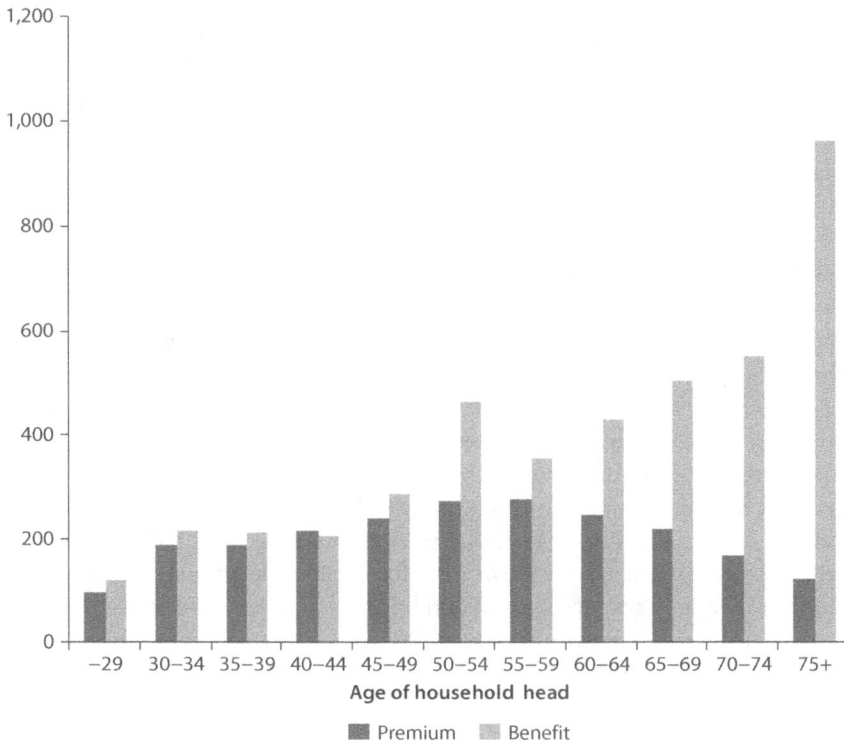

Source: MHLW 2013a.

basis, health insurance has become similar to pensions in that they have both led to large income transfers from the young to elders. The age group from which benefits exceed contributions is 45–49 (figure 2.13).

The government has tried to reduce the fiscal burden on the general budget by forcing social health insurance programs to contribute to elders' health expenditures. However, it has faced increasing resistance from employers and employees who are members of the employment-based programs because they are already contributing nearly half their premium revenue to the pooling fund to finance the health expenditures of elders. Their demands have led to increased financing from taxes (see figure 2.9).

Prospects for Improving Fiscal Space

The prime minister formally decided on October 1, 2013, to raise the consumption tax from 5 percent to 8 percent from April 2014 (Prime Minister of Japan and His Cabinet 2013), with programs to take it to 10 percent in October 2015. The government has promised that revenues from these tax hikes will be earmarked for social security, but only 20 percent would be allocated to any "improvement" of social security, the balance going to "stabilize" social security (mainly decreasing the deficit financing of social security benefits).

As a first step, the Diet passed the "Act to promote the reform for establishing a sustainable social security system" on December 5, 2013. The act has set a timeline for social security reform, including health care. However, reform as written in the act is vague, and details will be determined in separate bills.

The government faces two challenges. First, to mitigate any downturn in the economy due to the consumption tax increase, it plans to lower the corporate tax rate and allocate funding for investment in key growth areas—but such measures may negate any improvement in fiscal space. Second, to balance the present elder-biased social security system, it has revealed unpopular programs to lower their benefits. Gradually increasing the copayment rate of elders aged 70–74 from the present 10 percent to 20 percent (the age from which the 20 percent rate applies will go up by one year from 2014) is particularly disliked, as these elders would also be facing a higher consumption tax.

The government has admitted that even if the consumption tax were raised to 10 percent as planned and the economy were to grow at 2.1 percent a year, it would still not be possible to restore the primary balance for 2020 as had been planned in the comprehensive reform plan for social security and tax (Cabinet Office 2013). The only way to do so would be to have faster economic growth—and so, given the track record of the past 20 years, the prospects of increasing fiscal space do not seem that bright.

Insights

Social security programs that were designed and established during periods of rapid economic growth and a large working population provided the fiscal space to achieve UHC from the 1950s to the 1970s. Under the hybrid system of financing, the proportion funded from taxes was gradually increased, which allowed the disadvantaged to enroll and enjoy the same benefits as those who were advantaged (mainly the regularly employed). However, as the economy slowed and the aging process picked up, the continued reliance on funding from taxes has squeezed the diminishing fiscal space. Although the social security accounts had to balance increases in expenditures by raising their contribution rates, the general budget was not restrained because the deficit could be covered by issuing bonds. Aging has also changed the function of health insurance to resemble pensions': the effect is less to redistribute wealth from the rich to the poor, but more from the young to the old. As slowing economic growth and society's aging seem inevitable as countries mature, UHC programs should be designed with this in mind.

Notes

1. National medical expenditures do not include over-the-counter drugs, extra charges for beds with more amenities, and so forth (but include copayments). They have been consistently about 80 percent of total health expenditures of the countries in the Organisation for Economic Co-operation and Development (OECD) (see chapter 5).

2. Growth increased under the Income-Doubling Plan, designed by the economist Osamu Shimomura and introduced by Prime Minister Hayato Ikeda in 1960. The plan's goal was to double per capita income in 10 years by achieving annual GDP growth of 11 percent. In fact, national income doubled by 1967.

3. In OECD data (OECD 2013), benefits in kind are not included and household size is adjusted.

4. Long-term nursing care benefits in kind became part of social security after the program was implemented in 2000.

5. The decrease in the gradient cannot be attributed to the transfer of services to the public Long-Term Care Insurance system because it had been launched in 2000.

6. See chapters 5 and 6.

Bibliography

Cabinet Office. 2009. "Supplementary Report for the Revival of Middle Class—Working Group on the Japanese Economy and Policy Direction." http://www5.cao.go.jp/keizai2/keizai-syakai/k-s-kouzou/shiryou/wg3-4kai/pdf/2-2.pdf (accessed November 2013).

———. 2012. "Annual Reports on National Accounts." http://www.esri.cao.go.jp/en/sna/kakuhou/kakuhou_top.html (accessed November 2013).

———. 2013. "Mid-Long Term Fiscal Projection." http://www5.cao.go.jp/keizai-shimon/kaigi/minutes/2013/0808/shiryo_02.pdf (accessed November 2013).

MHLW (Ministry of Health, Labour and Welfare). 2011. "National Medical Expenditures by Age Group." http://www.mhlw.go.jp/toukei/saikin/hw/k-iryohi/10/dl/data.pdf (accessed November 2013).

———. 2013a. "Survey of Income Redistribution." http://www.mhlw.go.jp/stf/houdou/0000024829.html (accessed November 2013).

———. 2013b. "National Medical Expenditures FY2011." http://www.e-stat.go.jp/SG1/estat/List.do?lid=000001115498 (accessed November 2013).

———. 2013c. "National Medical Expenditures Database and Materials." http://www.mhlw.go.jp/bunya/iryouhoken/database/zenpan/dl/kokumin_roujin23.pdf (accessed November 2013).

MIC (Ministry of Internal Affairs and Communication). 2011. "Preliminary Sample Tabulation of the 2010 Population Census of Japan." http://www.stat.go.jp/english/info/news/1932.htm (accessed November 2013).

———. 2013. "Basic Resident Registration." http://www.stat.go.jp/data/idou/ (accessed November 2013).

MoF (Ministry of Finance) 2013. "Japan's Fiscal Condition." https://www.mof.go.jp/comprehensive_reform/gaiyou.pdf (accessed November 2013).

OECD (Organisation for Economic Co-operation and Development). 2013. "Economic Survey of Japan 2013." http://www.oecd.org/eco/surveys/japan-2013.htm (accessed November 2013).

Ohtake, F., and M. Saito. 1998. "Population Aging and Consumption Inequality." *Review of Income and Wealth* 44: 361–81.

Oshio, T. 2005. "Social Security and Intragenerational Redistribution of Lifetime Income in Japan." *Japanese Economic Review* 56 (1): 105–39.

Prime Minister of Japan and His Cabinet. 2013. "Decision on the Changes of Consumption Tax Rate and Regional Consumption Tax Rate." http://www.kantei.go.jp/jp/kakugik-ettei/2013/__icsFiles/afieldfile/2013/10/08/20131001-01.pdf (accessed November 2013).

United Nations 2010. "World Population Prospects." http://esa.un.org/wpp/ New York (accessed November 2013).

Zweifel, P., S. Felder, and M. Meiers. 1999. "Ageing of Population and Health Care Expenditure: A Red Herring?" *Health Economics* 8 (6): 485–96. http://www.ncbi.nlm.nih.gov/pubmed/10544314 (accessed November 2013).

CHAPTER 3

Fiscal Disparities among Social Health Insurance Programs in Japan

Reo Takaku, Shunichiro Bessho, Shuzo Nishimura, and Naoki Ikegami

Abstract

Japan has over 3,000 social health insurance (SHI) programs, broadly divided into employment- and residence-based programs. Despite different age and income distributions among enrollees, all programs provide the same statutory benefit package and access to virtually all health facilities. However, aging and changes in working patterns have eroded the fiscal basis of residence-based Citizens' Health Insurance (CHI) programs particularly, despite the subsidies from the national government and the introduction of transfers from other programs to pay for the health care costs of elders. Disparities in premium contribution rates (the share of income levied as premiums) exist among CHI programs because some of the subsidies are provided on a matching-fund basis (programs will be subsidized more if their expenditures are high). Such disparities exist and have increased among Society-Managed Health Insurance (SMHI) programs for employees of large companies. In hindsight, as the fiscal disparities between and within the two broad types of SHI programs are now likely to increase, a long-term goal of eventually merging the programs should have been considered some time ago, including standardizing the methods of levying premiums.

Objectives and Context

The objectives of this chapter are to analyze trends in the extent to which fiscal disparities between the CHI and employment-based programs have been mitigated by subsidies from taxes and transfers from employment-based programs to pay for the costs of elders, and the limitations encountered in maintaining equity in premium rates (the share of wage income levied as premiums) under multiple SHI programs.[1] These results may help provide positive and negative lessons for low- and middle-income countries that have established, or are about to establish, SHI programs.

Overview of SHI Programs

All permanent residents in Japan for three or more months must enroll in the SHI plan designated by the employer if employed, or by the local government if not regularly employed. There is no choice of programs, or of opting out and enrolling in private insurance. Dependents are covered by the insurance plan of the head of the household. All programs provide essentially the same comprehensive benefits,[2] unrestricted access to virtually all providers, and have the same cost-sharing rate (copayment) for those of the same age group (elders and children have lower rates). Administration costs have been reduced by the clearinghouses (SHI Payment Agencies) established in the 47 prefectures to which providers send their claims and from which insurance programs are billed. These agencies have helped to streamline claims processing and reduce the administrative burden on health care providers and insurance programs.[3]

However, although all three dimensions of universal coverage have been achieved and administrative costs have been decreased by unified clearinghouses, there are more than 3,000 SHI programs, each having a different income level, age, and other risk structure, and geographic access to health facilities for enrollees. The employment-based programs were implemented in 1927 for manual workers and have subsequently been expanded to all those formally employed. The residence-based programs were first legislated in 1938, primarily targeted at rural municipalities. Universal health coverage was achieved when the last municipalities implemented programs in 1961 and enrollment was made compulsory.

Reflecting differences in origin, premium contributions in the employment-based programs are levied as a percentage of wages as payroll deductions, regardless of the number of dependents; in residence-based programs, they are levied from households, basically half based on the household as a unit and on the number enrolled in each household, and the other half based on total household income and the household's property tax. The former are similar to a poll tax, but the amount is reduced by 20 percent, 50 percent, or 70 percent for those with incomes below the thresholds set for each. Each municipality has its own method for setting the premium amount based on the combination of these factors.[4] The ceiling from which premium contributions are made as a share of income is ¥14 million in employment-based programs and about ¥7 million in residence-based programs. Once employees retire, they must leave the employment-based plan and enroll in the residence-based plan where they live.

The above two broad groupings can be further divided into four tiers based on the proportion of their expenditures financed by taxes (figure 3.1). The first is composed of programs for those employed in large companies by SMHI and in public sector organizations by the Mutual Aid Association, neither of which receives any other revenue.[5] The second consists of the quasi-government National Health Insurance Association (NHIA) for those employed in small to medium companies, which receive 16.4 percent of benefit expenditures as subsidies from taxes.[6] The third is made up of residence-based CHI programs

Figure 3.1 Flow of Money in SHI Programs, 2011

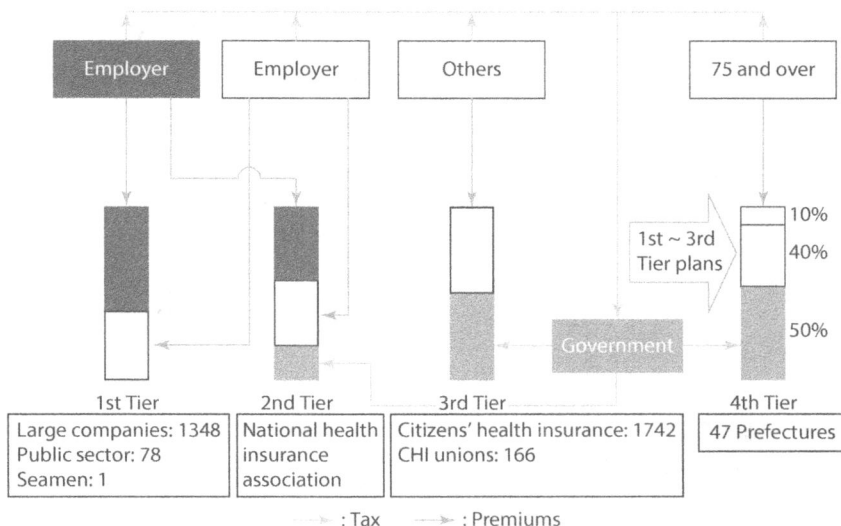

	Employer	Employer	Others		75 and over

1st ~ 3rd
Tier plans

10%
40%
50%

Government

1st Tier	2nd Tier	3rd Tier	4th Tier
Large companies: 1348 Public sector: 78 Seamen: 1	National health insurance association	Citizens' health insurance: 1742 CHI unions: 166	47 Prefectures

———► : Tax   ——►— : Premiums

Source: Ikegami et al. 2011 (updated).

managed by municipalities, enrolling the self-employed, the irregularly employed, nonworkers, and pensioners below the age of 75, which receive on average half their benefit expenditures from taxes. The fourth comprises the insurers organized at prefectural level for elders (aged 75 and over), which were established by the 2008 health system reform, and receive 50 percent as subsidies from taxes plus 40 percent from contributions (cross-subsidization) by programs in the other three tiers.[7] Expenditures for elders aged 65 to 74, who would mostly be enrolled in the CHI, are paid from a pooling fund, to which employment-based programs must contribute (Ikegami et al. 2011).

Of these four tiers, the CHI is the most fiscally and financially precarious for three reasons: it enrolls those not regularly employed, including retired elders below the age of 75; it is at risk of enrollees being unable or unwilling to pay premiums;[8] and the risk pools are small (57 percent of the programs had fewer than 10,000 enrollees in 2010) (MHLW *Annual Survey 2010*). Its fiscal situation has deteriorated for three reasons.

First, the population has aged, which has had particular impact on the CHI (rather than the SMHI) because it enrolls those who had been in employment-based programs (figure 3.2). Even after elders 75 and over were transferred to the new programs specifically established for this age group in 2008, the CHI has continued to have higher proportions of those aged 55 and over.

Second the occupation composition has changed: those working in agriculture, forestry, and fisheries accounted for more than 40 percent of enrollees in 1963, but only 3 percent in 2010 (figure 3.3). In contrast, the share of retired and nonworkers increased from 12 percent to 40 percent, even after the 2008

Figure 3.2 Age Distributions of Enrollees in CHI and SMHI, 1970 and 2010

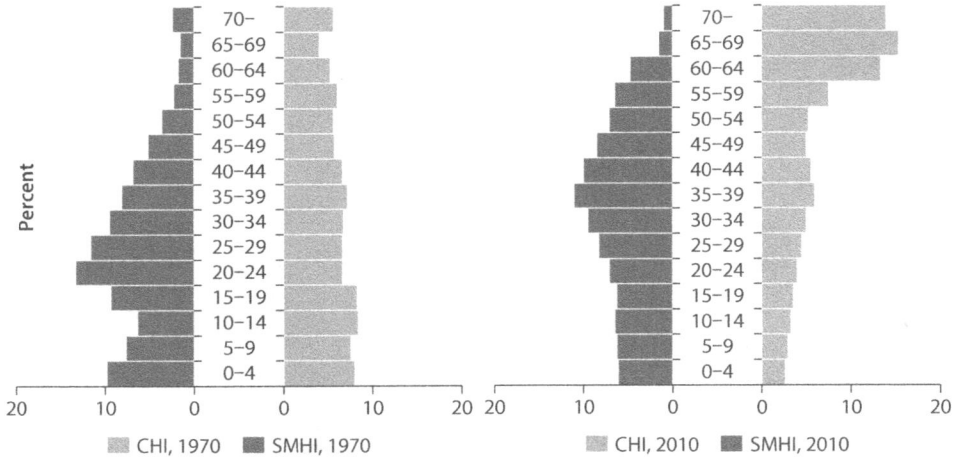

CHI, 1970   SMHI, 1970   CHI, 2010   SMHI, 2010

Source: National Institute of Population and Social Security Research.
Note: CHI = Citizens' Health Insurance; SMHI = Society-Managed Health Insurance.

Figure 3.3 Occupation Distribution of CHI Enrollees

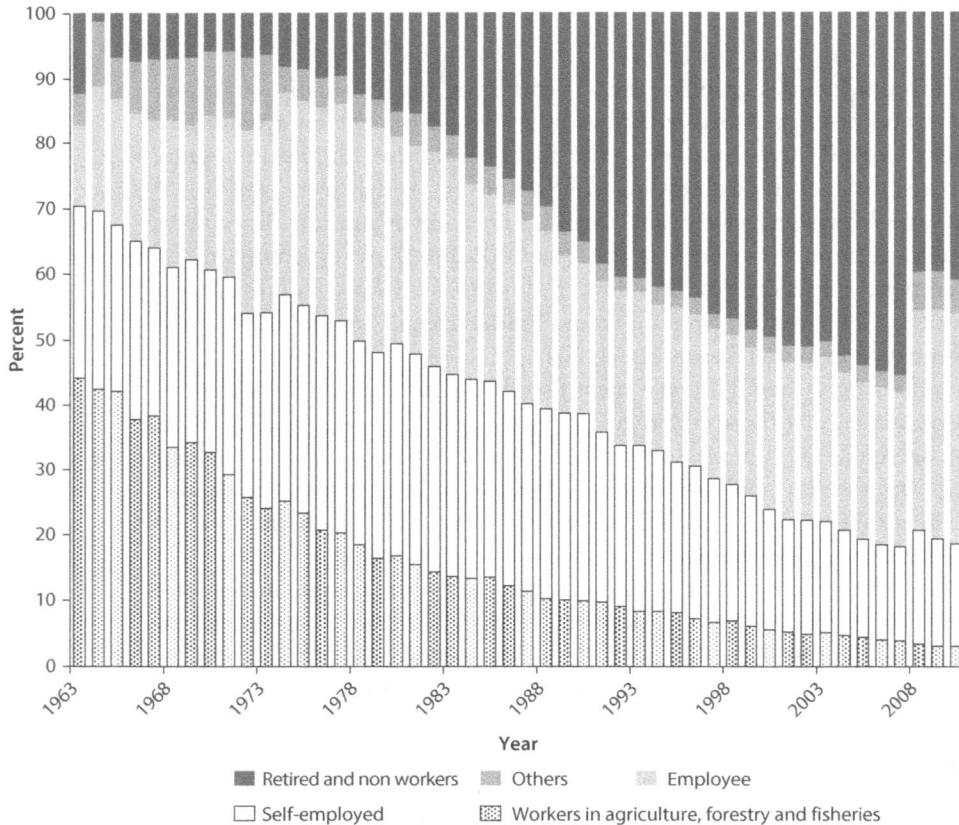

Retired and non workers   Others   Employee

Self-employed   Workers in agriculture, forestry and fisheries

Source: MHLW (1963–2010 Annual Surveys).
Note: There is discontinuity between 2007 and 2008 because of the introduction of the programs for those aged 75 and over.

move for those aged over 75. Aging and the increase in the proportion of retirees in society have had a compounding fiscal effect because health expenditures have increased as revenues fell, because pension income is subject to lower premium contribution rates.

Finally, the proportion of employees working fewer than 30 hours a week and not enrolled in an employment-based plan (who tend to have lower incomes) has risen.

The national government has increased allocations from its general expenditure budget to the CHI, elders, and the NHIA, from 2 percent in 1960 to 9 percent in 2010 (figure 3.4). This increase matches the increase in total expenditures: as a share of health expenditures, it was around one-fourth in both 1965 (24.9 percent) and 2010 (25.9 percent). This proportion rose to a peak of 30.6 percent in 1983, but subsequently declined because the government gradually introduced contributions (transfer payments) from all SHI programs to a pooled national fund to pay for the costs of all elders, 70 and over (see chapter 2).[9]

Figure 3.4 Subsidies from the National Government to SHI

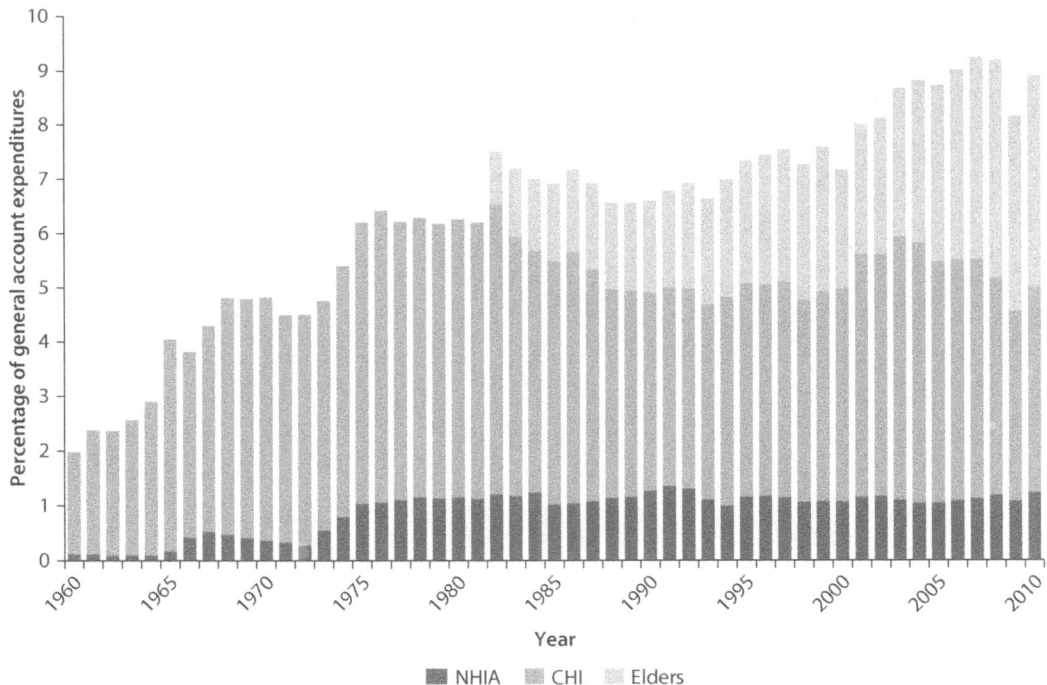

Source: Data for elders from Ministry of Finance (1983–2010 Surveys); data for CHI and NHIA from National Institute of Population and Social Security Research.
Note: The subsidies from the national government to the SMHI paying some of the administrative costs are negligible and are therefore excluded. CHI = Citizens' Health Insurance; NHIA = National Health Insurance Association.

Changes in the Fiscal State of CHI

Of the total CHI revenue for all its programs in 2010, 26 percent was financed by the national government, 25 percent by premiums from enrollees, 24 percent by employment-based programs (to finance health expenditures of elders 65–74 who are disproportionally enrolled in the CHI), 8 percent by municipal governments, 4 percent by prefectural governments,[10] and 14 percent by others.

The proportion of revenue from premiums initially decreased from 36.9 percent in 1965 but increased from 32 percent in 1974 to 41 percent in 1991. After then it continuously declined because of the increase in the transfers to pay for elders' expenditures (figure 3.5). The other changes that have occurred are as follows: first, subsidies from the national government have fallen from about one half to one quarter; second, this fall has been more than compensated for by increases in transfers from the employment-based programs to pay for the costs of elders (the proportion dropped to 26 percent in 2008 because programs for all elders 75 and over were implemented that year); third, the erosion of the fiscal position has forced municipal governments to increase funding from their general revenue budget.

Figure 3.5 Trends in the Composition of CHI Revenue

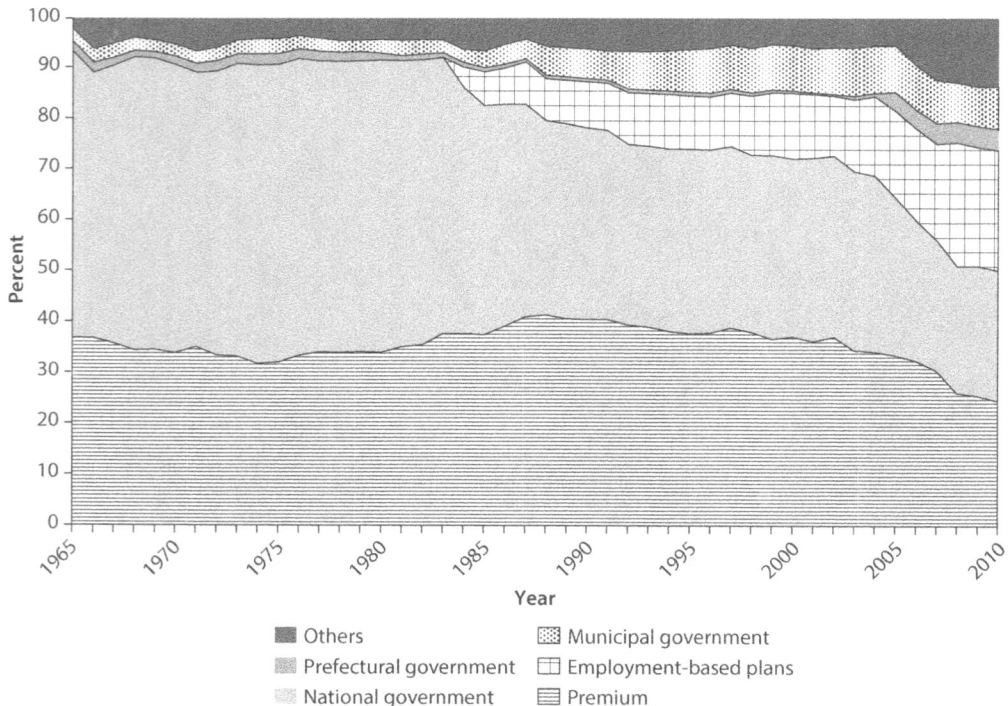

Legend:
- Others
- Prefectural government
- National government
- Municipal government
- Employment-based plans
- Premium

Source: National Institute of Population and Social Security Research.
Note: There is discontinuity between 2007 and 2008 because of the introduction of the programs for those aged 75 and over in 2008.

Figure 3.6 CHI Premium Rates, Taxable Income per Enrollee, and Benefit Expenditures

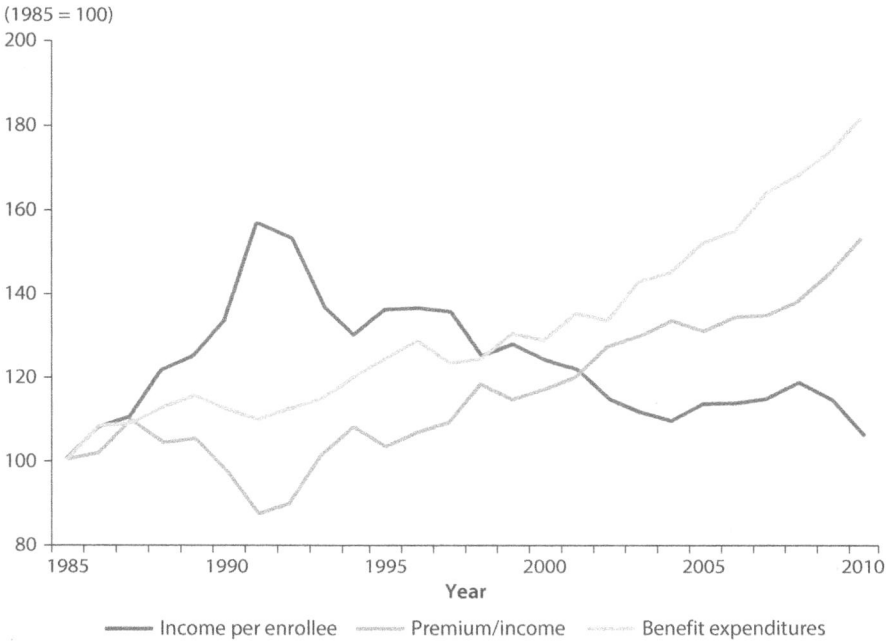

(1985 = 100)

Legend: Income per enrollee — Premium/income — Benefit expenditures

Source: Income per enrollee, premium, and benefit expenditures from MHLW (1985–2010 *Annual Surveys*); consumer price index data from Ministry of Internal Affairs and Communication (MIC).
Note: All variables are standardized as 100 in 1985. Health care benefit and taxable income are deflated by the consumer price index. There is discontinuity between 2007 and 2008 because of the introduction of the programs for those aged 75 and over in 2008.

However, although the share of CHI revenue financed by premiums has declined, because benefit expenditures increased much more than enrollees' incomes the proportion of income raised as premiums has risen (figure 3.6). Income fell from a peak of ¥1.2 million in 1991 to ¥0.8 million in 2010, while the proportion of premium to income climbed from 5.6 percent to 10.0 percent.[11]

Effects of Fiscal Transfers to Reduce Disparities in CHI Premium Rates

We examined the effect of fiscal transfers in reducing disparities due to income levels among the CHI programs by breaking down the revenue from premiums in each CHI plan using the following equation:

Revenue from Premiums = Expenditures − Transfers and Subsidies
= Health Care Expenditures + Transfer to Other Plans
+ Reinsurance Program (Contributions − Benefits)
− Matching Grant − Ordinary Adjustment Subsidy − Prefectural Adjustment Subsidy − Transfers from Municipal General Account
− Other Transfers and Subsidies

In each CHI plan, the revenue from premiums must equal its expenditures minus the transfers and subsidies it receives. The equation breaks down expenditures into Health Care Expenditures, Transfer to Other Plans (the pooling fund to pay for the costs of elders 75 and over) and the net costs (premium contributions minus the benefit amount received) of the Reinsurance Program.[12] Additional revenue is broken down into that coming from the national government in the form of the Matching Grant (*Ryoyou Kyufuhi Futankin*) and the Ordinary Adjustment Subsidy (*Futsuu Chousei Koufukin*), from the prefectural government in the form of the Prefectural Adjustment Subsidy (*Todoufuken Chousei Koufukin*), transfer payment from employment-based programs for the health expenditures of elders 65–74, Transfers from the Municipal General Account (*Ippan Kaikei Kuriire*), and Other Transfers and Subsidies.

Of these elements, the Matching Grant and the Prefectural Adjustment Subsidy are made on a matching fund basis.[13] Thus, only the Ordinary Adjustment Subsidy is focused on narrowing disparities in premium rates and its proportion ranges from zero to a maximum of 32.0 percent of benefit expenditures. This subsidy is based on the gap between Standard Demand, which generally corresponds to health care expenditures, and Standard Revenue, which generally corresponds to premium revenues. However, the latter has greater weight, so that CHI programs not receiving this subsidy are restricted to those having relatively high average incomes.

Table 3.1 shows how the variations in premium rates have been reduced, through calculating the coefficient of variation (CV) before and after each fiscal transfer. The CV of total expenditures is computed; then, the transfers to CHI programs are subtracted one by one, and the same procedure repeated, revealing that the transfers have reduced the CV from 0.38 to 0.22. The most effective transfers are the Ordinary Adjustment Subsidy, followed by the Reinsurance Program.

Table 3.1 Variation in Premium Rates Among CHI Programs before and after Adjustment

	CV	△ CV
Total expenditure	0.38	n.a.
Matching grant	0.39	0.01
Ordinary Adjustment Subsidy	0.33	△ **0.06**
Prefectural Adjustment Subsidy	0.33	0.00
Reinsurance program	0.28	△ **0.05**
Transfers from municipal government	0.26	△ **0.02**
Total Premiums	0.22	n.a.

Source: World Bank based on data from All-Japan Federation of National Health Insurance Organizations 2011.
Note: CVs are calculated using data from all CHI insurers. All variables are divided by average income. CV = coefficient of variation. n.a. = not applicable.

Fiscal Disparities among CHI Programs

To illustrate the extent of disparities in premium rates, we calculated the model premium rates of representative households in all the CHI programs in 2010 using the method set by each municipality.[14] Because premium rates differ by the number of enrollees in each household, we standardized that number to two: the head and the spouse. Because public pension income is substantially exempt when calculating premiums, we differentiated by the age of the household head: one of working age and the other elderly. Premium amounts were then calculated for the six annual income levels, from ¥2 million to ¥14 million.

As table 3.2 shows, there are three- to fourfold differences between the minimum and maximum premium rates for both nonelders' and elders' households across all income levels except for the highest. The median premium rate is much higher among nonelders' households than elders' households—with annual income of ¥2 million, for example, 10.9 percent vs. 6.1 percent—because pension income is largely exempted. By income, the premium rate is generally lower in households with higher incomes because there is a ceiling in which CHI premiums can be levied: at the 75th percentile, the premium rate in nonelders' households with an income of ¥7 million is 9.0 percent, but only 4.5 percent in those with an income of ¥14 million. Thus, the structure is regressive.

Table 3.2 Range of Premium Rates of Nonelders' and Elders' Households across CHI Programs, 2010

percent

Annual income	Min	p10	p25	Median	p75	p90	Max
				Non-elders' households			
¥2 million	4.6	8.5	9.8	10.9	12.3	13.4	18.6
¥3 million	4.2	7.6	8.9	10.0	11.4	12.5	17.7
¥5 million	3.8	6.8	8.0	9.3	10.5	11.5	12.8
¥7 million	3.6	6.5	7.4	8.4	9.0	9.0	9.0
¥14 million	2.9	4.2	4.5	4.5	4.5	4.5	4.5
				Elders' households			
¥2 million	2.7	4.6	5.4	6.1	6.7	7.2	9.2
¥3 million	2.9	5.3	6.0	6.8	7.6	8.3	11.3
¥5 million	3.1	5.6	6.6	7.5	8.5	9.4	12.6
¥7 million	3.0	5.5	6.3	7.3	8.1	8.8	9.0
¥14 million	2.9	4.2	4.5	4.5	4.5	4.5	4.5

Source: All-Japan Federation of National Health Insurance Organizations 2011.
Note: p10, p25, p75, and p90 denote percentiles in annual incomes. All calculations are based on the method set by the rules in 2010. In elders' households, the head is 65 or older, and receiving a public pension.

Figure 3.7 Health Care Expenditures Index and Premium Rates, and Average Income and Premium Rates, in Municipalities, 2010

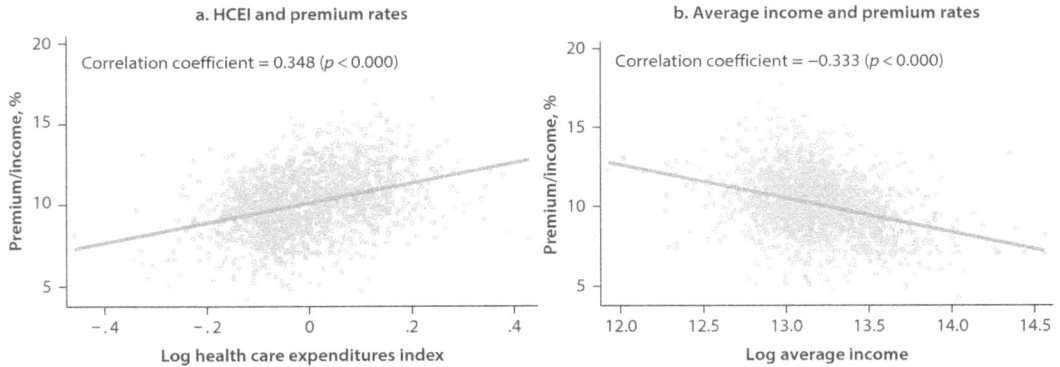

a. HCEI and premium rates

Correlation coefficient = 0.348 (p < 0.000)

b. Average income and premium rates

Correlation coefficient = −0.333 (p < 0.000)

Source: Health care expenditures index and average income from MHLW (2010); premium data from All-Japan Federation of National Health Insurance Organizations 2011.
Note: Amounts and rates are for nonelders' households with annual income of ¥3 million.

What are the determinants of premium rates in CHI programs across munici-palities? Figure 3.7 shows the distribution among municipalities for nonelders' households having an income of ¥3 million. The relationship between the pre-mium rates of nonelders' households and the age-standardized health care expenditures (health care expenditures index)[15] is significantly positive (0.348), that is, the insurance principle is being applied. However, the relationship of the former to average income is significantly negative (−0.333), even after health expenditures have been controlled for age. This confirms that the current mea-sures to reduce fiscal disparities among CHI programs are insufficient. We obtained the same results for nonelders' households at different incomes.

Fiscal Disparities within SMHI Programs

Although the SMHI and the Mutual Aid Association have the most secure source of funding, their fiscal position has eroded due to the transfer payment they must make for insurance programs for elders 75 and over and to the pooling fund for elders 65–74. Together, the transfer payments to these two programs make up nearly half (46 percent) of SMHI's expenditures in 2013 (National Federation of the Health Insurance Societies 2013). There are also disparities among the SMHI programs: in benefits, some programs provide supplementary (nonstatutory) benefits (*fuka kyufu*) in the form of health promotion and preven-tion programs and the partial reimbursement of the copayment. In addition, although the minimum proportion of the premiums paid by employers is legally set at 50 percent or more, most programs contribute more than that. However, the greatest inequity is in the differences in the premium rates. Here, we focus on 1960–2005 due to data limitations.[16]

The growth of health expenditures stemming from raised prices, population aging, and technological progress led over the period to increases in both the premium amount and rates (figure 3.8). The median premium per employee went up from ¥83,000 in 1960 to ¥404,000 in 2005.[17]

Premium amounts show a strong positive correlation (0.7 in 2005) with the per employee statutory benefit expenditures while the correlation with the supplementary benefit expenditures is relatively weak. And while the premium amounts per employee are strongly positively correlated with average wages of the insured in SMHI (0.6 in 2005), premium rates are negatively correlated with average wages (−0.4), suggesting that premiums in SMHI programs are levied regressively.

These relationships were relatively consistent from 1960 to the mid-2000s (figure 3.9). However, first, the correlations between the statutory benefit expenditures and both the premium amount and the premium rate fell somewhat from 1985 (probably due to the introduction of the program of elders in 1983, which required SMHI to transfer premium revenue to a nationally pooled fund for elders), and second, the negative correlation between the premium rates and income steadily rose, such that programs with enrollees on low incomes tend to have increasingly higher premium rates.

Figure 3.8 Trends in Premium Amount per Employee and Premium Rates in SMHI Programs

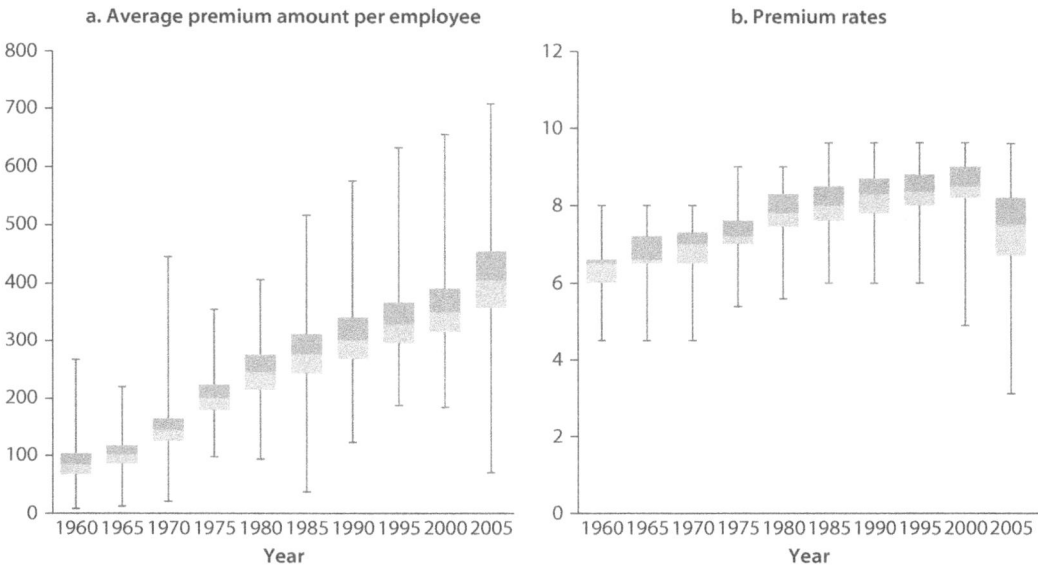

Source: Average premium amount per employee and premium rates from the National Federation of the Health Insurance Societies (1960–2005 Surveys); consumer price index data from MIC.
Note: The tops of whiskers are maximum values and the bottoms minimum values. The tops of boxes are 75th percentiles, the middle line medians, and the bottoms 25th percentiles. The vertical axis of left panel is premium per capita (¥1,000) including employer's premiums deflated by the consumer price index (FY2010 = 100). Premiums per employee are computed as the ratio of revenues from premiums to the number of the employee (dependents covered are excluded). The vertical axis of the right panel is the premium rate including the premiums paid by employers. Because the basis for calculating premiums was changed in 2003 from monthly to annual income, data for 2000 and 2005 are not comparable.

Figure 3.9 Trends in Correlations of Premium Amount per Employee and Premium Rates with Statutory and Supplementary Benefit Expenditures and Average Wage

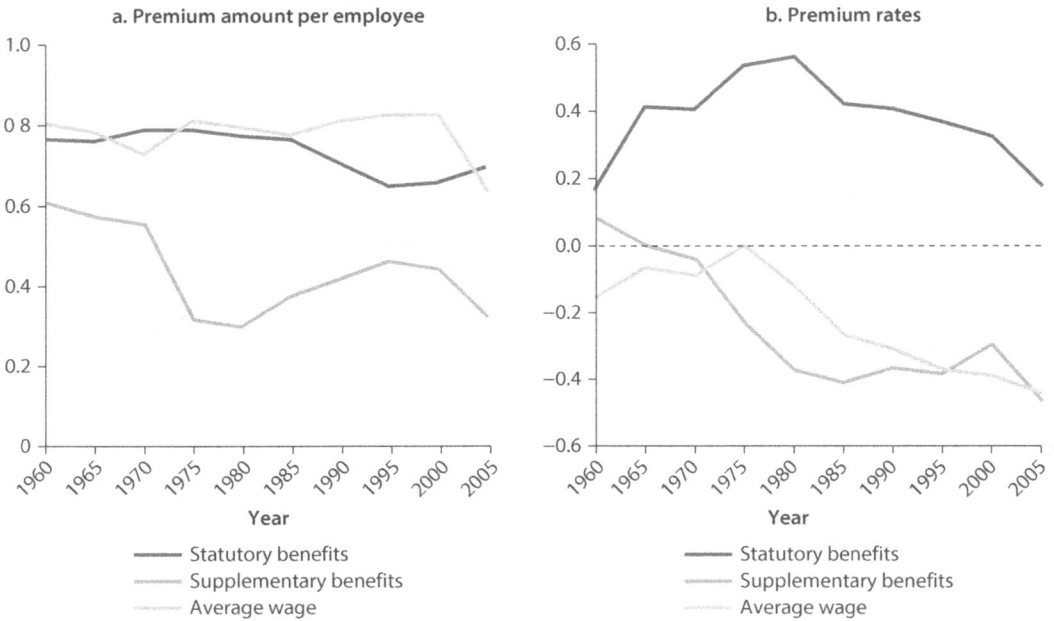

Source: National Federation of Health Insurance Societies (1960–2005 Surveys).
Note: The vertical axis marks correlation coefficients between variables selected and the premium amount per employee and the premium rates. Statutory benefits and supplementary benefits are converted to a per employee basis, excluding dependents. Because the basis for calculating premiums was changed in 2003 from monthly to annual income, data for 2000 and 2005 are not comparable.

Insights

Although SHI developed based on the principle of solidarity, this was limited to those enrolled in the same plan and is why both management and labor have bitterly complained about the transfer payments they have been forced to make from the employment-based programs. However, the national government had to rely on their contributions because, with the rapid aging of the population, it could not continue to afford funding the fiscal disparity between the employment- and residence-based programs from its general expenditure account. More radical solutions have not yet been implemented because any mergers would raise the premium rate of those programs with lower rates. Moreover, there is a logistical hurdle among the CHI programs because the method of calculating the premium amount varies by municipality. There are even greater obstacles in merging employment- and residence-based programs because of the fundamental differences in calculating premiums.

National government subsidies are needed to mitigate disparities in income among programs for the formal and informal sectors, and the above evidence shows that these subsidies are likely to increase, both because aging may progress more rapidly in rural than urban communities (due to migration of workers) and because the numbers of those irregularly employed are likely to increase (with the expansion of service industries). Yet, forcing programs that are better financially positioned to contribute more will face resistance.

In hindsight, a better solution would have been to develop a long-term goal of eventually merging the SHI programs so that the basis of solidarity could be broadened from just the plan's enrollees. As a start, the method of levying premiums would have to be standardized, which would require a national definition of "an equitable contribution."

In order to avoid problems akin to those Japan is facing, such as redistributing equitably across different programs and constituencies, countries that have, or are about to implement, SHI should aim to achieve equity not only in population, benefit, and cost coverage but also in the premium rate. Whether these rates should be uniform nationally or differ regionally would depend on the situation in each country. The advantage of the latter is that rates would reflect the region's health expenditures, so that more focused efforts could be made to develop facilities to improve access.

Notes

1. We did not focus on the NHIA because the prefectural level differences have only been gradually introduced from 2006. The differences in the programs for those 75 and over are also minor and only at the prefectural level. It was difficult to analyze contributions and expenditures for Mutual Aid Association programs because accounting is linked to pension benefits.

2. The benefit package in Japan covers in-hospital treatment at private hospitals and clinics, pharmaceuticals, and dental treatment. Balance billing is not allowed and extra billing is limited to extra room charges and new technology being evaluated in approved hospitals. While some programs provide additional nonstatutory benefits in health promotion and so forth, they do not serve to segment enrollees because there is no choice of plan.

3. SHI programs perform secondary audit of the claims and may deny payment. Nevertheless, clearinghouses had been criticized for not allowing direct exchanges between SHI programs and providers. Regulations were revised in 2002, allowing SHI programs to bypass them and directly reimburse providers. In 2008, the insurance programs of Toyota and NEC opted to do so.

4. These variations are a legacy of the voluntary development of residence-based programs. Each municipality designed its own method of levying premiums based on its notion of fairness. The income on which the calculation is made is that of the previous year, reflecting the fact that farmers would not know how much they have earned until after the harvest.

5. In fact, SMHI programs do receive a very small subsidy amounting to less than 0.1 percent of their expenditures for their administrative costs, which dates back to the implementation of SHI in 1927.

6. Benefit expenditures (*Kyufuhi*) is a term used in Japan to denote expenditures for the statutory benefits in the SHI. They exclude transfer payments to pay for the costs of elders, nonstatutory benefits such as screening, administrative costs, and so forth. They also exclude the copayment paid by patients.

Universal Health Coverage for Inclusive and Sustainable Development
http://dx.doi.org/10.1596/978-1-4648-0408-3

7. Premiums are levied in a way similar to the CHI, but on an individual, not household, basis.

8. The proportion of premium revenue in arrears has fluctuated from 3.53 percent in 1973 to 11.99 percent in 2009, and was 10.61 percent in 2011. The recent drop is probably due to a lowering of the rules to qualify for a decrease in the per capita portion of premiums. The proportion in arrears is financed by raising the premium rate of those contributing. These percentages tend to be higher in big cities than in towns and villages.

9. Expenditures for elders had surged after the introduction of "free" (no copayment) medical care in 1973.

10. The increase in the share of prefectural government from 2005 is part of a general transfer of responsibility from the national to prefectural governments. The latter can set the formula for allocating their prefectural adjustment subsidies to municipalities. However, as of 2011, 36 prefectures have continued to allocate the same share of benefit expenditures to all municipalities, and only 11 made adjustments to reflect the fiscal state in each municipality.

11. "Others" made up 13.5 percent of the revenue in 2010, of which 81 percent came from the benefits paid by the Reinsurance Program. This program is organized at prefectural level and is funded by CHI programs to pay for expenditures above ¥300,000. The CHI programs contribute half based on the number of enrollees and half based on their past health expenditures. The premiums paid would appear in expenditures so that if the denominator were actual net revenue, the proportions would be about 10 percent less.

12. Since this is financed by CHI, it does not appear in figure 3.5 because contributions would equal expenditures at the aggregate level.

13. Disasters are separately funded by Special Adjustment Subsidies (*Tokubetsu Chousei Koufukin*).

14. In municipalities that use property tax in calculating the premium amount, we assumed that all households pay the municipal average. The proportion derived from property is less than 10 percent of the total.

15. This index is released by the MHLW. Using it, we can compare health care expenditures by municipalities, excluding the difference in age structures.

16. Since the disparity in premium rates has apparently not changed in recent years, the findings in this section are probably still valid. The results are published two years after data collection.

17. The decrease in the premium rate from 2000 to 2005 is because the basis for levying premiums was changed in 2003 from monthly to annual earnings. Earlier a flat rate, referred to as "special premiums," was levied on bonuses.

Bibliography

All-Japan Federation of National Health Insurance Organizations. 2011. "Report on National Health Insurance (*Kokumin Kenkou Hoken no Jittai*) 2010." Tokyo.

Ikegami, N., B. K. Yoo, H. Hashimoto, M. Matsumoto, H. Ogata, A. Babazono, R. Watanabe, K. Shibuya, B.-M. Yang, M. R. Reich, and Y. Kobayashi. 2011. "Japanese Universal Health Coverage: Evolution, Achievements, and Challenges." *Lancet* 378 (9797): 1106–15.

Ministry of Finance. "Monthly Report on Financial Statistics (*Zaisei Kinyuu Toukei Geppou*) (1960–2010 Surveys)." http://www.mof.go.jp/pri/publication/zaikin_geppo/hyou03.htm (accessed October 23, 2013).

MHLW (Ministry of Health, Labour and Welfare). "Annual Survey on the National Health Insurance (*Kokumin Kenkou Hoken Jittai Chyousa*) (1963–2010 Surveys)." Tokyo.

———. "Geographic Disparities of Health Care Expenditure (*Iryouhi no Chiikisa*) 2010." http://www.mhlw.go.jp/topics/bukyoku/hoken/iryomap/ (accessed October 23, 2013).

MIC (Ministry of Internal Affairs and Communication). "Consumer Price Index." http://www.stat.go.jp/data/cpi/ (accessed October 23, 2013).

National Federation of Health Insurance Societies. "Reports on Society-Managed Health Insurances (*Kenkou Hoken Kumiai Jigyou Nenpou*) (1960–2005 Surveys)." Tokyo.

———. "Report on the Budget of Society-Managed Health Insurances 2013." Press release based on interim data. http://www.kenporen.com/include/press/2013/2013042202.pdf (accessed October 23, 2013).

National Institute of Population and Social Security Research. "Japanese Social Security Statistics." http://www.ipss.go.jp/ssj-db/e/ssj-db-top-e.asp (accessed October 23, 2013).

CHAPTER 4

Japan's Long-Term Care Insurance Program as a Model for Middle-Income Nations

John Creighton Campbell

Abstract

The number of frail older people in middle-income nations is relatively low compared with that in advanced nations, and so may not be recognized as a high-priority problem. Japan's early experience with long-term care offers cautionary lessons on how failing to confront the issue preemptively can allow makeshift and expensive practices to take root. Its Long-Term Care Insurance (LTCI) Program, which started in 2000, offers suggestions on how effective programs can be structured. The main argument of this chapter is that adoption of explicit long-term care programs is worth considering at any level of development.

Objective and Context

The objective of this chapter is to point up aspects of Japan's experience with long-term care policy that are distinctive and that are potentially relevant to middle-income countries.

In the past 20 years or so, most high-income nations have initiated or substantially reorganized programs for long-term care of frail older people.[1] All were responding to the same three trends that seem to be inherent to higher levels of economic development:

- *Population aging*: with improved health, the number of older people increases; with declining birthrates, their share in the population rises even more. The majority of older people are relatively healthy but a substantial minority need assistance to maintain a decent life.
- *Erosion of family support*: the number of potential family caregivers decreases as women are less willing to devote themselves to taking care of elders when they have more opportunities to work and when traditional attitudes about family responsibilities weaken.

- *Pressure on the health care and other systems*: the cost of hospitalizing older people without acute medical needs, and dealing with health problems exacerbated by inadequate care, increasingly strain health care finances and facilities. Social welfare and housing programs also have trouble dealing with frail older people.

Many middle-income nations are seeing similar trends, not so prominently so far but with a possibility of acceleration even beyond the pace of high-income countries.

Japan is the oldest country in the world and has been trying to deal with the problem of caring for frail older people nationally since 1962. In 2000, it launched its distinctive program of mandatory, social LTCI. It was aimed at the "socialization of care," with the government taking on a portion of the responsibility for caring for frail older people. The program has several goals:

- Improving the lives of older people with disabilities
- Easing the burdens of family caregivers
- Relieving strains on the health care system
- Establishing an efficient system to manage a growing social problem.

These goals have generally been met in the 14 years that LTCI has been operating, though of course problems remain. The program is now accepted as a necessary and popular component of Japan's social policy.

Current System Operations

Japan's LTCI system (*Kaigo Hoken*) is a social insurance–based system, although half its revenue comes from taxes. Everyone aged 40 and over pays premiums and everyone aged 65 and over (or 40 and over for "aging-related" disabilities) is eligible for benefits. Applicants are assessed by an objective questionnaire mainly measuring "activities of daily living" (a common list is bathing, dressing, toilet use, transferring in and out of bed or chair, urine and bowel continence, and eating); about 95 percent pass and are sorted into seven categories of need.[2] They receive institutional care or home- and community-based services, with no cash allowances. The value of the services they are entitled to use ranges from about US$500 to over US$3,000 a month. Many recipients use much less than their entitlement, partly because there is a copayment of 10 percent for nearly all services. Recipients can choose what services they want, how much, and from which provider, and they get advice and management support from a trained care manager. The client may change care managers and providers at will, which is an important mechanism for quality control.

In home- and community-based services, for-profit providers compete with nonprofits on an equal basis, getting the same fees for the same services. The insurers are municipal governments, which oversee services and manage finances under strict guidelines from the Ministry of Health, Labour and Welfare (MHLW).

Two Issues: High Expectations and Cost

Two problematic aspects of Japan's long-term care system stand out. First, family ideology (whether or not due to a Confucian heritage) is often seen as so strong in Japan that families are reluctant to put their aging parents into an institution—but the reality is that the opposite is the case. Of Japan's elderly (65 and over) population, 4.7 percent live in publicly supported institutions, a higher proportion than in many developed nations.[3] The reason is historical and political: in the early 1970s, the Japanese government responded to criticism from the political opposition (and its own worries about the next election) by making medical care essentially "free" for people aged 70 and over, by reducing their copayment from 30 or 50 percent to zero. The result over several years was a flood of older people into hospitals, many newly built to meet this demand. The problem of these "social admissions" into hospitals, with little or no medical justification, has plagued governments ever since. Moreover, because room and board costs in hospitals and nursing homes alike were covered, the out-of-pocket burdens for institutional care were quite low until recently. The public came to see 24-hour institutional care as attractive and normal, a perception that once ingrained, is hard to remove.

The second issue—also stemming from history and politics—is that Japan's public spending on long-term care for older people is relatively costly, at 1.4 percent of gross domestic product (GDP) at least, compared with 0.9 percent in Germany (the best comparison because it has the most similar LTCI system).[4] The story here, again as a response to electoral pressures, is that in 1989 the government announced a "Ten Year Strategy for Health and Welfare of the Elderly," called the "Gold Plan" for short. It promised a doubling or tripling of programs for frail older people, all administered by local governments and paid for from tax revenues. The Gold Plan was very popular but proved to be expensive and unwieldy; in particular there were no effective criteria for judging eligibility and need.

The initiation of LTCI in 2000 was partly aimed at imposing a more rational and efficient system for long-term care. However, because the government had already been providing generous benefits to people who sometimes had relatively light needs, it was politically impossible to backtrack on the earlier generosity. In contrast, when Germany had started its quite systematic program in 1995, it was providing rather low benefits to relatively few people, so it could start out with stricter eligibility rules and lower benefits (Campbell 2002).

High LTCI spending has become a significant political concern. Outlays rose rapidly in the early years, though since 2005 growth has been more moderate (figure 4.1). Still, by 2010, it had reached ¥7.3 trillion (over US$70 billion) and was seen as a serious fiscal problem. The government is discussing reforms in Japan's entire social security system, aimed at constraining spending despite population aging, and LTCI is on the agenda.

Figure 4.1 Total Government Spending on the LTCI Program

¥ trillion

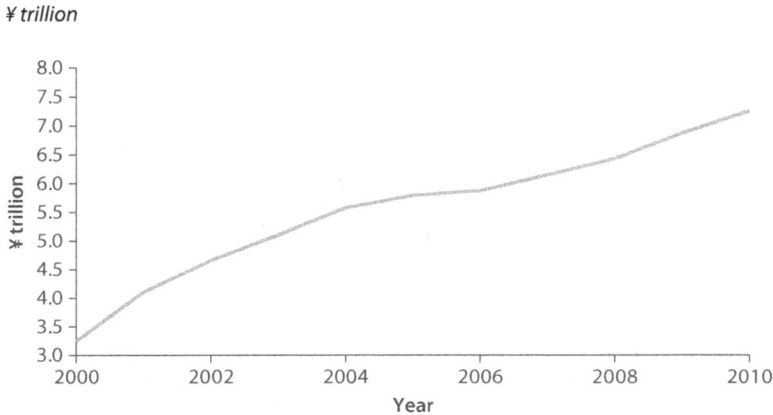

Source: MHLW 2011.

Figure 4.2 Per Capita Government Spending on the LTCI Program

¥1,000

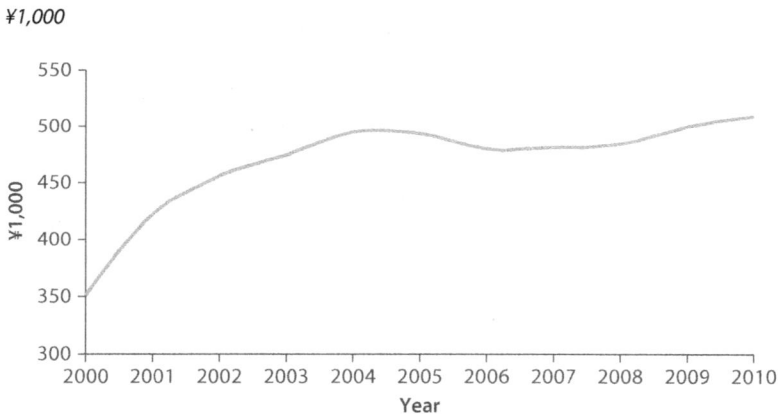

Source: MHLW 2011; Census of Japan.
Note: Divided by the population 75 years and over.

Two points should be noted: much of the increased spending was simply due to demographic change; and moderate reforms to control costs can be effective. Figure 4.2 shows public spending on long-term care per person aged 75 and over. The denominator includes all persons in the population over the age of 75, and not just the recipients of long-term care. Since this is the age group that uses nearly all the services, it is an important factor that influences the size of long-term care expenditures. The per capita expenditures rose by about 30 percent in the first five years of the program, but thanks in part to reforms in 2005–06 it leveled off for the next five years. The most important reforms were cuts to the number of institutional beds, particularly in hospitals, although restrictions on benefits for lighter-need recipients and other cost-cutting measures also played a role.

The issue is not just spending, though: many choices must be made when designing long-term care programs, as can be seen in the variety of provisions among the advanced nations. As well as strict vs. soft criteria for eligibility and minimal vs. generous benefits, the choices include (Ikegami and Campbell 2002) the following:

- Services-only vs. cash benefits
- Coverage for older people only vs. for younger disabled people as well
- Tax-based vs. social-insurance style financing and eligibility criteria
- Provision by for-profit companies vs. public or nonprofit agencies.

These four aspects of Japan's distinctive approach are now considered in more detail, as they may merit attention from nations considering long-term care programs.

Services, Not Cash

Unlike Germany, the United Kingdom, and many other countries, Japan provides only services, not "cash for care" allowances. The idea of cash for care rather than formal services in long-term care policy is attractive in some ways. It maximizes consumer choice. It rewards the efforts of family caregivers, and at the margin may encourage some families to provide more care. Case by case it can be less expensive than services: for example, Germany offers a choice of cash and services, and even though the value of the services is more or less double the cash allowance at the various levels of disability, most people take the cash.

Such positive points are outweighed by negative points, however, particularly for middle-income nations. Due to budget constraints, the cash amounts would have to be low, not enough to provide a decent income but perhaps enough to trap caregivers (mostly women) into a situation with few future prospects. And even if the amounts are relatively low, they would still be expensive for the government because many people would want it and would contrive to make a convincing application. Services (think of help in bathing and so on) are less attractive except when really needed, and demand is likely to be limited at least for several years in nations where traditional family caregiving is widely accepted as normal.

Of course, offering services requires the development of infrastructure, institutions like nursing homes on the one hand, and community-based services (home help, day care, "respite care" to give family caregivers a break, assistive devices) on the other. Nursing homes are expensive to build and operate, but because the government is likely to control capital expenditure, it can control the pace of expansion. Community care agencies do not require much new construction but they do need trained staff and good management, which need investment. However, they too can be developed gradually. A long-run benefit is that the training and work experience will raise the quality of the female work force. In short, the cash option may appear less expensive and easier to implement, but in the long run may not be as effective as Japan's services-only model.

Universal Health Coverage for Inclusive and Sustainable Development
http://dx.doi.org/10.1596/978-1-4648-0408-3

Older People Only, Not Disabled Younger People

Japan's long-term care system is exceptional among high-income nations in targeting only frail older people rather than including younger people with physical or mental disabilities. Including everyone who meets a given criterion of disability may seem fairer than an arbitrary age criterion. It is certainly a reasonable policy for a nation that relies on cash allowances for caregiving, since it is simple and fair just to give similar amounts for disabled people regardless of age. Also, very severely disabled younger people, who require 24-hour care, can be accommodated in nursing homes alongside older people, although it can lead to management problems (particularly for those with mental illness).

However, the needs of frail older people and disabled younger people are mostly quite different for home and community-based services. For all but the most severely disabled younger people, the goal is for them to participate in economic and social life as actively as possible. The key services are skill training and providing supportive environments for working and leading active social lives. For most older people, the goal is to help them lead a comfortable and satisfying life and to relieve burdens on their family caregivers. Home help and day care are the core services. If a services-only strategy is adopted, as in Japan, it is best to have separate programs for older and younger people.

Eligibility by Social Insurance Criteria, Not Case by Case

In many countries where long-term care services are paid from taxes, including the United Kingdom and Scandinavian nations, eligibility is determined by case workers employed (or contracted) by municipal governments. They evaluate the physical and mental condition of the potential clients, plus their income and assets, and the extent to which family care is available. The caseworker draws up a personalized care plan for services to be provided by the municipality, determining the amount of benefits to be offered within the constraints of the municipal budget. An advantage of this system is that it allows the benefits to be tailored flexibly to individual situations; moreover, if a means test for income or assets is included, public resources do not go to people who could afford care on their own.

Municipal case-by-case evaluations also present disadvantages. For this approach to work, each municipality needs trained officials in a well-organized bureaucracy that is trusted by residents to have high ethical standards. Even when that is true, differences in the financial situations among municipalities bring regional variations in eligibility criteria and benefit levels that may be seen as unfair, or even as a geographic lottery. There will also be variations among people in whether they are eligible or among the benefits they get; also, the chances of being accepted can be lower toward the end of the budget year if funds have been used up.

The alternative is to decide on eligibility and degree of disability through a national standardized instrument, associated with a social insurance approach (although it is possible with tax-based financing as well). The test usually measures how well applicants can perform the standard activities of daily living. Japan uses a 74-item questionnaire that is administered by a moderately trained public servant in a home visit of an hour or so. The numerical results are analyzed with a statistical algorithm to sort people into eight categories (independent; two grades of "needs support" at a relatively low level; and five grades of "needs care"). The computer's decision is reviewed by a local committee, which also looks at a brief report on the applicant's medical condition from the family physician, and may move the grade up or down one level.

Whatever process is adopted, it is essential that anyone who stands to gain, such as a family doctor or a potential service provider, be excluded from eligibility decisions. Establishing the legitimacy of the system in the eyes of the public is crucial.

Mixed Provision

One fundamental aspect of long-term care is having enough providers, whether nursing homes and other institutions or home care agencies. Ensuring quality requires a set of rules, licensing procedures, and an effective governance structure. A key issue is whether provision in a public long-term care system should be opened to for-profit companies, or restricted only to not-for-profit organizations.

Japan has always excluded for-profit companies from the institutional sector that provides 24-hour care, including accommodations for a set fee.[5] Over the years, nursing homes were built and operated by charitable organizations that were usually well connected to local governments, with public financial assistance for capital costs that was later phased out. Such close relationships can have both positive and negative implications for quality regulation. Under LTCI, in principle institutions compete for clients, but in reality, high demand plus government restrictions on building new facilities have brought waiting lists instead.

For home- and community-based services, many countries rely on public or contracted-out bodies to provide services, and recipients have little or no choice among them. In Japan, for-profit companies compete with established social service organizations and other not-for-profits. This approach, which started in 2000, was a big departure in Japanese social policy. The competition is limited—services are tightly defined, local governments license and oversee providers, and fees for each service are fixed nationally (corrected only for cost differences across municipalities). In particular, every three years the government reviews the program after analyzing providers' financial records and adjusts the fees for specific services up or down. But despite these constraints, competition is real because providers' income depends on attracting enough clients, and as fees are fixed, they can appeal only on the basis of "quality"—that is, reputation, convenience, and performance from the recipients' perspective.

Of course, competition is most intense in urban areas where the market is big enough to be attractive. In the countryside, there are likely to be only two or three agencies competing to deliver the most popular services, home help and day care, and perhaps just one for services with fewer users like rehabilitation. Nonetheless, with few exceptions all the listed services are available everywhere in Japan. In areas where for-profit companies or new-style nonprofit organizations like cooperatives have not been attracted, nonprofit agencies that had been active from well before LTCI was enacted are the main providers. Mostly, these are of two types: hospitals, public or private, which have the experience and resources to set up long-term care agencies easily, and Social Welfare Councils in every municipality, which are closely tied to local officials and for many years dominated any social services not directly provided by government.

Compared with a monolithic public system, the great variety of providers in Japan has allowed flexibility, avoided straining government managerial resources (the national government can analyze system performance and local governments oversee provision rather easily), and encouraged competition. Competition in turn brings efficiency, innovation, and quality control. Unlike simply subsidizing or encouraging private provision, the government can guide the program in the interests of national coverage, equity and fairness, high quality, and—particularly—efficiency. And as has long been evident in Japan's health care field, a strong public role is crucial for holding down expenditures.

Insights

Middle-income countries should consider early adoption of government policies to establish systematic long-term care programs before their number of frail older people or the decline in traditional support mechanisms has really taken hold. For example, Israel established the world's first LTCI system in 1988, when under 10 percent of its population was aged 65 and over, and it has succeeded in keeping costs down and the number in institutions very low (Asiskovitch 2013). The Republic of Korea established a system largely based on the Japanese model in 2008 when only 9.1 percent of its population was 65 or older; the costs have been quite moderate (Duk 2012). Japan's first effort at systematic long-term care policy came in 1989 with the Gold Plan; at that time, the 65 and over population was just 11.6 percent of the total. Because of earlier misguided policy on institutionalization and poor controls in the Gold Plan itself, spending was higher than it could have been.

These multicountry experiences suggest three general lessons for early consideration of systematic long-term care programs:

If a comprehensive system is established before there is much evolution of other solutions to the problem, serious difficulties can be headed off. One example of a serious difficulty is that, faced with doing something about more and more frail older people with inadequate family support, local governments or charities and other welfare groups (perhaps with government subsidies) will build a lot of nursing homes to house them. Worse still, more and more frail older people may enter hospitals, the most expensive form of care. Gerontologists agree that home- and community-based services to allow people to stay home are preferable to institutional care for all but the most serious cases. But if institutional care comes to be seen as normal by the public and if an increasing number of public or quasi-public nursing homes—orworse still, hospital owners—band together to protect their interests politically, it will be difficult to change course and adopt more rational programs.

Another case that is at present a worry in many nations is the importation of immigrants from less-developed nations to provide care, as is the case in Austria, Italy, Singapore, and so on. In most cases, these are untrained women, often with dubious immigration status, who live in the household to provide full-time care for a frail elder and cook and clean for the family as well. As their numbers grow, tricky problems emerge: quality of care, issues of fairness and exploitation, abuse on both sides, a stunting of the development of more professional long-term care, and demands for heavy and growing government subsidies of the practice. These problems are hard to deal with when a big constituency of families has a vested interest in the system. Some high-income nations have tried to regularize recruitment, training, and employment conditions of migrant caregivers, but without much success so far.

Japan is unusual in the extent to which it relies on trained careworkers employed by agencies in providing long-term care. An advantage of early establishment of a formal long-term care system in middle-income nations is that training and certification programs can be built up gradually as demand expands.

Initiating a Good Long-term Care System Is Good Politics and Good Economics

It might be thought that there would not be much pressure for long-term care programs in nations with few frail older people needing care. However, the problem of caring for them is not a worry only for government. Even at an early stage in population aging, it is acutely felt by more and more ordinary citizens who are concerned about what will happen to their parents and ultimately themselves—some combination of leading a miserable life and imposing great burdens on family members. Virtually, everyone would welcome any help that a new program would provide.

The earlier a long-term care system is started, the lower is the cost. When the number of qualifying older people is relatively low, and traditional family supports are still working fairly well, the demand for public programs will not be very high. Moreover, when no public services had previously been available, even modest benefits will be welcomed. The government can decide a decade or more later whether coverage or benefits should be upgraded.

Initiating a Good Long-term Care System Is Good Public Policy

Early adoption of long-term care makes sense from the government's point of view for three reasons:

- If care for frail older people—qualitatively different from other social problems—can be handled by a dedicated system, the health care system can focus on acute care and prevention, while other social programs can concentrate on pressing needs like poverty, urban housing, and helping young people to succeed.

- An early start allows a gradual learning curve for training staff and seeing what works.
- Good long-term care will lead to real savings in health care provision. Frail older people who get good day-to-day care are less likely to get sick, and particularly are less likely to relapse after being hospitalized. Long-term care is inherently less costly than medical care as it uses staff with lower wages and does not lead to open-ended benefits.

Most fundamentally, as the experience of high-income nations demonstrates, a well-designed long-term care system delivers good benefits at moderate cost—a key yardstick for all public policies.

Notes

1. Long-term care was defined by the Institute of Medicine in the United States (1986) as "a variety of ongoing health and social services provided for individuals who need assistance on a continuing basis because of physical or mental disability. Services can be provided in an institution, the home, or community, and include informal services provided by family or friends as well as formal services provided by professionals or agencies."

2. Independent older people can participate in services offered directly by local governments, including, exercise, recreation, and so forth. Services for frail older people and their caregivers that are not included within LTCI, such as meal delivery, alarms, transportation, counseling, and so forth are also provided directly by local governments.

3. "Institution" means facilities that take responsibility for 24-hour care of residents over a period of several months at least; it refers primarily to nursing homes, although hospitals, group homes, and other types can be included. See Rodrigues, Huber, and Lamura (2012). This figure includes older people in hospitals for three months or more.

4. Estimates from circa 2010, by Organisation for Economic Co-operation and Development (OECD) (Colombo et al. 2011). This is Japan's formal LTCI system; if spending from health insurance for long-term elderly residents of hospitals is included, the figure is 1.7 percent of GDP. Using a different measure, in 2005 public long-term care spending for each person 65 and over was about US$1,750 a year, compared with US$1,185 in Germany (Campbell, Ikegami, and Martin 2010).

5. Old-age housing projects with attached services are being developed rapidly; they are almost always on a for-profit basis with accommodation costs borne by residents and services provided through the public LTCI system.

Bibliography

Asiskovitch, Sharon. 2013. "The Long-Term Care Insurance Program in Israel: Solidarity with the Elderly in a Changing Society." *Israel Journal of Health Policy Research* 2 (3). http://www.ijhpr.org/content/2/1/3.

Campbell, John Creighton. 2002. "How Policies Differ: Long-Term-Care Insurance in Japan and Germany." In *Aging and Social Policy—A German-Japanese Comparison*, edited by Harald Conrad and Ralph Lutzeler, 157–87. Munich: Iudicium.

Campbell, John Creighton, Naoki Ikegami, and Mary Jo Martin. 2010. "Lessons from Public Long-Term Care Insurance in Germany and Japan." *Health Affairs* 39 (1): 87–95.

Colombo, Franceso, Ana Llena-Nozal, Jérôme Mercier, and Frits Tjadens. 2011. "Help Wanted? Providing and Paying for Long-Term Care." OECD Health Policy Studies, OECD Publishing. http://dx.doi.org/10.1787/9789264097759-en.

Duk, Sunwoo. 2012. "The Present Situation and Problems of the Long-term Care Insurance in South Korea: From Comparative Perspectives between South Korea and Japan." *Japanese Journal of Social Security Policy* 9 (1): 49–60. http://www.ipss.go.jp/webjad/WebJournal.files/SocialSecurity/2011/spring/Web%20Journal_Dr%20Sunwo.pdf.

Ikegami, Naoki, and John Creighton Campbell. 2002. "Choices, Policy Logics and Problems in the Design of Long-Term-Care Systems." *Journal of Social Policy and Administration* 36 (7): 719–34.

Institute of Medicine. 1986. *Improving the Quality of Nursing Homes*. Washington, DC: National Academy Press.

MHLW (Ministry of Health, Labour and Welfare). 2011. "Heisei 22 nen Kaigo Hoken Jigyou Joukyou Houkoku (Nenpou)." http://www.mhlw.go.jp/topics/kaigo/osirase/jigyo/10/index.html (accessed March 3, 2013).

Rodrigues, Ricardo, Manfred Huber, and Giovanni Lamura, eds. 2012. *Facts and Figures on Healthy Ageing and Long-term Care*. Vienna: European Centre for Social Welfare Policy and Research.

Tamiya, Nanako, Haruko Noguchi, Akihiro Nishi, Michael R Reich, Naoki Ikegami, Hideki Hashimoto, Kenji Shibuya, Ichiro Kawachi, and John Creighton Campbell. 2011. "Population Aging and Wellbeing: Lessons from Japan's Long-Term Care Insurance." *The Lancet* 378: 1183–92.

Tsutsui, T., and N. Muramatsu. 2007. "Japan's Universal Long-term Care System Reform of 2005: Containing Costs and Realising a Vision." *Journal of the American Geriatric Society* 55 (9): 1458–63.

CHAPTER 5

Controlling Health Expenditures by Revisions to the Fee Schedule in Japan

Naoki Ikegami

Abstract

Japan's health expenditures are relatively low for a high-income country with gener-ally excellent health indicators. One of the main reasons for this cost containment is the system of revising the fee schedule (shinryo houshu) every two years. The two-step approach of setting a "global" (or overall) revision rate and then fine-tuning item-by-item revisions and setting conditions of billing (seikyu youken) provides a unique model for containing costs under fee-for-service (FFS) payments. Small increases in medical services prices have been financed mainly by reducing pharmaceu-tical prices to reflect their volume-weighted market prices. Item-by-item revisions have prevented the full feed-thorough of increases in expenditures of items that have rapidly increased in volume and/or that can be delivered at lower cost by providers, maintain-ing an equitable balance of revenue and expenditures across types of hospitals, and have provided bonus incentives to physicians by listing new items, thereby helping to achieve policy goals. Aspects of Japan's fee schedule could serve as a model in countries or sectors within each country where the institutional capacity exists or could be devel-oped and where services are rapidly expanding and costs must be contained.

Objectives and Context

Despite its essentially FFS form of payment—an approach that often lifts health care costs—Japan's health expenditures are relatively low for a high-income country, at 9.6 percent of gross domestic product (GDP) in 2010 (OECD 2013). This ratio is impressive because it must be considered in light of Japan's stagnant economy of the past 20 years and the country's rapid aging to become the oldest in the world: those 65 and over made up 25 percent of the population in 2013 (MIC 2013). And cost containment seems not to have undermined quality: not only does Japan have excellent macro health indexes of life expectancy at birth, but its outcomes in acute inpatient treatment appear to be on a par with those in the United States (Hashimoto et al. 2011).

The key mechanism for containing expenditures is the fee schedule administered by the Ministry of Health, Labour and Welfare (MHLW). With over 4,000
medical services (physician and hospital) items and 130,000 pharmaceutical
products, it sets prices and the conditions of billing for medical services, pharmaceuticals, and devices for virtually all providers.[1] Adherence to the conditions is
monitored by a claims review process and on-site inspections. "Balance billing"
(charging more than the fees set in the fee schedule) is prohibited. "Extra billing"
(billing services and pharmaceuticals not listed in the fee schedule together with
those listed) is strictly restricted to items such as extra room charges and a few
new technologies still being evaluated for efficacy and safety.

Thus, the fee schedule determines the following:

- Over 95 percent of how physicians and hospitals earn their revenue
- The statutory benefits package of all permanent residents in Japan
- Over 95 percent of out-of-pocket (OOP) expenditures of all patients (OOP
  is effectively limited to the prescribed copayment rate).

In analyzing how the fee schedule is revised very two years, it is useful to see
the processes operating at two levels: first, *macro*—the health care sector as a
whole; and then *micro*—one item at a time, or multiple items in the same
category.

Macro: The Global Revision Rate

Process

The revision process starts with the Ministers of Finance and of the MHLW, with
top civil servants, deciding on the global rate of price increase or decrease of all
medical services and pharmaceuticals combined listed in the fee schedule—the
volume-weighted global revision rate. This rate is based on their evaluation of the
political and economic situation.[2] By setting this rate, and taking into account the
extent to which expenditures will increase due to nonprice factors (such as volume increases in, or greater use of, more expensive medical services and pharmaceuticals) from the past three years' data, they determine a de facto global budget. These decisions must be made at the top level because the national government's subsidies to the social health insurance account for about 10 percent of
the budget. At the same time, because these subsidies are a fixed one-quarter of
total health expenditures, budgetary control is exercised.[3]

Another key factor in this rate decision is the extent of reductions in pharmaceutical prices, which are primarily based on the MHLW's survey of the market
price of each product (which are generally lower than in the fee schedule
because of competition among sellers). These reductions are not based on the
government procuring and negotiating discounts on behalf of all providers, but
are set mainly according to actual sales prices that have been determined by
market competition. The MHLW conducts the Pharmaceutical Price Survey
(*Yakka Chousa*),[4] which looks at the price and volume of each product as listed

in wholesalers' books. Based on these data, the volume-weighted market price of each product is calculated. Then the pharmaceutical price revision rate is set by summing the volume-weighted differences between the amount based on the market price and the current fee schedule price of every product listed.

Next, within the budgetary limits set by the global rate and the funds made available by pharmaceutical price reductions, the revision rates of the medical services prices are set.[5]

Trends in Health Expenditures

The national medical expenditures (NME) include all medical expenditures in the benefit package of the social health insurance plans, government expenditures in medical care, and the copayments set by the government. They are the amount used for all decisions on revising the fee schedule.[6] Although the nominal NME nearly doubled over 1990–2011 (figure 5.1), the real increase was 5 percent less because of deflation. Pharmaceutical expenditures increased less than the NME, remaining stagnant in the 1990s. As we are focusing on the budget impact of the revision rates, we look more at nominal growth rates. Growth in the NME can be decomposed into two components: price and nonprice factors.

The *price factor* is determined by the biennial fee schedule revision. While the global rate does not necessarily have a one-to-one impact on the NME, the two

Figure 5.1 Trends in the Fee Schedule Revision Rates and Medical Expenditures, 1990–2010

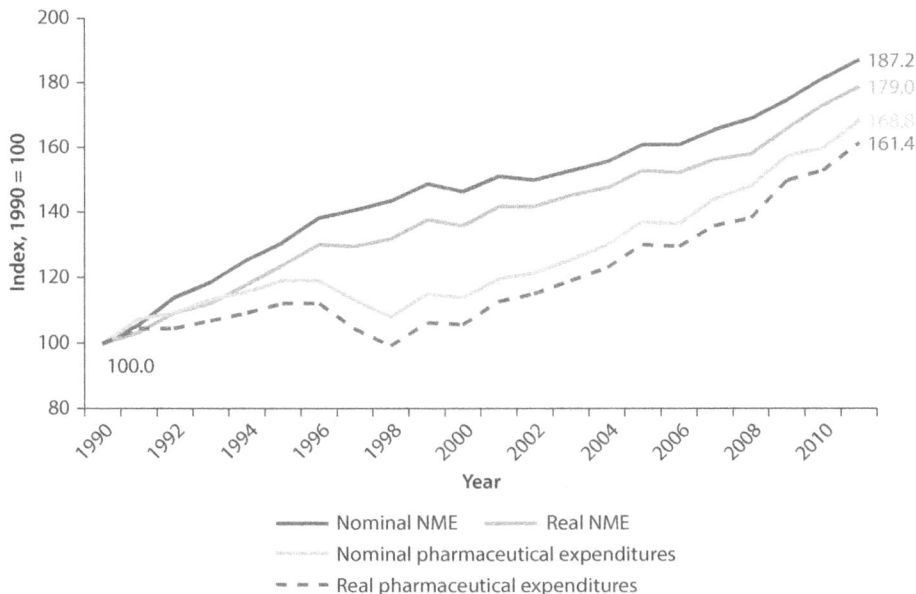

Sources: NME from MHLW 2013; pharmaceutical expenditures—estimated based on IMS JPM March MAT 2002–13 (Copyright 2014 IMS Health. All rights reserved); consumer price index data from Ministry of Internal Affairs and Communications.
Note: NME = national medical expenditure.

Universal Health Coverage for Inclusive and Sustainable Development
http://dx.doi.org/10.1596/978-1-4648-0408-3

Figure 5.2 Trends in the Fee Schedule Revision Rates and Medical Expenditures, 1990–2012

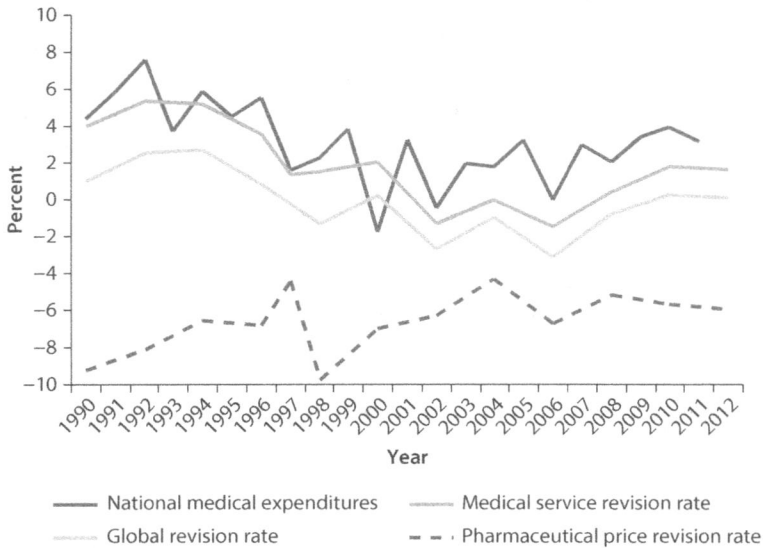

——— National medical expenditures   ——— Medical service revision rate
········· Global revision rate   — — · Pharmaceutical price revision rate

Source: MHLW 2013.

are closely related (figure 5.2). Between 1990 and 2013, the pharmaceutical price revision rates have been negative, in the range of -4 percent to -10 percent. In contrast, the only years in which the medical services rate decreased were 2002 and 2006.

The *nonprice factors* in the growth of the NME are increases in volume (largely reflecting demographic changes), and introduction and greater use of more expensive services—such as first computed tomography (CT), then magnetic resonance imaging (MRI) and later positron emission tomography (PET) scans—or new pharmaceuticals listed in the fee schedule. The impact of such nonprice factors is estimated at 2–3 percent a year over the past two decades (MHLW 2013), as it has been mitigated by the processes described in the next section. Beyond these supply-side controls, the effects of increases in volume have been suppressed on the demand side by raising the copayment rate. For employees, they were gradually raised from none in 1983 to the current 30 percent in 2003, but with provision for catastrophic coverage. Although the higher copayment has not over the long-term suppressed demand, it has mitigated increases in benefit expenditures.

Micro: Item-by-Item Revisions

Objectives and Processes

After the numbers for the overall revision rate and the average price revision rates for both medical services and pharmaceuticals are decided, item-by-item revisions of service prices and the conditions of billing are made within the budgetary limits set by the global rate and the additional funds made available through reductions in pharmaceutical prices.[7] These decisions are officially made by the Central Social Insurance Medical Council of the MHLW, but most of the negotiations are made between provider organizations and the ministry's civil servants (who are primarily physicians) because the details are very complex.

The revision rates of prices for pharmaceuticals and medical services are not applied across the board as conversion factors, as said, but on an item-by-item basis, the objectives differing between pharmaceuticals and medical services. For pharmaceuticals, prices are mainly revised to reflect the market price of each (explained later).

For services, price revisions are made to achieve the following policy objectives. First, to hold down expenditure increases by lowering prices in items which have shown rapid increases in volume and/or can be delivered at lower costs by providers. Second, to maintain appropriate and equitable margins in revenue and expenditures across the various types of hospitals. Third, to provide bonus incentives to physicians to achieve policy goals by listing new items or raising their prices.

If the revision does not achieve these objectives and there are unforeseen outcomes, they could be remedied in the next revision. Unlike an across-the-board conversion rate, which would affect all providers similarly (and with a reduction probably unite them), the item-by-item revision divides providers into those who gain and those who lose, which can facilitate the negotiation process for the government.

The budget impact of making a change to the price of each item in the NME on the global rate is calculated from the item's volume. Even small changes would have a big impact if the volume is large (such as repeat consultations), and vice versa (with complicated surgical procedures). The price changes would continue to be adjusted until their cumulative impact is made equal to the overall medical service revision rate.[8] The budget impact of a newly listed item would also be included in this process by adjusting its price and estimating its volume from expert opinion.

Importance of Conditions of Billing in Containing Costs

Setting and resetting the conditions of billing are equally important for containing costs because, by doing so, they restrict the provision of services and contain costs increasing due to nonprice factors. Conditions can be set, not only at the time of the revision, but also ad hoc by MHLW directives, if there are reports of inappropriate usage or in response to queries made by providers. For example, when PET scan was first listed, the conditions restricted its use to patients who had a confirmed diagnosis of cancer so that it could not be used for screening purposes.

Conditions of billing are also set, or revised, to ensure quality. For example, in order to bill for rehabilitation therapy, the hospital must have the required minimum number of therapists, physical facilities, and so forth (*shisetsu kijun*). These conditions (*shisetsu kijun*) on staffing and facilities, focusing on facility inputs and structure, have been the main mechanism for assuring quality in Japan, given the paucity of data on processes and outcomes.

Universal Health Coverage for Inclusive and Sustainable Development
http://dx.doi.org/10.1596/978-1-4648-0408-3

To monitor adherence to these conditions and directives, claims are sent to the prefectural clearinghouse where they are electronically screened and then audited by a peer review committee.[9] In addition, on-site inspections are periodically carried out to validate a random sample of claims with the patient's medical records.[10] If the documentation is found to be insufficient, providers must retrospectively pay back the cumulative amount of the items that they had billed inappropriately in say the last 6 or 12 months, according to how serious the omission was. For providers with a bad local reputation, the claims review process is more rigorous and on-site audits more frequent.

Box 5.1 Setting the Price Low and Lowering it Further for New Procedures: The Case of MRI Scans

When new procedures are included in the fee schedule, prices are set after comparisons of their efficacy with existing technologies, and not based on cost calculations. The price of an MRI scan, for example, was set at twice that of the CT scan in 1982, despite the fact that the difference in the price of purchasing the equipment was more than 10 times at that time (Hisashige 1994). Still, the number of MRI scans exploded because manufacturers came out with less expensive models and were willing to give big discounts on the list price, and because hospitals competed to purchase or lease the equipment to attract patients and physicians. As a result, spending on MRI scans rose quickly.

The government responded by cutting the fee per scan in 1996, 1998, and 2000, but these cuts were less than 10 percent. In contrast, the cut made in 2002 was 31 percent. Volume did go up that year, but only by 9 percent, about half the pace of the previous year. The following year, with the price at the same level, volume actually declined sharply. As a result, total spending on MRI scans dropped by 25 percent in 2002 and an additional 14 percent in 2003. Although other factors no doubt influenced the volume and expenditure figures, it appears that reducing prices led physicians to cut back on ordering MRIs. After 2003, volume and expenditure both rose roughly in parallel, with spending going up at a slightly slower pace. As the box figure shows, during 1994–2010,[a] while the volume of MRI scans increased by a factor of five, total spending increased by only a factor of three.[b] Thus, Japan has the highest per capita number of MRI machines in the world (as of 2012 or nearest year, OECD 2013), but the prices of scans may be lowest: in 2012, the price for an MRI scan was ¥13,330, or US$150 (MHLW 2012b), compared with US$363 in France and US$1,121 in the United States. (The pattern is similar for CT scans: ¥9,000 or US$100 [16–64 multislice], compared with US$183 in France and US$566 in the United States, as of 2012 [IFHP 2012; MHLW 2012b].)

It has also been possible to absorb increases in costs resulting from the development of more advanced models by changing the way prices are set. In the 2006 revision, prices were set according to the type of equipment, and not by the part of body as before. This change was found to be budget neutral when expenditures were calculated using 2005 volume-weighted prices based on body parts. Increases in spending caused by the higher price of high-density MRI (1.5 Tesla or more) were offset by savings due to the lower price of low-density MRI scans. In the 2012 revision, the introduction of a still higher-density MRI (3.0 Tesla or more) was offset by further lowering the price of low-density MRI (less than 1.5 Tesla).

box continues next page

Box 5.1 Setting the Price Low and Lowering it Further for New Procedures: The Case of MRI Scans *(continued)*

Figure B5.1 MRI: Number of Scans and Expenditures, 1994–2010

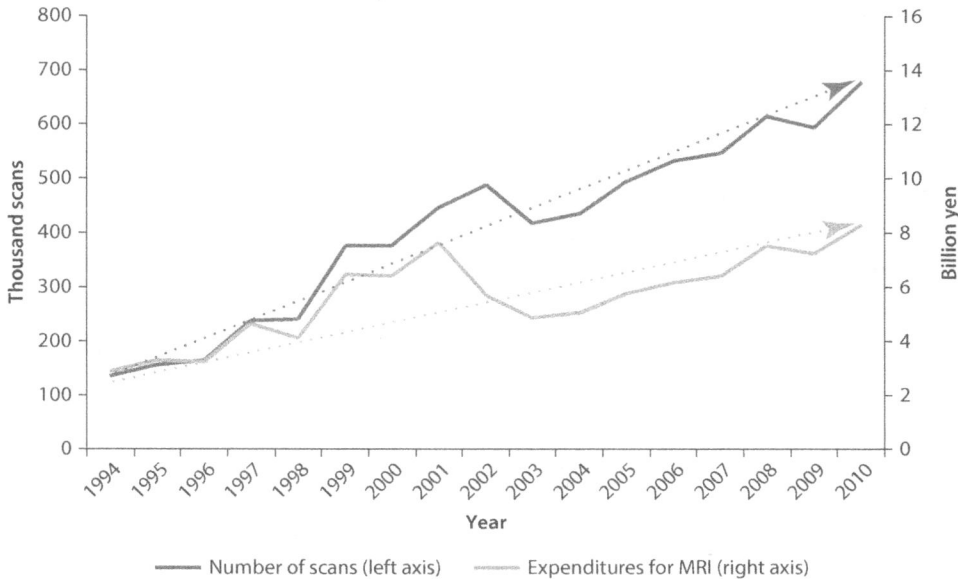

——— Number of scans (left axis) ——— Expenditures for MRI (right axis)

Source: MHLW 2011a.

Note: MRI = Magnetic resonance imaging.

a. We focused on changes in volume of simple (without contrast) MRI scanning after confirming that the proportion using contrast medium to the total was constant for the years investigated (averaging about 2.0 percent for MRI) (MHLW 2011a).

b. The MHLW survey data do not include MRI scans for inpatients in hospitals paid under Diagnosis Procedure Combination (DPC), a Japanese version of Diagnosis Related Groups. However, their exclusion would not affect the expenditures and have only a marginal impact on volume because hospitals paid by DPC have tended to shift their MRI scans to outpatient care because they can then be billed FFS (Matsuda 2008).

The cost of making these audits has been estimated at about 0.44 percent of the NME in 1990 (Ikegami, Wolfson, and Ishii 1996). This small proportion has been made possible by the use of only one price and one condition of billing for all items set by the MHLW and concentrating the review process at prefectural level.

Adherence to the prohibition of balance billing and the restrictions on extra billing is also strictly monitored, mitigating the insidious pressure to include in the fee schedule pharmaceuticals and services that have not yet been evaluated for efficacy and safety.

Maintaining Balanced Financial Status among Providers

In making the item-by-item revisions, the need to maintain a balanced financial status among the various types of hospitals (general, chronic, and psychiatric) is considered. The MHLW conducts a survey of providers' financial status in the year before the fee schedule is revised. For hospitals, the results are tabulated by type and by ownership (MHLW).[11] Since the facilities sampled differ in each survey, the results are not used to analyze longitudinal trends, but to compare the current level of balance across the various types of hospitals so that any major imbalance can be rectified in the next revision.

In the 2005 survey, for example, data showing that the revenue exceeded expenditures by 7 percent in chronic hospitals compared to deficits in general hospitals were one factor that led to a decrease in their hospitalization per diem fees by 10 percent in the 2006 revision. However, the extent to which the decision was made based on the survey result is not clear. It may have been used to justify a decision that had already been made by the MHLW to reduce the number of chronic care hospital beds by lowering inpatient hospital fees to below costs (Ikegami 2009).

For clinics (*shinryoujo*), the results are also tabulated by the type (with or without inpatient facilities) and by ownership. We will focus on offices without inpatient facilities and physicians' sole proprietorships as they form the majority.[12] Almost all of these offices are solo practices so that the balance between revenues and expenditures is equivalent to the physician's pretax income. Since the services provided by clinics are limited to those that can be delivered in primary care settings, their income should be more directly affected by the item-by-item revisions.

However, the survey results have not been used as a basis for such revisions, even when their income has decreased, albeit with fluctuations, from a high of ¥2.4 million per month in 2001 to a low of ¥1.8 million in 2011. This may be because the government's main purpose of surveying offices lies in revealing the relative high income of their physicians compared with the specialists employed by hospitals.[13] For these reasons, the Japan Medical Association—the most powerful organization among providers and one that has championed the interests of physicians in clinics—has chosen to ignore these results in its negotiations with the government, thus preventing it from using the data as a basis for demanding increases in prices provided primarily by physicians in clinics.

Incentivizing Physicians

New services that have been added to the fee schedule sometime include incentive bonuses to encourage provision by physicians. To give one example, in order to expand the provision of end-of-life care at home, a bonus payment of ¥100,000 was introduced in the 2006 fee schedule revision if the facility met the conditions for a "home care supporting clinic or hospital" (such as being accessible to patients at all times) and the physician had made a home visit on the day of the patient's death. This bonus payment was subsequently refined in the 2012 fee schedule revision: the amount was divided into a ¥50,000 for making a visit to a patient at end of life, and an additional fee of ¥30,000 if the registered patient either died at home or died within 24 hours of being hospitalized, so that the physician could claim the former even if the patient had not died at home and was hospitalized on the day of death.

Pharmaceutical Expenditures
Lowering Prices
According to the Itemized Survey of Social Medical Care, pharmaceutical expenditures amounted to 38.7 percent of the NME in 1982 (MHLW 2013). From

about that year, containing pharmaceutical expenditures and decreasing their share of the NME have been major policy goals in Japan. This has mainly been pursued by gradually decreasing the profit margins that providers can earn from dispensing drugs—clinics, hospitals, and pharmacies.[14] This profit came from the difference between the fee schedule price and the actual price paid to buy the product. Because providers prefer to purchase products for which bigger discounts can be negotiated and earned, market mechanisms have led to a downward spiral of prices. (The launch price of a new product is set by the MHLW mainly by marking up the price of the comparator based on its relative efficacy and innovativeness, or by calculating its costs based on the government's formula for products that do not have a comparator.)[15] Once approved for efficacy and safety, the product is automatically listed without undergoing any health economics evaluation. Thus, cost containment is achieved by attempting to set the launch price of new products low, not by limiting their introduction.

The process for revising pharmaceutical prices in the fee schedule system starts with the MHLW conducting the Pharmaceutical Price Survey of market prices as recorded in wholesalers' books, carried out in the year before the fee schedule revision. The method for revising the fee schedule price of each product has evolved over time as follows:

- The bulk-line method (1967–92) works by listing the market price of each product from the highest to the lowest, and then setting the new fee schedule price at a certain percentile within that range. The percentile was changed from the 90th to the 81st in 1983, and then from 1987, the percentile came to be weighted by the volume of the product sold at that price.
- The reasonable zone method (since 1994) sets the new fee schedule price by adding a percentage ("reasonable zone") to the volume-weighted average market price of each product as calculated from compiling the results of the survey of market prices. The reasonable zone was initially set at 15 percent but was gradually reduced to the present 2 percent in 2000.

Two additional methods that do not depend on the survey have also been used to lower fee schedule prices. First, from 1994, prices have been cut based on the changes that have occurred in the sales volume of new products. For example, one condition was that if the total sales of a product were more than twice the amount projected by the manufacturer and the sales came to more than ¥15 billion, its price would be reduced. The extent to which conditions are met and the size of the cuts are subject to heated negotiations between the manufacturer and the MHLW. Second, starting in 2002, the price of the brand is cut when its patent expires, and these cuts have been gradually deepening.

We will show the impact of these price reductions on total pharmaceutical expenditures (and their share of the NME) and by functional groups. First, some important methodological points:

Universal Health Coverage for Inclusive and Sustainable Development
http://dx.doi.org/10.1596/978-1-4648-0408-3

- These analyses use IMS Health data, which are based on real-time sales data from the greater majority of wholesalers. The sales amounts have been calculated according to the prices set by the fee schedule, not by actual sale prices. Consistent and reliable data on total expenditures are available from 1988, and these data are divided into functional groups from 2001.[16]
- Although the MHLW has disclosed aggregated pharmaceutical expenditure estimates, we found their data to be inconsistent because they do not appropriately reflect the changes in the way pharmaceuticals have been billed.[17]
- We could not compare Japan's expenditures with other countries by using pharmaceutical expenditure data from the Organisation for Economic Co-operation and Development (OECD) because the OECD data exclude inpatient pharmaceutical expenditures, but include over-the-counter drugs. This is the converse of how data are compiled in Japan.

Trends in Expenditures

Pharmaceutical expenditures have increased less than the NME in the last two decades (see figure 5.1). The ratio of pharmaceutical expenditures to the NME declined from 27.4 percent in 1990 to 20.6 percent in 1998, then plateaued before increasing again.

Without the cumulative decreases in prices from 2001 to 2012, pharmaceutical expenditures would have been 28.0 percent higher in 2012 (figure 5.3). Thus,

Figure 5.3 Effects of Pharmaceutical Price Reductions, 2001–12

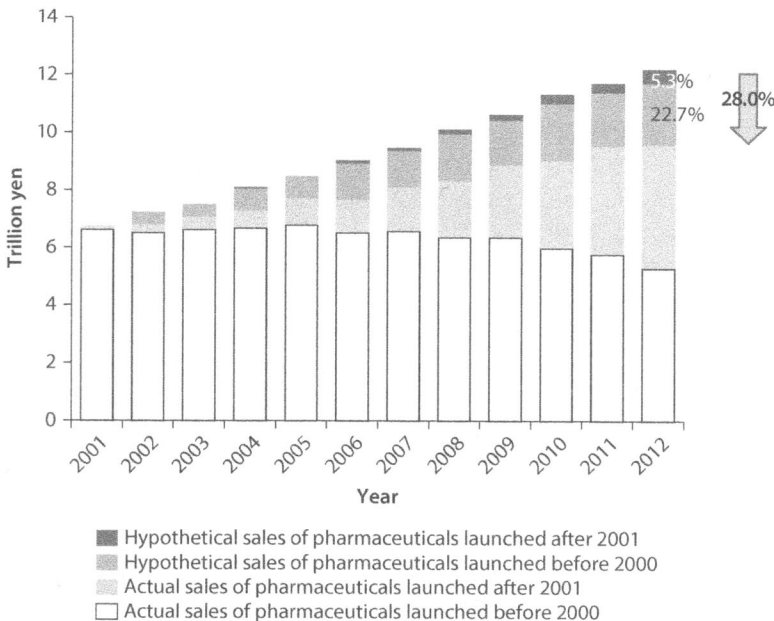

Hypothetical sales of pharmaceuticals launched after 2001
Hypothetical sales of pharmaceuticals launched before 2000
Actual sales of pharmaceuticals launched after 2001
Actual sales of pharmaceuticals launched before 2000

Source: Copyright 2014 IMS Health. All rights reserved. Estimated based on IMS JPM March MAT 2002–13.
Note: Hypothetical refers to the sales amount if pharmaceutical prices had not been decreased.

price reductions have been effective in containing costs. However, these decreases resulted more from reduction in prices of old products launched before 2000 than from reductions in prices of new products launched after 2001. Since these old products are very unlikely to be protected by patents, this implies that the price reductions have not been as effective as they may appear.

Cutting Expenditures by Increasing the Share of Generic Drugs?

There would have been greater decreases in pharmaceutical expenditures if more generics had been prescribed instead of brands. Although the share of existing brands launched before 2001 in sales fell by 22.7 percent from 2002 to 2012, their share in volume declined by only 6.6 percent (figure 5.4).

If the share of generics could be increased from 2011's 17 percent in Japan to the United States' 84 percent (IMS Institute for Healthcare Informatics 2013), and the price of generics be lowered to 10 percent of the brands, pharmaceutical expenditures could be decreased to about half the current amount.[18] An example of how expenditures could be decreased is given in figure 5.5. Not only is the replacement of brands by generics much slower in Japan, but the price of generics is also higher. This is because the price of the first generic launched is set at 70 percent of the brand's, with the price of those introduced later declining by a set percentage. Although their prices will subsequently decline—reflecting results of the survey of market prices—the price of each generic will remain unique to the manufacturer. Some molecular compounds show a more than fivefold price difference among generics, but under FFS there is no incentive to prescribe or dispense the least expensive product.

Figure 5.4 Trends in Volume and Sales of Brands Launched after 2002 and before 2001, and Generics, 2002–12

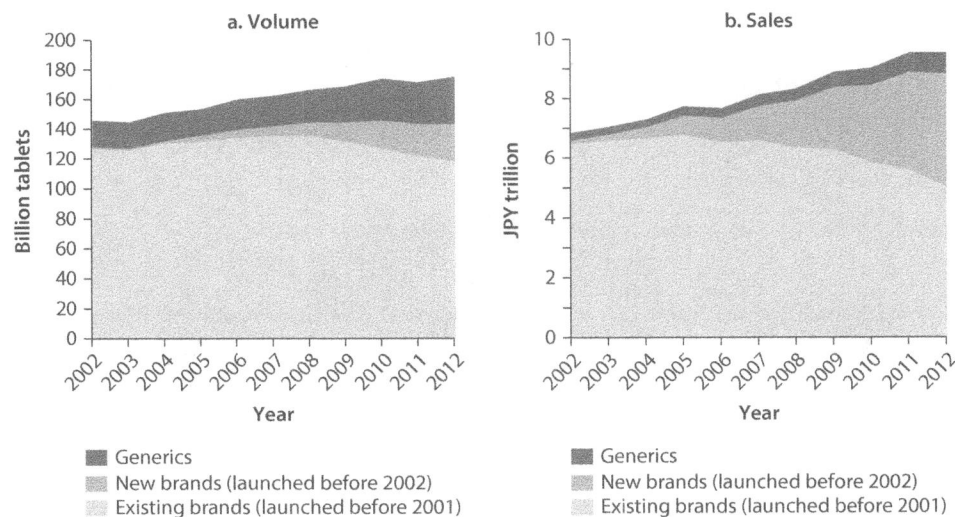

Universal Health Coverage for Inclusive and Sustainable Development
http://dx.doi.org/10.1596/978-1-4648-0408-3

Figure 5.5 Comparison of the Composition of Brands and Generics in Platinum Containing Agent for Anticancer in Japan and the United States, Volume and Sales, 2002–12

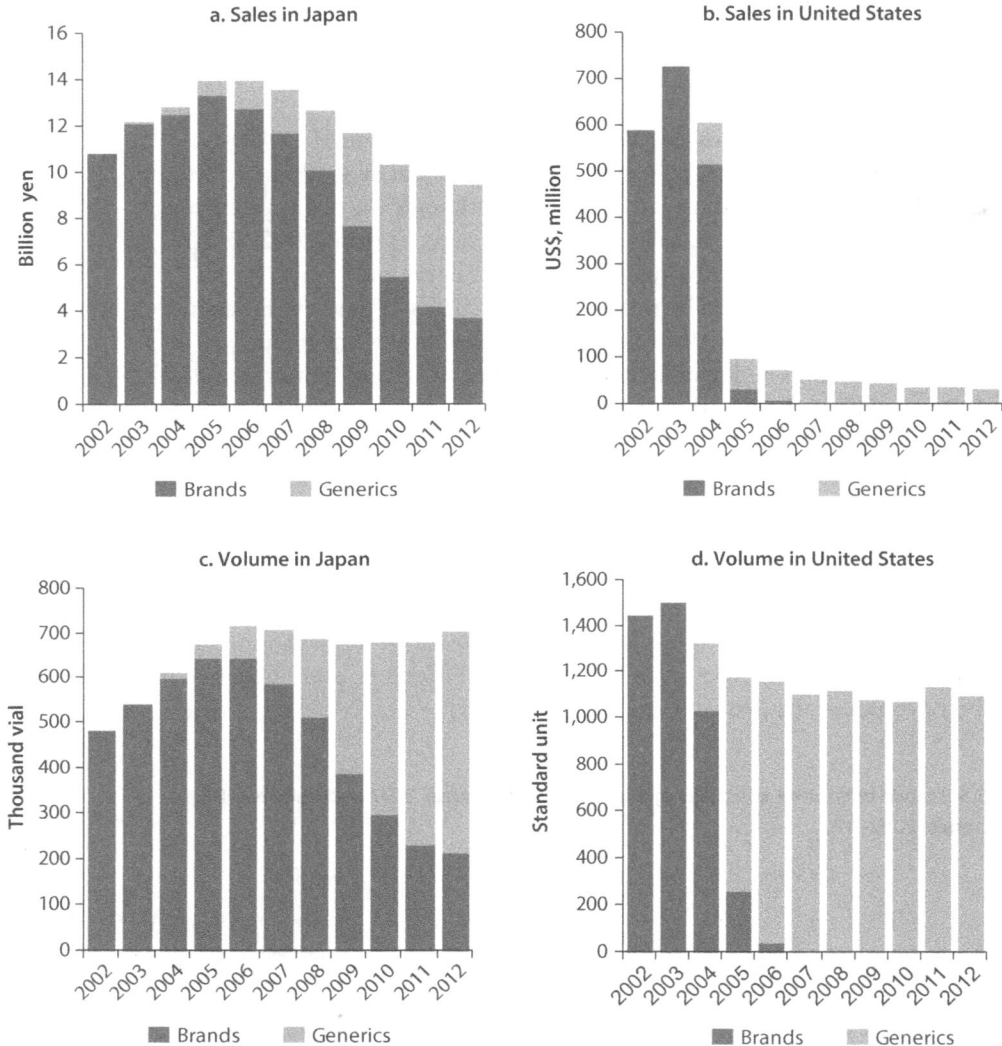

Source: Copyright 2014 IMS Health. All rights reserved. Estimated based on IMS JPM March MAT 2002–13.

Instead, the incentive lies in the product with the biggest margin between the fee schedule price and the market price, which could be the brand because a small reduction would allow a greater margin than a big reduction in a low-priced generic. Bonus incentives in the fee schedule for physicians to prescribe generics, and for pharmacies to substitute, have generally been insufficient to offset the profit from prescribing brands. More radical reforms, such as the introduction of reference pricing and the expansion of bundled payment, will be needed to expand the use of generics and lower their prices.

Universal Health Coverage for Inclusive and Sustainable Development
http://dx.doi.org/10.1596/978-1-4648-0408-3

Recent Trends

Although the fee schedule appears to be functioning relatively well, three recent developments may threaten its sustainability as a way for meeting policy goals.

First, at macro level, will it be possible to continue the current cost-containment policy but at the same time also promote the health care industry as one of the "three new pillars of economic growth" (Prime Minister of Japan and His Cabinet 2013a)?

One solution would be to revoke the current prohibitions on balance billing and the restrictions on extra billing, though this faces potential problems, as this deregulation could lead to the provision of services and pharmaceuticals of unproven efficacy and safety. Moreover, in the long run, deregulation will lead to cost escalations on the publicly funded health care system because the pressure to cover these services and pharmaceuticals will increase. Because it is extremely hard to explicitly deny services based on a patient's inability to pay, deregulation should be made only after a careful review of its ramifications. Opportunities for industries to develop are more likely to lie in long-term care where egalitarian provision is not the social norm, unlike health care (Ikegami and Campbell 2002).

Second, will targeted item-by-item revisions remain effective?

The answer is no for the majority of acute inpatient care, because of the introduction and expanded use of DPC.[19] Initially introduced only at the 82 special function hospitals (the main hospitals of the 80 medical schools plus the two national centers on cancer and cardiovascular diseases) in 2003, it has expanded to cover more than 1,200 hospitals that together account for half of all acute care beds. These hospitals have voluntarily opted to be paid under DPC, primarily because it would increase their revenue. DPC sets a conversion factor specific to each hospital that guarantees the same revenue if the hospital delivers the same services as before adopting DPC. However, hospitals have lowered their inpatient costs by transferring services such as imaging to outpatient care (where they are billed FFS) (Matsuda 2008). Thus, contrary to what payers had expected, there is no evidence to show that DPC has lowered expenditures (Kondo and Kawabuchi 2012). While average length of stay and bed occupancy rates have declined, they have been offset by higher per diem revenue and increases in admissions.

To resolve these issues and introduce policy-directed incentives, the MHLW is gradually phasing out hospital-specific coefficients and replacing them with new ones applied across the board to all DPC hospitals, such as for providing emergency care and for being the regionally designated cancer center. However, these coefficients may be inappropriate for meeting local needs because they have been uniformly set at national level. In order to resolve this issue in turn, some of the MHLW's authority must be devolved to prefectural governments.[20] More local initiative is also needed to monitor upcoding as this could not be detected by inspecting individual claims during the claims audit process and would require comparing the composition of case-mix groups across hospitals.

Universal Health Coverage for Inclusive and Sustainable Development
http://dx.doi.org/10.1596/978-1-4648-0408-3

Third, will it be possible to continue financing small increases in medical service fees by reducing pharmaceutical prices?

This may become less feasible because of the new rule introduced in the 2010 revision,[21] under which pharmaceutical companies have the option of applying for a waiver on price reductions while the product's patent remains active. This waiver will remain in force provided that the product's price reduction rate, as revealed in the Pharmaceutical Price Survey, is less than the weighted average of all products. When the patent expires, its price will be cut to reflect its market level. This decrease could be considerable because it would be the accumulated reductions as revealed in past surveys. A greater switch to generics when the patent expires is also expected. These assumptions should make this waiver option budget neutral, but it would not apply to products, such as some for cancer, that have a short shelf life.[22]

More aggressive incentives to dispense generics must therefore be introduced and their launch price further lowered to offset the costs of maintaining the high price of brands still on patent.

Insights

Japan's method of setting the global revision rate and then fine-tuning revisions item by item presents a unique—and largely successful—example of managing costs under an FFS payment structure.

- This is not an open-ended FFS whereby providers are permitted to claim as many procedures without any constraints. Rather, there is a soft global cap as agreed by the Ministry of Finance and the MHLW based on the size of the total government subsidies. As the government funds a set one-quarter of the NME, it controls not just the proportion it funds, but the entire NME.
- The fee schedule includes not only prices but conditions of billing that prescribe various service standards which set boundaries on the volume and quality of services. This is reinforced by the prohibition on balance billing, which prevents providers to charge a higher rate than the rate set by the national fee schedule.
- The FFS is implemented and *enforced* through a monthly claims review and adjudication process that includes medical audits by professional peers. Providers who do not comply with the conditions of billing face financial consequences.
- The biennial FFS review process allows health policy makers to introduce and implement new policy measures directly through the FFS by adjusting, in considerable detail, the financial incentives. This process also involves reviewing the trends in the price and volume of health services, and enables policy makers to make adjustments to correct or compensate for unexpected results. The system would not function without this regular and continual adjustment of the fee schedule.

- The FFS review process requires substantial technical capacity to collect and analyze large volumes of current data on service utilization and prices, as the necessary information basis for negotiating the fee schedule. The validity of these datasets and analyses are important features for setting a reliable basis for negotiations.

Most of these features are quite distinct from those in other countries' FFS systems. Similarly, the complex governance structure, as well as the technical capacity required to manage all these functions simultaneously, may not be readily replicable in lower-income countries.

What is particularly unique about Japan's system is that the fee schedule revision is much more than a price setting and price negotiation process, and the integration of multiple functions in one process. It also effectively defines the benefits covered because all covered medical procedures, medicines, and technologies are included in the fee schedule; it establishes certain levels and standards for utilization of services by defining the conditions for billings; and by setting them as conditions for reimbursement, it mitigates increases in expenditures due to nonprice factors. Through this process, policy makers are provided with an instrument not only for containing costs but also for creating incentives to promote policy goals and disincentives (as through reduced reimbursement rates) to curb undesirable practices.

While each country must develop its own policy levers for achieving and maintaining universal health care, in countries that are contemplating (or have started) the transition from global budgets to activity-based financing, the primary task should be to develop the institutional capacity to prospectively revise the payment system, control volume by setting conditions of billing, and impose penalties for violations. The details of each must be negotiated with the key stakeholders, such as physician and hospital associations, as governance has to be a shared responsibility.

Universal Health Coverage for Inclusive and Sustainable Development
http://dx.doi.org/10.1596/978-1-4648-0408-3

Annex

The figures in this annex provide further detailed information on the effects of pharmaceuticals price reductions, drivers of pharmaceuticals costs changes, and replacement by generics, as shown in figure 5.3 and figure 5.4 in the main text. Although figures 5.3 and 5.4 are most illustrative, in this annex the results of all the analyses made would be of interest to researchers.

Figure 5A.1 Sales of Drugs, 2001–12

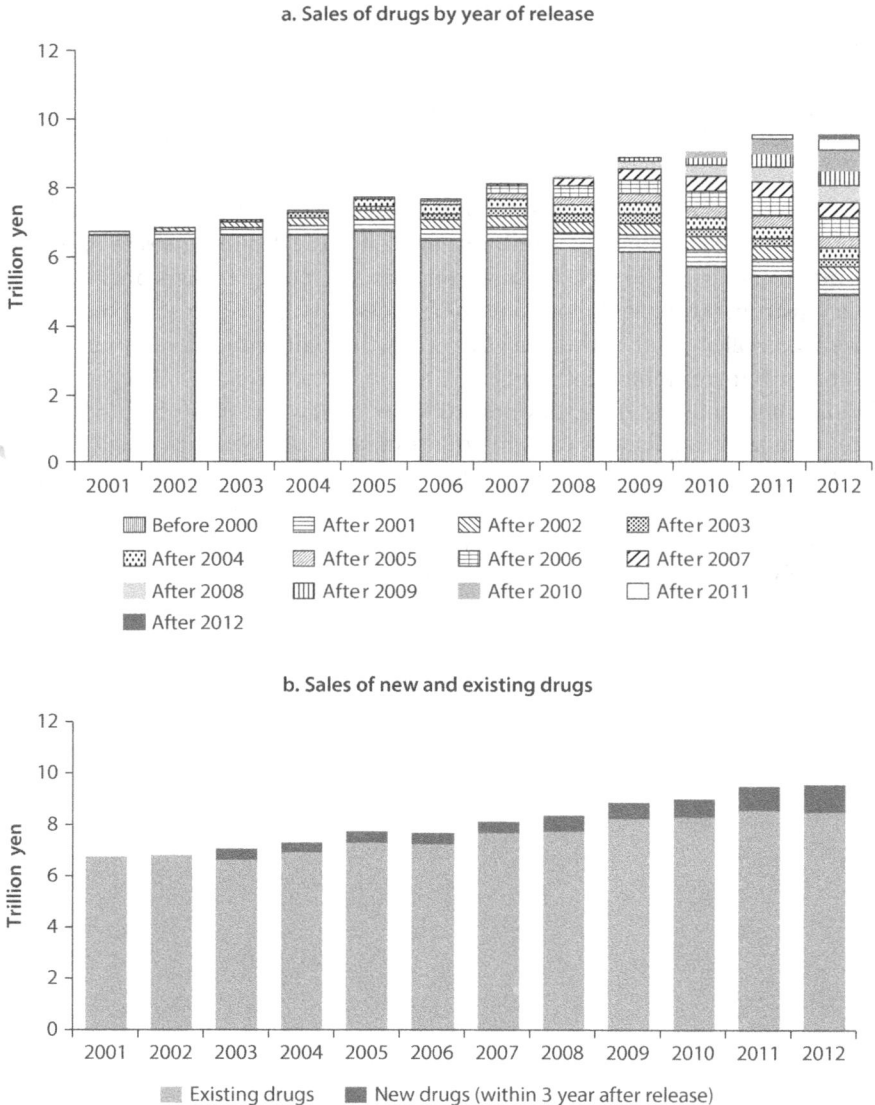

a. Sales of drugs by year of release

Legend: Before 2000, After 2001, After 2002, After 2003, After 2004, After 2005, After 2006, After 2007, After 2008, After 2009, After 2010, After 2011, After 2012

b. Sales of new and existing drugs

Legend: Existing drugs, New drugs (within 3 year after release)

Source: © 2014 IMS Health. All rights reserved. Any alteration of the figures and tables which are copyrighted by IMS Health is not permitted. If reproduced, the copyright of IMS Health must be clearly written and acknowledged. Estimated based on IMS JPM March MAT 2002—13.

Figure 5A.2 Hypothetical Sales of Drugs, 2001–12

a. Hypothetical sales of drugs by year of release
(price is fixed as of 2001)

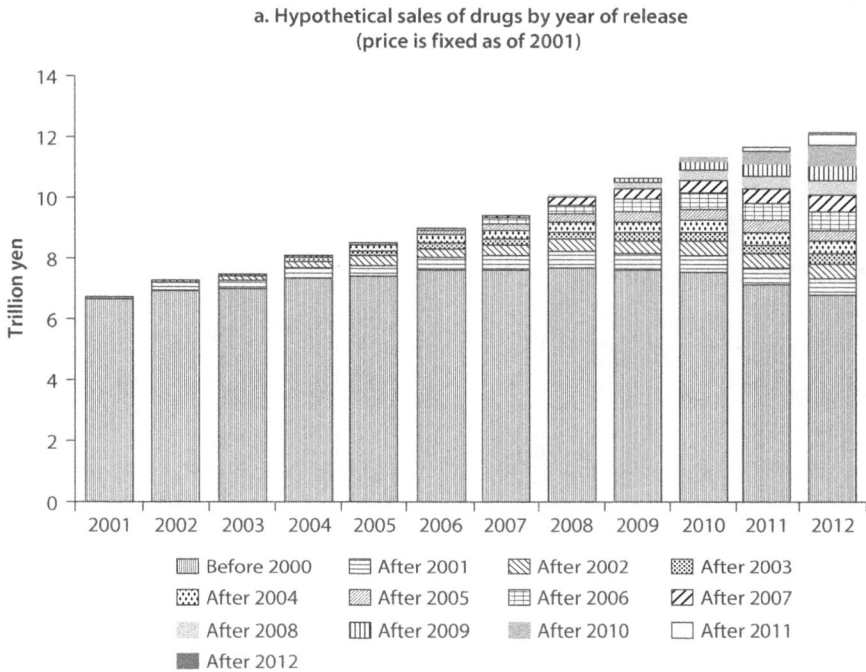

Before 2000 · After 2001 · After 2002 · After 2003 · After 2004 · After 2005 · After 2006 · After 2007 · After 2008 · After 2009 · After 2010 · After 2011 · After 2012

b. Hypothetical sales of new and existing drugs
(price is fixed as of 2001)

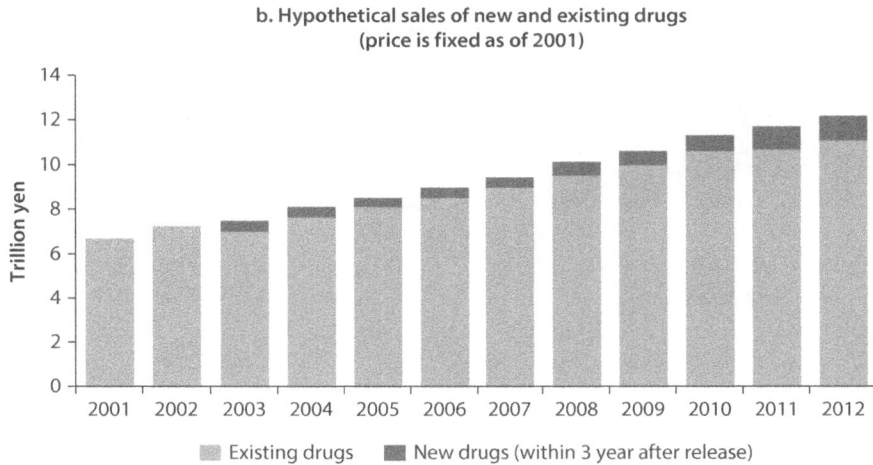

Existing drugs ■ New drugs (within 3 year after release)

Figure 5A.3 Sales Volume, Sales, Hypothetical Sales, and Decomposing Sales of Anticancer and Antibiotics in Japan, 2001–12

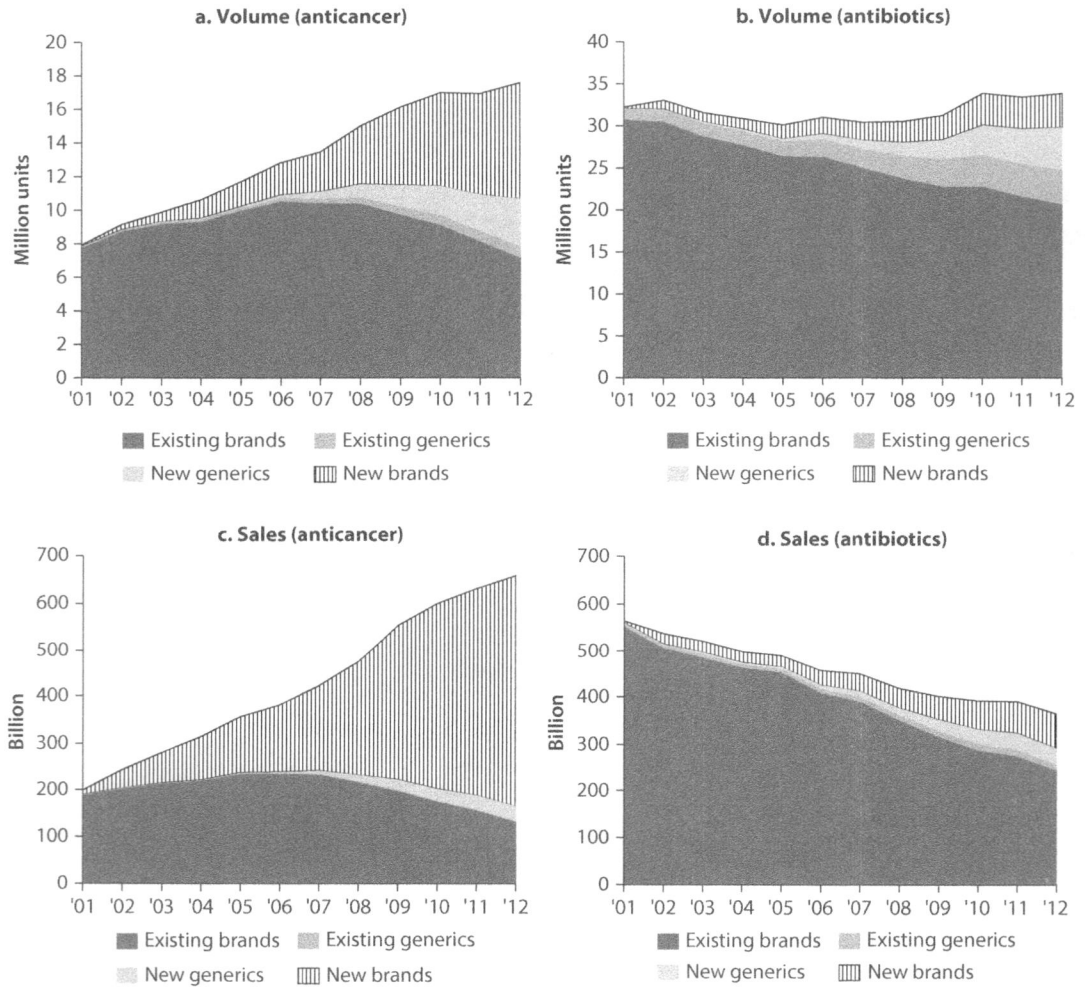

a. Volume (anticancer)

Legend: Existing brands | Existing generics | New generics | New brands

b. Volume (antibiotics)

Legend: Existing brands | Existing generics | New generics | New brands

c. Sales (anticancer)

Legend: Existing brands | Existing generics | New generics | New brands

d. Sales (antibiotics)

Legend: Existing brands | Existing generics | New generics | New brands

a. Hypothetical sales if price cuts had not been made (anticancer)

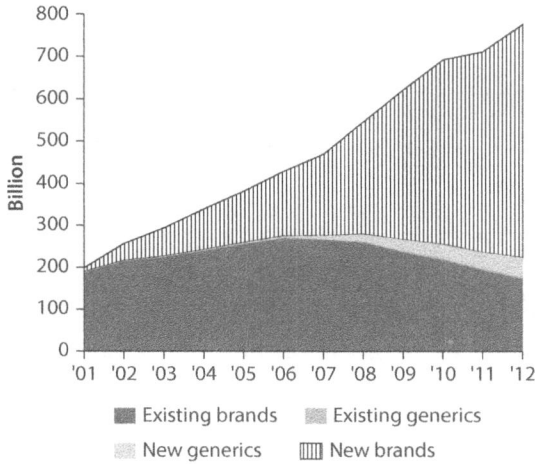

Billion

800
700
600
500
400
300
200
100
0

'01 '02 '03 '04 '05 '06 '07 '08 '09 '10 '11 '12

■ Existing brands   ▨ Existing generics
▨ New generics   ▥ New brands

b. Hypothetical sales if price cuts had not been made (antibiotics)

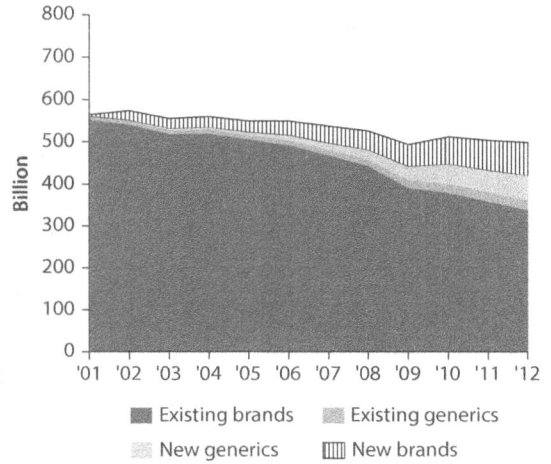

Billion

800
700
600
500
400
300
200
100
0

'01 '02 '03 '04 '05 '06 '07 '08 '09 '10 '11 '12

■ Existing brands   ▨ Existing generics
▨ New generics   ▥ New brands

c. Decomposing changes in the sales (anticancer)

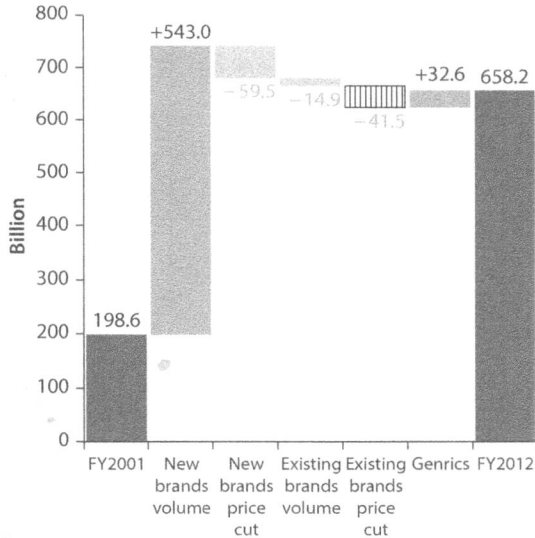

Billion

+543.0
−59.5 −14.9
−41.5
+32.6   658.2
198.6

FY2001 | New brands volume | New brands price cut | Existing brands volume | Existing brands price cut | Generics | FY2012

d. Decomposing changes in the sales (antibiotics)

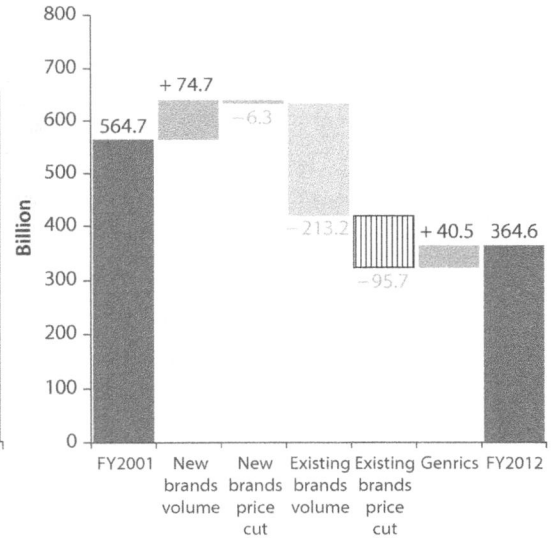

Billion

564.7
+ 74.7   −6.3
−213.2
−95.7
+40.5   364.6

FY2001 | New brands volume | New brands price cut | Existing brands volume | Existing brands price cut | Generics | FY2012

Source: © 2014 IMS Health. All rights reserved. Any alteration of the figures and tables which are copyrighted by IMS Health is not permitted. If reproduced, the copyright of IMS Health must be clearly written and acknowledged. Estimated based on IMS JPM March MAT 2002–13.

Note: "New" drugs are those launched after 2002. "Existing" drugs are those launched before 2001
1. "FY2001" denotes sale as of fiscal year 2001 (April 2001–March 2002)
2. "New Brands Volume" denotes hypothetical new drug sales through increased sales volume
3. "New Brands Price Cut" denotes sales decrease of new brands through their price reduction
4. "Existing Brands Volume" denotes sales decrease of existing brands through decreased sales volume
5. "Existing Brands Price Cut" denotes sales decrease of existing brands through their price reduction
6. "Generics" denote sales of generics (which has same efficacy of existing and/or new drugs)
7. "FY2012)" denotes sale as of fiscal year 2012 (sum of 1–6)

Figure 5A.4 Drugs of Largest Sales Increase and Decrease by ATC

Largest Sales Increase

		2001 (Thousand Yen)	2012 (Thousand Yen)	△ 2012-2001 (thousand yen)	Growth Rate (2012/2001, %)
	Market Total	6,763,591,608	9,560,127,661	2,796,536,053	41.3%
1	L01 Antineoplastic Agents	198,576,339	658,243,652	459,667,313	231.5%
2	C09 Agents acting on Renin-Angiotensin System	265,390,697	632,067,374	366,676,677	138.2%
3	L04 Immunosuppressants	37,954,207	298,349,734	260,395,527	686.1%
4	A10 Drugs used in Diabetes	185,187,076	427,450,748	242,263,672	130.8%
5	N07 Other Nervous System Drugs	84,513,120	268,334,895	183,821,775	217.5%
6	J07 Vaccines (including toxioid)	40,916,194	220,866,754	179,950,560	439.8%
7	B01 Antithrombotic Agents	222,714,746	379,298,997	156,584,251	70.3%
8	N05 Psycholeptics	171,536,765	314,258,663	142,721,898	83.2%
9	R03 Drugs for Obstructive Airway Diseases	188,116,020	308,400,299	120,284,279	63.9%
10	J05 Antivirals for Systemic Use	60,482,652	168,822,896	108,340,244	179.1%
11	T02 Diagnostic Reagents	108,165,168	208,230,512	100,065,344	92.5%
12	N06 Psychoanaleptics	58,856,582	148,984,929	90,128,347	153.1%
13	M05 Drugs for Treatment of Bone Diseases	72,832,057	161,849,244	89,017,187	122.2%
14	G04 Urologicals	111,915,560	193,573,654	81,658,094	73.0%
15	N03 Antiepileptics	28,154,429	106,805,038	78,650,609	279.4%
16	V03 All Other Therapeutic Products	134,233,905	210,301,299	76,067,394	56.7%
17	L02 Endocrine Therapy	129,127,060	202,066,370	72,939,310	56.5%
18	R06 Antihistamines for Systemic Use	141,094,556	211,505,258	70,410,702	49.9%
19	S01 Ophthalmologicals	190,097,036	257,514,193	67,417,157	35.5%
20	H04 Pancreatic Hormones	106,995,517	167,235,118	60,239,601	56.3%

Largest Sales Decrease

		2001 (Thousand Yen)	2012 (Thousand Yen)	△ 2012-2001 (tho usand yen)	Growth Rate (2012/2001, %)
	Market Total	6,763,591,608	9,560,127,661	2,796,536,053	41.3%
1	J01 Antibacterials for Systemic Use	564,652,564	364,623,757	−200,028,807	-35.4%
2	C01 Cardiac Therapy	241,555,013	134,687,305	−106,867,708	−44.2%
3	C08 Calcium Channel Blockers	323,135,884	228,049,856	−95,086,028	−29.4%
4	L03 Immunostimulants	126,242,829	50,991,020	−75,251,809	−59.6%
5	T01 Radiocontrast Agent	149,993,318	100,125,826	−49,867,492	−33.2%
6	C04 Peripheral Vasodilators	55,979,509	21,718,207	−34,261,302	−61.2%
7	K01 Intravenous Fluids	147,794,357	122,596,551	−25,197,806	−17.0%
8	A11 Vitamins	122,375,986	104,536,348	−17,839,638	−14.6%
9	C02 Antihypertensives	34,955,578	18,351,729	−16,603,849	−47.5%
10	D08 Antiseptics ans Disinfectants	29,874,467	13,630,272	−16,244,195	−54.4%
11	J02 Antimycotics for Systemic Use	71,951,706	58,769,094	−13,182,612	−18.3%
12	K03 Whole Blood and Plasma Replacements	28,094,506	15,546,469	−12,548,037	−44.7%
13	K06 Dyalisis Fluid	61,813,566	49,491,873	−12,321,693	−19.9%
14	A05 Bile and Liver Therapy	44,417,186	32,574,898	−11,842,288	−26.7%
15	R05 Cough and Cold Preparations	69,023,019	59,383,251	−9,639,768	−14.0%
16	B02 Antihemorrhagics	124,283,249	114,737,388	−9,545,861	−7.7%
17	C07 Beta Blocking Agents	80,331,696	72,057,862	−8,273,834	−10.3%
18	D01 Antifungals for Dermatological Use	22,855,369	16,294,132	−6,561,237	−28.7%
19	H02 Corticosteroids for Systemic Use	29,591,398	23,513,591	−6,077,807	−20.5%
20	A03 Drugs for Functional Gastrointestinal Disorders	47,763,020	42,254,830	−5,508,190	−11.5%

Figure 5A.5 Sales Volume, Sales, Hypothetical Sales, and Decomposing of Sales of Renin-Angiotensin in Japan, 2001–12

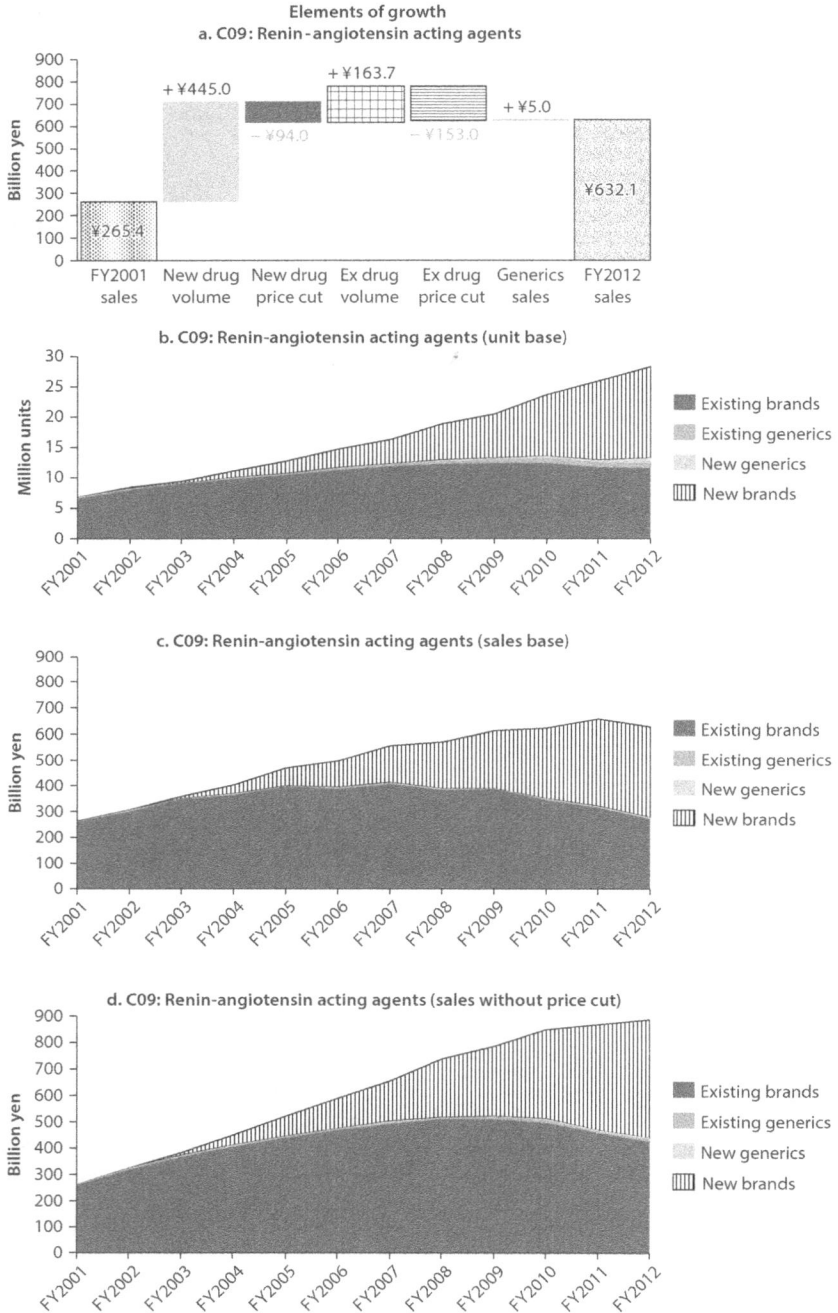

Elements of growth
a. C09: Renin-angiotensin acting agents

b. C09: Renin-angiotensin acting agents (unit base)

c. C09: Renin-angiotensin acting agents (sales base)

d. C09: Renin-angiotensin acting agents (sales without price cut)

Source: © 2014 IMS Health. All rights reserved. Any alteration of the figures and tables which are copyrighted by IMS Health is not permitted. If reproduced, the copyright of IMS Health must be clearly written and acknowledged. Estimated based on IMS JPM March MAT 2002–13.
Note: "New" drugs are those launched after 2002. "Existing" drugs are those launched before 2001.

Figure 5A.6 Sales Volume, Sales, Hypothetical Sales, and Decomposing of Sales of Immunosuppressants in Japan, 2001–12

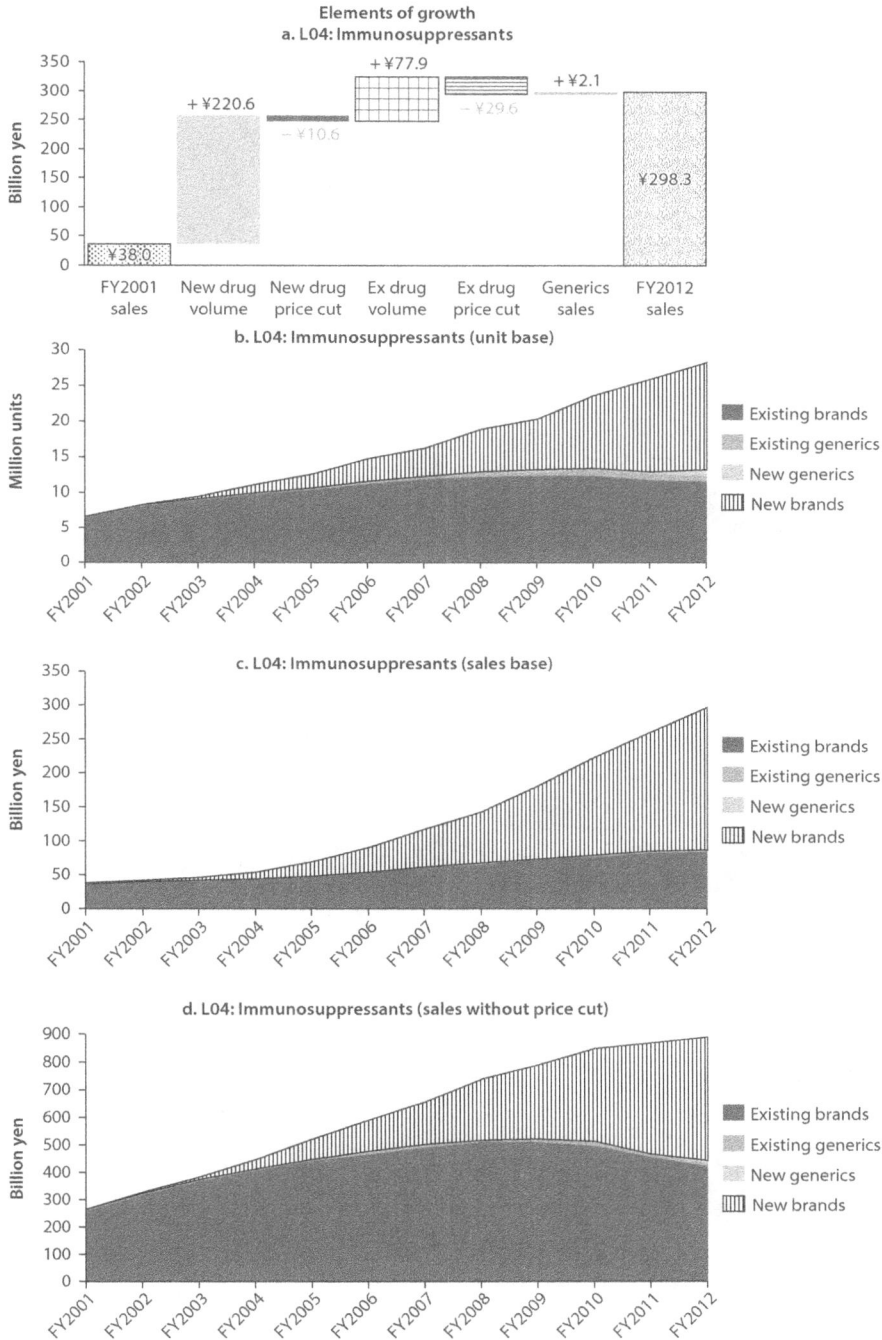

Note: "New" drugs are those launched after 2002. "Existing" drugs are those launched before 2001.

Figure 5A.7 Sales Volume, Sales, Hypothetical Sales, and Decomposing of Sales of Diabetes Drugs in Japan, 2001–12

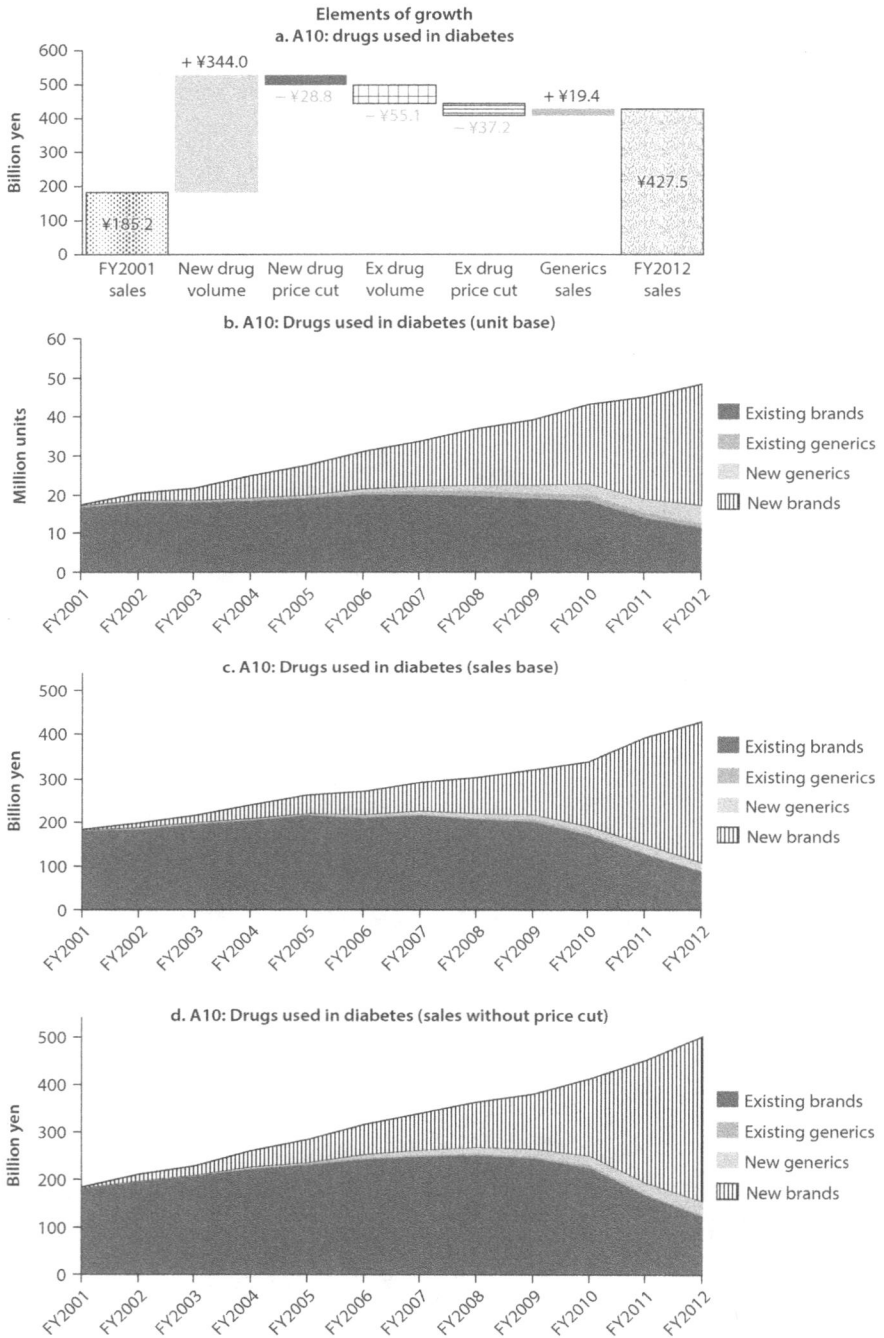

Elements of growth
a. A10: drugs used in diabetes

b. A10: Drugs used in diabetes (unit base)

c. A10: Drugs used in diabetes (sales base)

d. A10: Drugs used in diabetes (sales without price cut)

Note: "New" drugs are those launched after 2002. "Existing" drugs are those launched before 2001.

Figure 5A.8 Sales Volume, Sales, Hypothetical Sales, and Decomposing of Sales of CNS Drugs in Japan, 2001–12

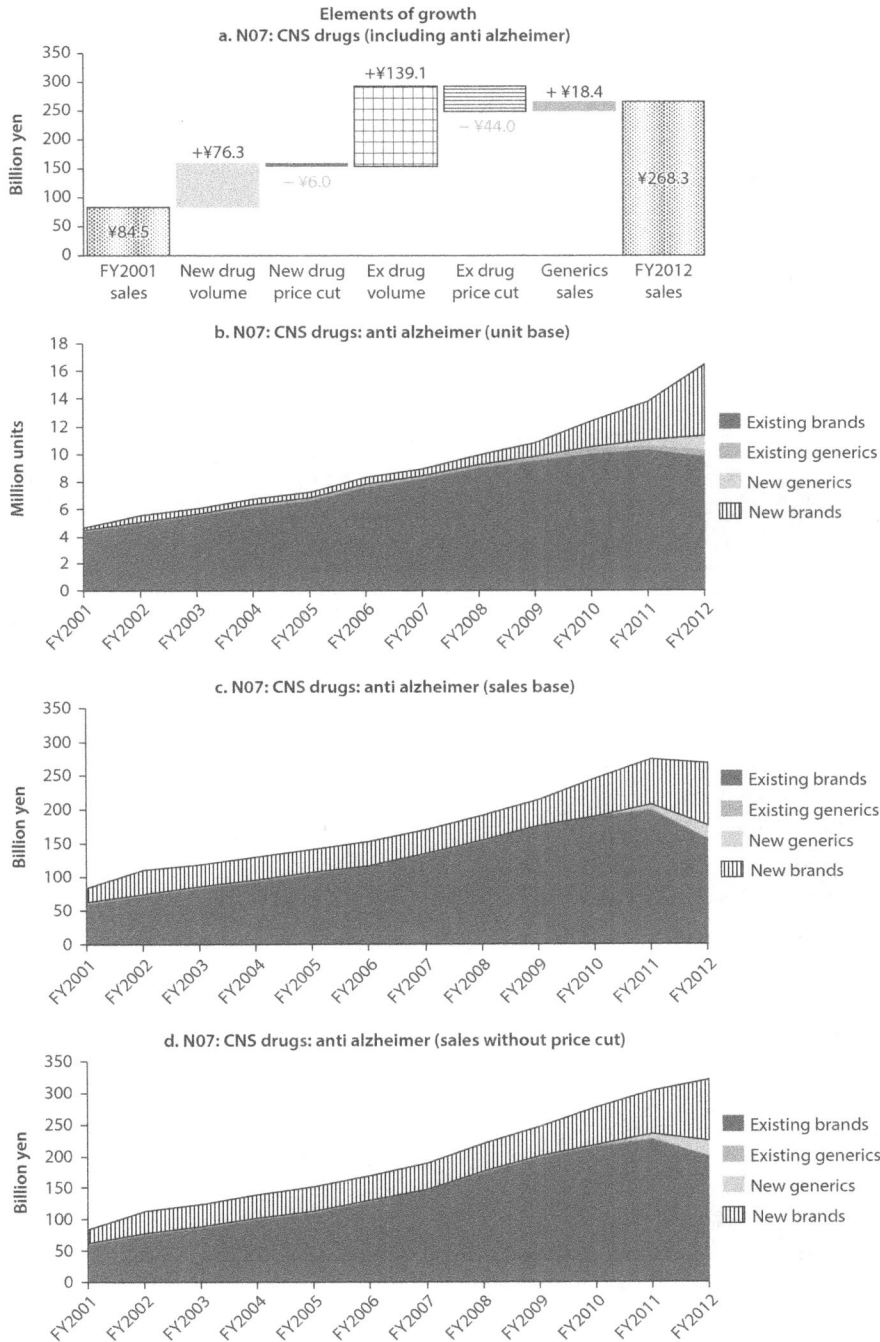

Elements of growth
a. N07: CNS drugs (including anti alzheimer)

b. N07: CNS drugs: anti alzheimer (unit base)

Existing brands
Existing generics
New generics
New brands

c. N07: CNS drugs: anti alzheimer (sales base)

Existing brands
Existing generics
New generics
New brands

d. N07: CNS drugs: anti alzheimer (sales without price cut)

Existing brands
Existing generics
New generics
New brands

Source: © 2014 IMS Health. All rights reserved. Any alteration of the figures and tables which are copyrighted by IMS Health is not permitted. If reproduced, the copyright of IMS Health must be clearly written and acknowledged. Estimated based on IMS JPM March MAT 2002–13.
Note: "New" drugs are those launched after 2002. "Existing" drugs are those launched before 2001.

Universal Health Coverage for Inclusive and Sustainable Development
http://dx.doi.org/10.1596/978-1-4648-0408-3

Figure 5A.9 Sales Volume, Sales, Hypothetical Sales and Decomposing of Sales of Cardiac Therapy Drugs in Japan, 2001–12

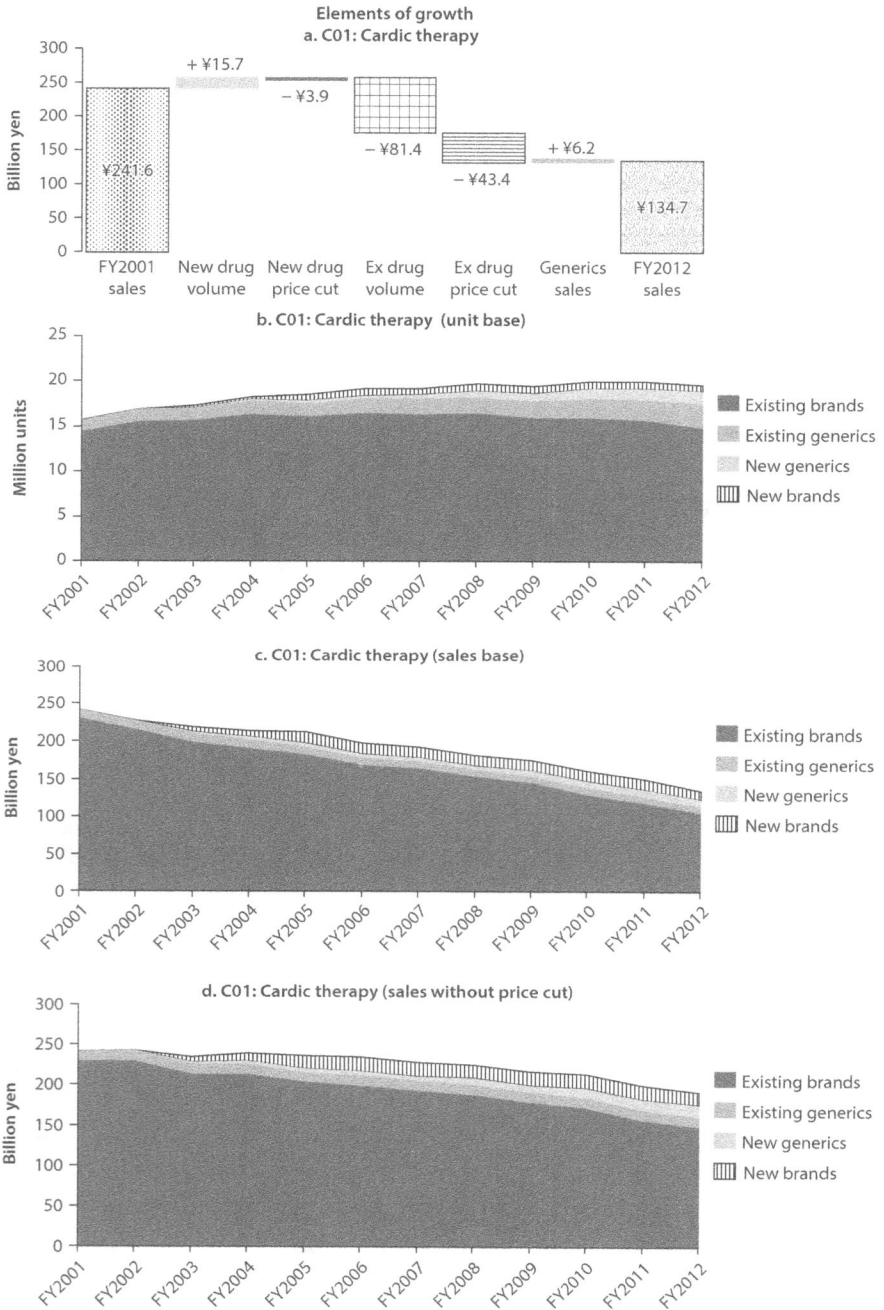

Elements of growth
a. C01: Cardic therapy

b. C01: Cardic therapy (unit base)

c. C01: Cardic therapy (sales base)

d. C01: Cardic therapy (sales without price cut)

Note: "New" drugs are those launched after 2002. "Existing" drugs are those launched before 2001.

Figure 5A.10 Sales Volume, Sales, Hypothetical Sales, and Decomposing of Calcium Antagonists in Japan, 2001–12

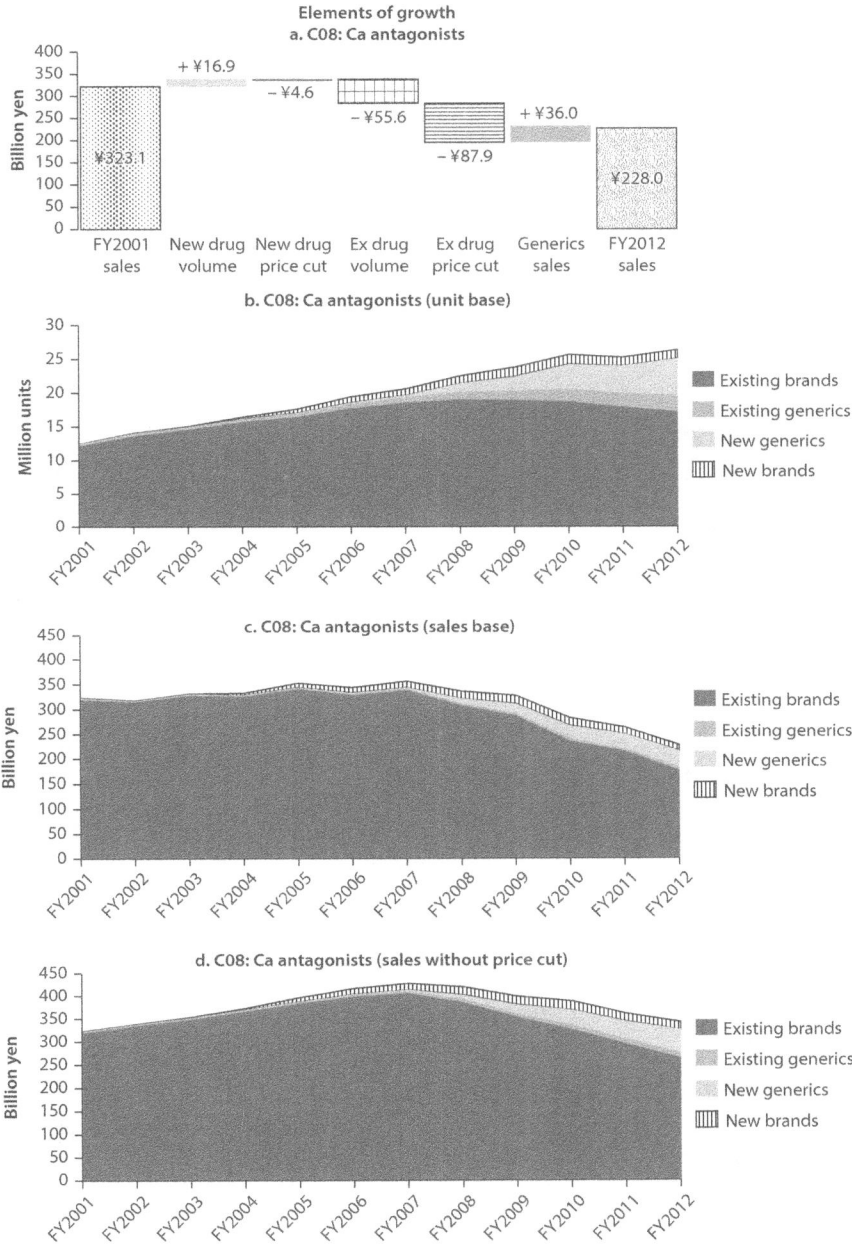

Elements of growth
a. C08: Ca antagonists

b. C08: Ca antagonists (unit base)

c. C08: Ca antagonists (sales base)

d. C08: Ca antagonists (sales without price cut)

Note: "New" drugs are those launched after 2002. "Existing" drugs are those launched before 2001.

Figure 5A.11 Sales Volume, Sales, Hypothetical Sales, and Decomposing of Immunostimulating Agents in Japan, 2001–12

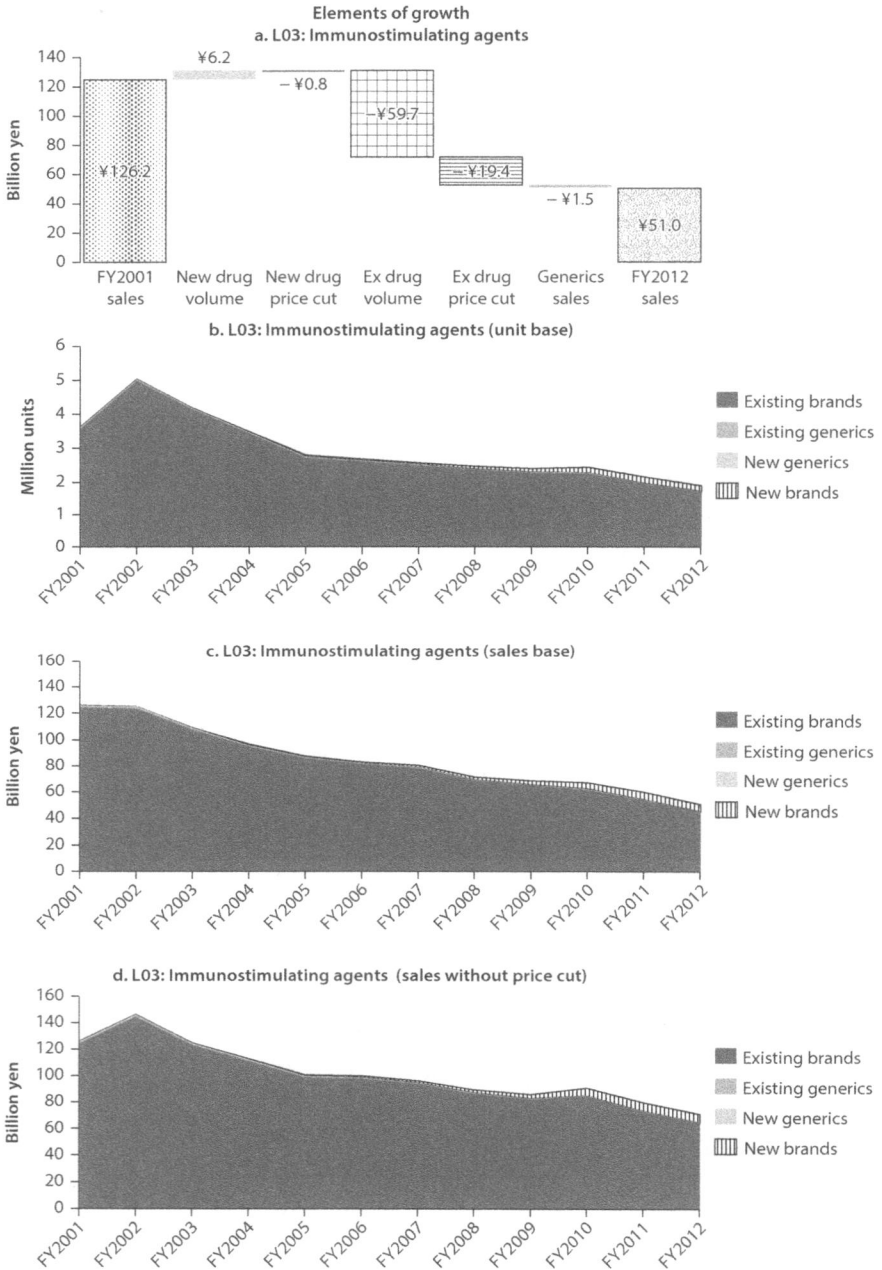

Elements of growth
a. L03: Immunostimulating agents

b. L03: Immunostimulating agents (unit base)

c. L03: Immunostimulating agents (sales base)

d. L03: Immunostimulating agents (sales without price cut)

Note: "New" drugs are those launched after 2002. "Existing" drugs are those launched before 2001.

Figure 5A.12 Sales Volume, Sales, Hypothetical Sales, and Decomposing of Diagnostic Imaging Drugs in Japan, 2001–12

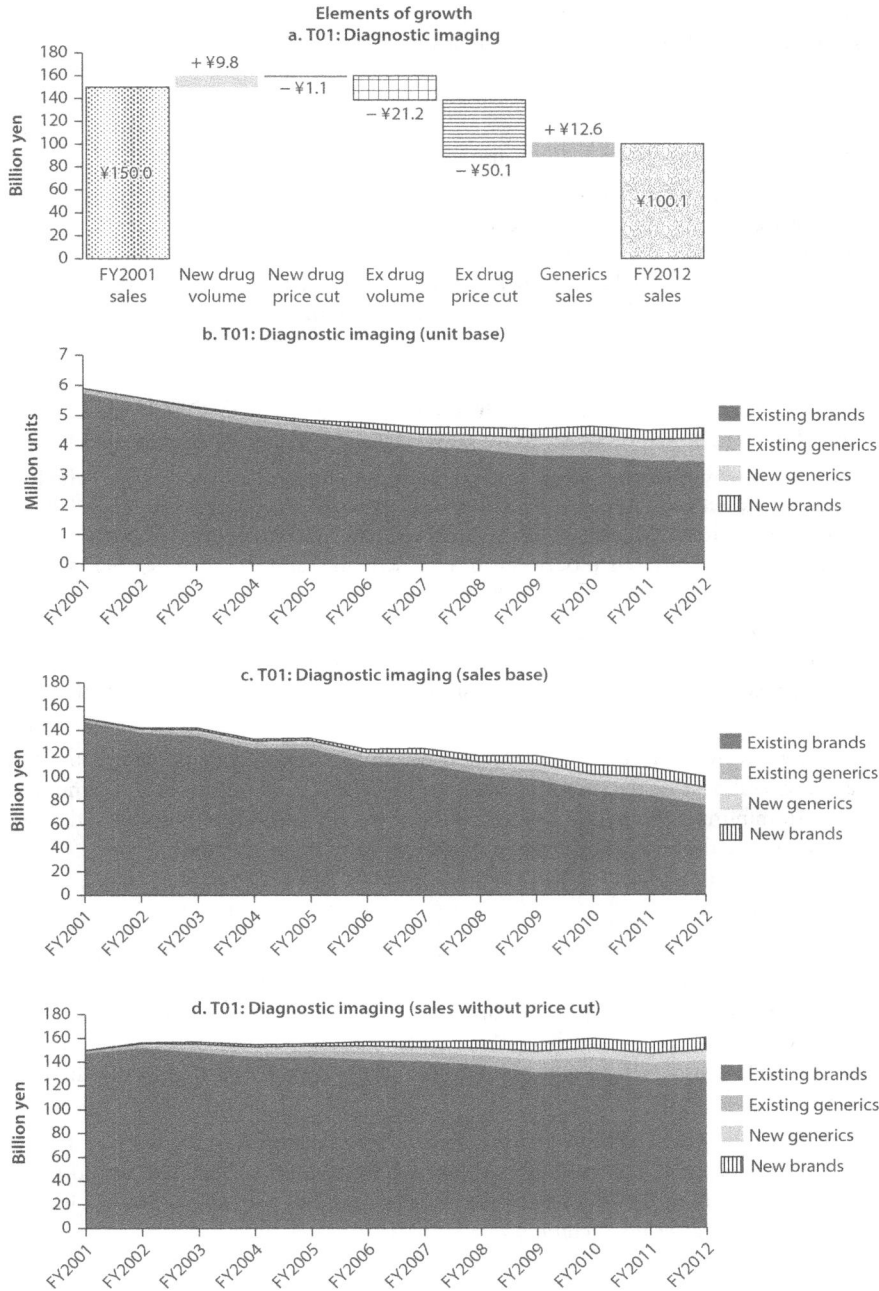

Elements of growth
a. T01: Diagnostic imaging

b. T01: Diagnostic imaging (unit base)

Existing brands
Existing generics
New generics
New brands

c. T01: Diagnostic imaging (sales base)

Existing brands
Existing generics
New generics
New brands

d. T01: Diagnostic imaging (sales without price cut)

Existing brands
Existing generics
New generics
New brands

Note: "New" drugs are those launched after 2002. "Existing" drugs are those launched before 2001.

Notes

1. Devices are listed separately in the fee schedule under 212 functional groups because there are so many variations by manufacturer The prices are reduced in a similar way as pharmaceuticals, but according to their functional groups.

2. See chapter 6.

3. See chapter 3.

4. This survey is not published, and is used as an internal document at MHLW.

5. Revisions in the two other service categories, dental and dispensing, are made by the same process: the savings made from the cumulative pharmaceutical price revision rates in each category are added to the global rate. The prices of medical devices are revised in a method similar to pharmaceuticals, but they are set by functional groups, rather than on an item-by-item basis, because of the many variations.

6. NME exclude expenditures for over-the-counter drugs, screening and other preventive health measures, and normal delivery, and so on, which are not included in the benefit package of the social health insurance. Compared with OECD total health expenditures that include these items, NME remain consistently 20 percent less.

7. One reason why pharmaceutical price revisions are integrated into the fee schedule revision for services is because dispensing was performed by physicians, especially in their office clinics. A large share of the providers' income was derived from the profits coming from the difference between the fee schedule and the market price, so that revising both within the same fee schedule has been regarded as a normal procedure.

8. The volume of each service or pharmaceutical is derived from claims data. They were based on a sample survey, the Itemized Survey of Social Medical Care, but are in the process of being gradually transferred to that of all claims in the National Dataset from 2012.

9. The peer review committee is composed of clinicians who are appointed to audit claims several days of the month. Claims are reviewed by clinicians of the same specialty. To minimize the personal inclinations of the reviewers, the hospital audits are rotated among the review committee members every three months.

10. The nurses' daily working record is also audited to check whether the hospital had met the staffing requirements for the staffing level of nursing that they had billed.

11. The national government, local governments, quasi-public organizations such as the Red Cross and social health insurance plans, medical corporations, other corporations, and individuals own hospitals. Two-thirds are owned by medical corporations. Deficits in public sector hospitals have been financed by subsidies. The survey's valid response rate has been just over half, with the rate for clinics about 5 percent lower than for hospitals.

12. Clinics are allowed to have 19 or fewer beds. Those having 20 or more beds are categorized as hospitals. The margin in clinics without inpatient facilities would more appropriately reflect the physician's income because they would require less investment from their after-tax income.

13. See chapter 7.

14. In 1990, about four-fifths of the hospitals and clinics dispensed. The profits generated amounted to 7 percent of the net revenue for hospitals and 12 percent for clinics. However, the percentage of prescriptions dispensed in hospitals and clinics declined to 37 percent in 2010, as the profit margin declined and the fee for prescribing to an independent pharmacy was increased.

15. International prices have also come to be used as benchmarks from 2002. The launch price is set so that it would not be more than 25 percent higher than the average of the list prices in United States, Germany, United Kingdom, and France (product is available in these countries).

16. Note that IMS Health data include vaccines which are not included in NME. They could not be excluded before 2001, but constituted only 0.6 percent of total pharmaceutical expenditures in 2001.

17. For example, the Itemized Survey of Social Medical Care excludes pharmaceuticals that have been prescribed for patients paid for by DPC.

18. Caution is needed in making direct comparisons with the United States because the share of generics is made based on the number of pills prescribed in Japan, but of prescriptions in the United States. The IMS Health figure of 17 percent in volume is less than the government figure of 23 percent (MHLW 2011b) because they include only about 70 percent of all generic products sales.

19. Unlike Diagnosis Related Groups, DPC rates are set on a per diem basis with the amount declining in four stages as the length of stay increases. Furthermore, procedures, surgical operations and devices priced at more than ¥10,000 continued to be billed FFS so that bundling is limited to pharmaceuticals, diagnostic tests, and imaging.

20. Devolution has also been advocated by the Council on Social Security System Reform (Prime Minister of Japan and His Cabinet 2013b), with allocation of new funds based on need analysis in the regional health plan (see the chapter 1).

21. This new rule is applied not only for new products, but also for any expansion of its approved use. New clinical trials must be performed for any expansion of use because off-label prescribing is prohibited in Japan.

22. The extent to which manufacturers would take this option remains uncertain because, by not doing so and giving bigger discounts, they might be able to sell more and earn greater profits overall.

Bibliography

Gaihoren (Association of Surgical Specialties Social Insurance Committees). "Preliminary Fee Schedule by Gaihoren 2011." http://www.gaihoren.jp/gaihoren/public/book/book.html (accessed October 2013).

Hashimoto, H., N. Ikegami, K. Shibuya, N. Izumida, H. Noguchi, H. Yasunaga, H. Miyata, J. M. Acuin, and M. R. Reich. 2011. "Cost Containment and Quality of Care in Japan: Is There a Trade-Off?" *Lancet* 378 (9797): 1174–82.

Hisashige, A. 1994. "The Introduction and Evaluation of MRI in Japan." *International Journal of Technology Assessment in Health Care* 10 (3): 392–405.

IFHP (International Federation of Health Plans). 2012. "Comparative Price Report 2012." http://tinyurl.com/krhhgmb. London, United Kingdom (accessed October 2013).

Ikegami, N. 2009. "Games Policy Makers and Providers Play: Introducing Case-Mix-Based Payment to Hospital Chronic Care Units in Japan." *Journal of Health Politics, Policy and Law* 34 (3): 361–80.

Ikegami, N., and J. C. Campbell. 2002. "Choices, Policy Logics and Problems in the Design of Long-Term Care Systems." *Social Policy & Administration* 36 (7): 719–34.

Ikegami, N., J. Wolfson, and T. Ishii. 1996. "Comparison of Administrative Costs in Health Care between Japan and the United States." In *Containing Health Care Costs in Japan*, 80–93. Ann Arbor: University of Michigan Press.

IMS. "Data on Japan and US Pharmaceuticals". 2013. Copyright 2013 IMS Health. All rights reserved. Estimates based on IMS JPM March MAT 2002–13. Edited by IMS Japan. Tokyo, Japan.

IMS Institute for Healthcare Informatics. 2013. "Avoidable Costs in U.S. Healthcare." http://www.imshealth.com/portal/site/imshealth/menuitem.18c196991f79283fddc0 ddc01ad8c22a/?vgnextoid=0711e590cb4dc310VgnVCM100000a48d2ca2RCRD&v gnextfmt=default (accessed October 2013).

Kondo, A., and K. Kawabuchi. 2012. "Evaluation of the Introduction of a Diagnosis Procedure Combination System for Patient Outcome and Hospitalisation Charges for Patients with Hip Fracture or Lung Cancer in Japan." *Health Policy* 107 (2–3): 184–93.

Matsuda, S. 2008. "Diagnosis Procedure Combination: The Japanese Approach to Case-mix." In *The Globalization of Managerial Innovation in Health Care*, edited by J. R. Kimberly, G. de Pouvourville, and T. D'Aunno. New York: Cambridge University Press.

MIC (Ministry of Internal Affairs and Communications). 2013. "Population Estimates." http://www.stat.go.jp/data/jinsui/pdf/201310.pdf (accessed October 2013).

MHLW (Ministry of Health, Labour and Welfare). 2011a. "Itemized Survey of Social Medical Care." http://www.mhlw.go.jp/toukei/list/26-19.html (accessed October 2013).

———. 2011b. "Survey on Generic Pharmaceuticals Usage." http://www.mhlw.go.jp/ bunya/iryou/kouhatu-iyaku/dl/111205-01.pdf (accessed October 2013).

———. 2012a. "Central Social Insurance Medical Council." http://www.mhlw.go.jp/stf/ shingi/2r98520000008ffd.html (accessed October 2013).

———. 2012b. "Fee Schedule Revisions." http://www.mhlw.go.jp/stf/seisakunitsuite/ bunya/kenkou_iryou/iryouhoken/iryouhoken15/index.html (accessed October 2013).

———. 2013. "National Medical Expenditures." http://www.mhlw.go.jp/toukei/list/37-21.html (accessed December 2013).

OECD. 2013. "OECD Health Data 2013." http://www.oecd.org/health/health-systems/ oecdhealthdata.htm (accessed October 2013).

Prime Minister of Japan and His Cabinet. 2013a. "Speech on Growth Strategy by Prime Minister Abe." http://www.kantei.go.jp/jp/headline/seicho_senryaku2013.html (accessed October 2013).

———. 2013b. "Summary of the 15th Round, Council of Social Security System Reform." http://www.kantei.go.jp/jp/singi/kokuminkaigi/dai15/gijisidai.html (accessed October 2013).

CHAPTER 6

The Political Economy of the Fee Schedule in Japan

John Creighton Campbell and Yasuo Takagi

Abstract

Japan's biennial revision of the fee schedule (shinryo houshu) *is an important tool for health policy in general and spending control in particular. It operates at two levels, macro and micro, and is less an economic calculation than a political negotiation among competing interests. Central is the battle between, on the one hand, the Ministry of Finance and the Ministry of Health, Labour and Welfare (MHLW), seeking to hold down spending; and on the other, medical providers led by the Japan Medical Association (JMA) and backed by the majority political party, seeking higher fees. The process is predictable and quite incremental for the most part, except when the political leadership takes a direct role, leading to more dramatic outcomes.*

Japanese Characteristics

The preceding chapter 5 is about the technical process and impact; here, we focus on the political process: how Japan's distinctive approach to cost containment works.[1]

That approach dates back to the early days of universal health care—the early 1960s—if not earlier. Its techniques were modified and improved in the early 1980s as a reaction to high growth in medical spending. It seeks to carry out three objectives: restrain spending, protect the viability and quality of the health care delivery system, and maintain political consent—that is, prevent dissatisfaction by the various participants from getting out of hand.

Many nations set prices and conditions in health care, but three characteristics of the Japanese system are distinctive. First, the fee schedule[2] applies to all providers and in all parts of Japan. Second, it is revised through an elaborate process every two years. Third, each service and product is evaluated individually, so the prices of some will go up, some will go down, and some will remain unchanged, depending on specific factors.

Three sets of factors influence these price changes. One set can be called *economic* factors, when prices are moved up or down based on their cost impact. For example, the cost of provision may have changed due to technological change or the price of supplies. One indicator is that if usage has risen sharply over the previous two years, the item may have become more profitable for providers, so the price can be cut; a drop in usage may indicate that the price should be increased. Or the acute hospital sector may have started running a deficit (or a big surplus). The underlying principle is maintaining an appropriate level of provision at minimum cost.

Another set of factors is *policy driven*, a reallocation of resources to bring changes in levels of provision of something. More home care or less use of a costly technology may be desired and can be achieved by manipulating prices or the conditions for use. At the broadest level, resources can be moved between inpatient care and outpatient care, between surgery and internal medicine (or pediatrics), or even between services and pharmaceuticals. Here the government in not just keeping the system going in a straight line, it is trying to steer policy in desired directions.

A third set of factors can be called *political*, maintaining consent and minimizing protest from powerful actors within the health care system (doctors, hospitals, pharmaceutical companies, insurers) or outside it (political parties, big interest groups, voters). Changes in the balance of power among actors pursuing their interests will bring changes in the allocation of resources—again, through price changes.

It is helpful to see these three sets of factors as operating through processes at two levels: macro, that is, the health care sector as a whole, and micro, that is one item at a time, or a number of items in the same category (even broad categories like hospital care).

In making such calculations, the government mainly focuses on the gross income of providers—doctors, hospitals, manufacturers of products, and so on. Their income depends almost entirely on the payments they get from health insurance. Change in provider revenue is seen as two types. The first depends on changes in the number of treatments and products provided. It is assumed that this will increase due to population aging (requiring more medical care) and technological advances (leading to shifts to more expensive services and medications, including those newly introduced). This is called the "natural expenditure increase" (*shizenzou*). The other type of revenue change is caused by changes in the fee schedule—our concern in this chapter. In principle, the combination of these two types adds up to the change in total medical expenditures.

The Macro Process

The most highly publicized and—at least superficially—contentious aspect of fee schedule revision is deciding the growth rate of the average price for health care over the next two years. It refers to how much medical spending would go up (or down) if the system continued to provide exactly the same amounts of the same services and products for another two years, but with different prices. It is thus a hypothetical number that does not pertain directly to the real world. In reality, the services and products on offer will change somewhat over the two years, and their volumes will change considerably. And so the calculation is not really an estimate, let alone a ceiling, for the growth of total public spending on health care.[3] This overall revision rate can be seen as comprising two components: the rise or fall in the weighted average prices paid both for pharmaceuticals and for medical services.[4]

The Normal Process

The following presents a brief account of the macro process in "normal" years since the mid-1980s (all except 1998, 2002, and 2010, which are discussed below under *Exceptional Processes*). The key participants are the Budget Bureau (BB) of the Ministry of Finance (MOF); the Health Insurance Bureau (HIB) of the Ministry of Health and Welfare (MHW; from 2001 the MHLW); the majority Liberal Democratic Party (LDP); and the JMA. Other actors—organizations of hospitals, associations of nurses and dentists, insurance carriers for big company employees, municipal governments (the carriers for nonemployees), pharmaceutical manufacturers—may be active and influential but are not direct participants, at least in the macro process.

How do the active participants relate to each other? On the side of spending restraint in the biennial debate are the BB and the HIB; these two agencies rarely differ very much in their approach to the fee schedule revision.[5] The HIB's most immediate concern is that it is responsible for managing the finances of the biggest health insurance program, which covers employees of small firms.[6] Its premium revenue is limited so it needs to keep spending down. The BB's number one concern is the subsidy from the general account budget (that is, tax revenues, plus government borrowing), which is a fixed proportion of total health care spending. Minimizing spending is the key to the problems of both agencies, which unites them in opposition to the JMA and the LDP.

On the provider side, physicians, hospitals, dentists, pharmaceutical companies, and so forth naturally hope for higher prices to increase their income. The JMA in particular has been regarded as one of the most powerful pressure groups in Japan since the days of its legendary chairman, Tarou Takemi (1904–1983). Its strength stems partly from its financial and electoral support for the LDP at both the local and national level. JMA interests are strongly represented by a specialized division (*Bukai*) of the LDP's Policy Board (*Seichoukai*) and by many rank-and-file LDP politicians with ties to the JMA chapters in their electoral districts.

Between the BB–HIB alliance and the LDP–JMA alliance stand some mediators, who may have preferences for one side or the other but are mainly interested in seeing that a deal comes about on schedule and without too much disruption. Interestingly, in the normal fee schedule revision process, actors whom one might expect to play this role are mostly absent: cabinet ministers, the prime minister, and the *Kantei* (the executive staff office). Most important are the director of the LDP's Policy Board, a senior leadership post in the party, and an informal group of influential LDP Dietmen who have a long connection with both the MHLW and the JMA, called "family" (*zoku*) politicians. For many years, the Health and Welfare *zoku* was led by Ryuutarou Hashimoto (1937–2006), a very powerful politician.[7]

The process begins in every odd-numbered year in the spring, with conversations between the director of the HIB and the budget examiner (*shukeikan*) assigned to the MHLW in the BB. The point is to get a general sense of problems and likely outcomes; their conversations continue throughout the year. The JMA, with backing from the LDP, also starts early in the revision process to make its arguments about why the financial situation of providers requires more money.

The MHLW has some objective data to counter the claims of the JMA. On the cost side, in June of every odd-numbered year, it carries out a survey of a large sample of doctors and hospitals to determine their spending on labor and materials—the Empirical Survey of Medical Care Economics (*Iryou Keizai Jittai Chousa*). This snapshot of the current year's costs is combined with estimates of how macroeconomic trends will affect providers' costs in the following two years. On the revenue side, the MHLW estimates the "natural revenue increase" caused by volume and technological change as described earlier (under the assumption that prices stay the same). This estimate derives from data of payments from health insurance to providers in the three previous years, as compiled in the annual calculation of national medical expenditures (*Kokumin Iryouhi*).

In principle, subtracting the estimated natural revenue increase from the estimated cost increase would produce the amount to be made up with price increases in the fee schedule revision for medical services. In practice, the process is far from being so cut-and-dried because all the rough estimates leave plenty of room for argument, and the JMA plus the LDP are capable of making their case for higher spending vigorously. But before attempting a more realistic account we can turn to determination of the amount for revising pharmaceutical prices.

In February of each odd-numbered year, the MHLW makes preliminary estimates of the economic situation for the upcoming fee schedule revision. Behind-the-scenes negotiations are held with other participants, including pharmaceutical manufacturers, to get a sense of the politics. Then in September, it carries out the Pharmaceutical Price Survey (*Yakka Chousa*), based on wholesalers' sales records, to determine the market prices of all pharmaceuticals.[8] These data are mainly used in the micro part of the fee schedule revision, but they also make it possible to reach a rough estimate of the difference between prices in the current fee schedule and actual market prices. That means that by early November HIB officials, along with their colleagues in the BB, can estimate the amount of savings derived from reducing the pharmaceutical fee schedule that could be used to finance an increase in the medical services fee schedule.

Arithmetically, subtracting the savings by cutting pharmaceutical prices from the amount necessary to raise medical service prices gives the amount of the overall fee schedule increase (or decrease). In reality, the reverse can be more important. The first two numbers may be adjusted up or down to come out to the preferred number for the overall fee schedule percentage change. That is because, politically, the overall number is the most important, the one the public as well as the medical care world takes as indicative of how tough or generous the government is.

A key point, not often acknowledged, is that such signaling is in reality the main purpose of all three of the macro numbers. The reason is that the changes in the fee schedule do not have a direct, immediate relationship with any of the key measures of actual spending: total medical expenditures, the amount to come from the Treasury or health insurance premiums, or the revenues of doctors, hospitals, and pharmaceutical manufacturers. In fact, the rates of price revisions are decided on the basis of quite uncertain assumptions and estimates.

Because the numbers are likely to change (even if slightly), the process remains lively to the end. It always concludes in mid- to late December, just in time to produce a number for the Treasury contribution, which is necessary for finalizing the national budget. The final day begins with the vice-director of the BB and the director of the HIB attending the final negotiating meeting, which is conducted mainly by the budget examiner and the responsible HIB division chief, who had been talking for months and actively negotiating for weeks. Then comes the last stage in the formal process, a ceremonial meeting of the Ministers of Finance and Welfare, where they sign a document that includes all the price-change numbers; also present is the LDP Policy Board chairman.[9]

This account is of the formal negotiation, and since, as noted earlier, the two ministries rarely have big differences, their interactions are generally not very contentious. Not so the informal negotiation between the real contenders, which line up as follows:

JMA	LDP *Bukai*	LDP Leaders	MHLW	MOF

The JMA pushes its supporters in the LDP to be more aggressive, and the MOF pushes the MHLW to be more aggressive. In the middle are two LDP leaders who are more concerned with reaching a deal than with how it comes out. One is the Policy Board chairman, the person most responsible for making deals in disputes about almost any policy issue. The other is the chief health and welfare *zoku* leader. When he is powerful, as Ryuutarou Hashimoto was in the earlier part of the period, he can dominate (when "boss" rather than leader might be the more appropriate term); when less so, as true of Yuuya Niwa later on, he still has to help broker the deal.

A participant offers a good account of the end game of the 1996 revision. In December 1995, after agreement had been reached between the BB vice-director and the HIB director, they visited Hashimoto's office together. He had recently been elected LDP president, was serving as the Minister of International Trade and Industry, and would become prime minister in a month.[10] All these

responsibilities did not preclude his playing the role of welfare *zoku* leader. He
endorsed the deal and telephoned the heads of the medical, dental, and pharmaceutical associations. "Without those phone calls," the participant said, "the deal
would not have been possible."

The informal process is a negotiation in the sense that the contenders take
strong positions and then narrow them down by bargaining, but it is not conducted by people sitting at opposite sides of a table in a meeting room (as are the
formal negotiations). Rather, it is a series of statements to reporters, punctuated
by quiet talks among various participants, perhaps at a restaurant. For example,
the budget examiner might go out for drinks with the HIB division chief in
charge and the head of the LDP health and welfare *bukai*. Meetings with top
JMA officials occur too. The term *nemawashi* (literally wrapping twine around
tree roots before transplanting) refers to how agreements are reached by individuals talking informally on many occasions. Of course, when differences are
narrow and the outcome is already anticipated, the meetings are fewer and easier,
but the process always works this way none the less.

We may conclude this discussion of the "normal" macro process by examining
the relationship of fee schedule changes to changes in the growth rate of total
health expenditures (figure 6.1). The growth rate of national medical expenditures (the dark blue line) is higher in the earlier part of the period, corresponding
to higher growth rates in the global revision rate (the green line). That national
medical expenditures grew at a slower pace from 1996 on is partly because the
fee schedule growth rate was negative on average those years.

**Figure 6.1 Annual Growth Rate of National Medical Expenditures and the Global, Medical
Service, and Pharmaceutical Price Revision Rates, 1990–2012**

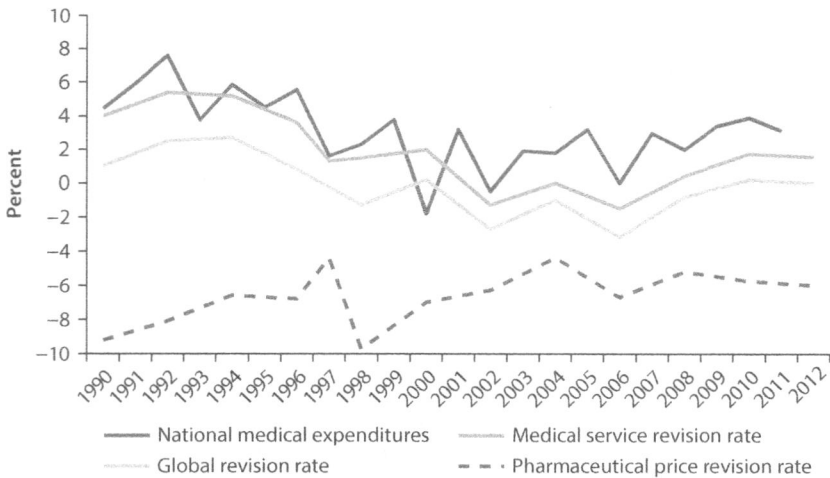

Sources: MHLW. 2012. "Central Social Insurance Medical Council." http://www.mhlw.go.jp/stf/
shingi/2r98520000008ffd.html; MHLW. 2013. "National Medical Expenditures." http://www.mhlw.go.jp/toukei/
list/37-21.html.

Although revisions of the global rate are not always directly reflected in the national medical expenditures, constricting the fee schedule has held down total health care spending in the long run. And as said, the signaling itself is quite important, especially in the "exceptional" years when the changes were more dramatic and real issues were at stake.

Exceptional Processes

Although the normal macro process appears to be quite portentous, certainly as covered by the newspapers including quotes from key participants, in fact it is mostly quite routine—even predictable. Everyone involved will have an accurate view of the outcomes early on, and in effect follow the same script as two years earlier.

Yet, there are exceptions. Some revisions brought marked changes from the previous one, as figure 6.1 shows: 1998, when the overall growth rate went below zero for the first time and pharmaceutical prices were cut sharply; 2002, when even medical service fees were reduced (the period 2004–06 is also interesting); and 2010, when the global revision rate went back into positive territory—just—for the first time in a decade.[11] Why were these years different? Because they saw real changes in public policy, which entailed somewhat different processes.

The First Exceptional Case—1998

Before the 1998 revision, a sharp recession and resulting perceived fiscal crisis had brought on drastic austerity measures. The Hashimoto administration imposed a Fiscal Structural Reform plan in November 1997 that required all ministries to constrain their budget requests. The ministry could ask for no more than ¥300 billion above its current level, sharply lower than it had planned, and it had to decide how to do it in about a month. Because most of its budget (such as pensions and public assistance) could not be constrained, at least in the short run, the bulk of savings had to come in the fee schedule revision. Accordingly the ministry enforced a 10 percent cut in average pharmaceutical prices, which it accomplished by changing the formula for calculation.[12]

The process in the 1998 revision was not particularly distinctive: the usual participants made the usual arguments in the usual sequence. However, the imposition of a governmentwide expenditure cutback—an exogenous shock—meant that the overall revision rate had to be negative; rather than confront the power of the JMA (one might note that the medical service revision was positive and indeed slightly higher than in the previous revision), the BB and HIB took the easier path of an unprecedented cut in pharmaceutical prices.

The Second Exceptional Case—2002

Jun'ichirou Koizumi became prime minister in April 2001, and he made the health care system—along with highway construction and the post office—one of his signature "structural reform" targets. For him, this meant overcoming resistance from entrenched interest groups and their allies in the LDP, particularly the *zoku* leaders. Many ideas for "radical reform" (*bappon kaikaku*) of health care were floated, including linking the growth of medical spending to gross domestic product (GDP) growth. The radical proposals in the end did not succeed, but the fee schedule revision was unprecedentedly drastic, and the process leading up to it the most contentious in years.

Prime Minister Koizumi and the MOF had the bad economic situation on their side. Public finances were very tight in the global recession of the early 2000s, and Japan was in the fourth year of deflation. By September 2001, JMA leaders were willing to confide to reporters that the prospect of a hike in medical service fees was dim and the best they could do was "hold the line."[13]

The prime minister adopted an aggressive strategy under the slogan *san-pouichiryouson*, an old Japanese tale that amounts to three sides sharing the pain of a loss. He said that patients would have the pain (*itami*) of an increase in the copayment for employees from 20 percent to 30 percent (and an increase for high-income older people as well); doctors and hospitals would have the pain of the first cut ever in medical service prices; and employers and employees would have the pain of an increase in premiums (for government-managed health insurance, the only plan where the government set the premium). Of course, the drug companies would have the pain of a big price cut as well, but they were used to it.[14]

Fighting back, the JMA focused on the medical services price cut, which it claimed would make hospitals and clinics impossible to manage, but the appeal was less effective than usual. For one thing, when the Medical Economics Survey came out in December, it showed that private practice doctors were actually doing well in the midst of the national recession.[15] For another, Koizumi's "three pains" strategy divided the LDP. The *bukai* and other strong sympathizers remained loyal to the JMA, but party leaders and many ordinary members were more concerned with the copayment increases and premium hikes, because they affected voters directly.

The biggest difference in the process was the very active role played by the prime minister himself, who made many strong public statements. The Prime Minister's Office (*Kantei*) was also unusually active, led by Assistant Chief Cabinet Secretary Kazuhiko Takeshima. According to a BB official at the time, Takeshima represented the prime minister so effectively that instead of the usual conflict of the HIB and BB vs. the JMA and LDP, it became a confrontation of the *Kantei* vs. the JMA and then the LDP, which meant in effect that the usual BB–HIB negotiations were superseded.[16] In the fall, the general feeling had been that a reduction in medical service prices would be impossible to achieve, but the tenacity of the prime minister and his staff prevailed and they were cut for the first time in history, with the global revision rate cut to below minus 2 percent, also the lowest ever (see figure 6.1).

Did this revision establish a new pattern? Not really—but the next two revisions were still interesting for policy watchers (box 6.1).

Box 6.1 Ebb and Flow in 2004 and 2006

The process for the next, 2004 revision started out similarly to that for 2002, with Prime Minister Koizumi determined to cut medical service prices again. However, the JMA was equally determined not to repeat its embarrassment of two years earlier.

The JMA leadership was under pressure from opposition factions and there was an election for a new chairman coming up. So was a national election for the Upper House, scheduled for July 2004, and the threat that the JMA might withhold support seemed quite real to LDP leaders. Three of them—the Secretary-General and the Policy Board Chief, plus the head of the Upper House LDP delegation—met with Prime Minister Koizumi in December and convinced him to ease up. Medical service fees were raised by a hair over zero percent.

Two years later, the 2006 revision went back to the 2002 pattern, and the efforts of Koizumi and the BB–HIB once again prevailed: medical service fees were cut back appreciably and the global revision rate was well under minus 3 percent, another new record.

The three instances—2002, 2004, and 2006—demonstrate the impact of powerful actors coming into the process who previously had not gotten much involved in fee schedule revision. In 2002 and 2006, the prime minister himself and his staff succeeded in forcing record-breaking cuts. In 2004, top LDP leaders, this time playing more than a broker role, responded to threats from the JMA and intervened to prevent a similar outcome in order to protect their party in an upcoming election.

The Third Exceptional Case—2010

In the general election of August 2009, the Democratic Party of Japan (DPJ) won a landslide victory.[17] The long-ruling LDP had become unpopular for many reasons: one the DPJ emphasized was a "collapse of medical care" (*iryou houkai*), which had gotten great attention in the media after 2007. The term referred to an assortment of inadequacies centering on the hospital sector. The DPJ's election manifesto promised to help hospitals, and more generally to end the LDP's health care austerity policies and spend an extra ¥900 billion to fix the system.[18]

As the fee schedule revision process was getting under way, the Diet came into session and Prime Minister Yukio Hatoyama delivered the policy speech:[19]

> We will change the policy pursued so far of single-mindedly containing medical and nursing care outlays purely from the perspective of fiscal rectitude and set about building a system that can supply high-quality medical services on an efficient and stable basis. As well as securing fine human resources, we must rebuild the system of providing medical care in such areas as regional medical care, emergency care, obstetrics and pediatrics.

The process for making that decision was new in that three of the usual key actors played much diminished roles.[20] The two bureaus that had handled much of the negotiations—HIB and BB—were now subordinated to the political leadership of their ministries. This was a governmentwide rule for the DPJ; it was particularly the case in the MHLW where relations between the bureaucrats and their new minister, Akira Nagatsuma, were mutually antagonistic.[21] The third diminished role was that of the JMA, which naturally suffered from having had so long and intimate a relationship with the defeated LDP; it had its position in a key MHLW advisory body reduced and also was rent by internal battles over strategy on whether to transfer its support from the LDP to the DPJ.

The main debate over the overall revision rate was clearly exposed in two press conferences. MOF vice-minister Yoshihiko Noda on November 19 said he favored a minus revision rate, as justified by recession and deflation, which had severely strained resources and also eased the costs problems of providers. Minister Nagatsuma replied the next day that resources were needed to improve hospital care and that the DPJ's manifesto mandated a positive revision rate. On December 10, Parliamentary Secretary Shinya Adachi (a surgeon before election to the Diet in 2004) and two colleagues in the MHLW political leadership called on vice-minister Noda at the MOF to start negotiations, and argued that Japan needed to raise overall medical spending from 8.1 percent of GDP up to the average in the Organisation for Economic Co-operation and Development of 8.9 percent. Adachi came up with concrete figures to support a hike in medical service fees of 1.73 percent at a press conference on December 15.

The following week, Chief Cabinet Secretary Hirofumi Hirano took on the role of broker. On December 23, just as the overall budget draft was about to be finalized, he invited Minister Nagatsuma and Finance Minister Hirohisa Fujii to the prime minister's residence for a final negotiation. Nagatsuma asked for an overall revision of plus 0.36 percent, and Fujii demanded a negative figure. Hirano proposed plus 0.19 percent; Fujii initially refused, but Hirano persuaded him and the deal was done.[22]

That the overall revision was a positive number for the first time since 2002, and indeed that medical service fees were raised by nearly 2 percent for the first time since 1998, was a real achievement for the DPJ. However, the magnitude of the price hike was hardly enough to transform the health care system, as the DPJ platform had intimated.

A Routine with Touches of Theater

To summarize, the main variation in the macro process was who was actively participating. In the normal process, detailed discussions were carried out by the BB and HIB, which came up with the government view of how much prices should be revised—in general decreased to reflect deflation and wage levels. The JMA and its allies in the LDP argued that they should be increased. At the last stage, when a final number for the total general account contribution to the system was required by the budget process, a compromise would be reached with the help of the LDP leadership and particularly the *zoku* leader. While contentious on the surface, the process in the normal years was highly routinized in that any of the participants could guess the outcome with great accuracy early on, and that the results were not much different from the previous review.

In the exceptional years, bigger changes were caused by interventions from outside this cozy group. For 1998, it was not an actual participant but the imposition of a strict ceiling on budget requests that compelled the MHW leadership to demand a cut in the general account contribution and therefore in overall prices—the process itself was not altered. In 2002, Prime Minister Koizumi demanded big reductions and intervened personally and via his staff to get what he wanted. In 2010, the newly elected DPJ brought the political leadership to the fore—and for the moment pushed out the JMA—and broke an eight-year austerity pattern.

Such changes in the process thus did have important effects on prices and to a lesser extent on the annual growth of national medical expenditures. More generally, it is the broad effect of having this biennial review—a process of political bargaining among powerful participants—that has kept growth in health care spending moderate, despite rapid population aging.

The Micro Process

After the numbers for the overall revision rate and the average price hikes for both medical services and pharmaceuticals are decided in December, the process of allocating the total among all the thousands of individual items begins.[23]

Smoke-Filled Rooms

The main arena for making these decisions is the Central Social Insurance Medical Council (Chuuikyou, for short), an official advisory body to the MHLW minister and staffed by the HIB. It is a tripartite committee. The seven payer members represent all the public insurance programs (including a mayor for the municipally managed system) plus representatives of business and labor. The seven provider members represent physicians (3), hospitals (2), dentists (1), and pharmacists (1). The six public interest members are university professors of law, economics, and public policy, plus a board member of the National Cancer Society (as of 2013). The JMA used to dominate Chuuikyou: its national organization named five of the (then) eight members of the provider side. Its power was reduced in 2004 following a bribery scandal, and then decimated in 2009 after the DPJ victory—Minister Nagatsuma picked three dissident physicians to replace the JMA-named members.[24]

Chuuikyou has an advisory role in health insurance and provision more generally but fee schedule revision is its main function. It meets through the year, and in the fall before a fee schedule revision, it discusses the macro issues in the form of a debate between payers and providers. It usually makes rather vague recommendations (although in 2009 the disagreement was so strong it could not agree on anything) that do not have much effect. Its real process starts when the global revision rate has been decided, or in practice after the New Year holiday, and ends in early March when all the new fees have to be decided in time to be published and then go into effect on April 1.

The medical service fee schedule has over 3,000 separate fees covering virtually everything a physician or hospital (or dentist or pharmacist) might do, along with detailed conditions. The staff—the Medical Economics Division of the HIB—makes the initial proposals. For old items, the great majority of items will be modified slightly if at all, mainly to adjust to economic or technical changes since the last review. The staff looks at changes in volume (based on an annual survey of health insurance claims by item) and may lower a fee if a sudden increase indicates the procedure may have become more profitable. Multiplying the price by the volume gives the expenditure for that item, which shows how any price revision will be reflected in total health care expenditures. These decisions are officially made by Chuuikyou, but most of the negotiations are made between provider organizations and the ministry's bureaucrats because the details are very complex.

New items or big price increases are more complicated. One type is called "technical" (*gijutsukei*), where many requests come from specialist associations, along with supporting evidence. These are examined by the Medical Technology Evaluation subcommittee of Chuuikyou and then discussed by the members and the staff; some 300 or so might be approved for inclusion or a price increase. The other type is "programmatic" (*seidokei*), such as incentives to increase home visits or end-of-life care. These are policy changes that are initiated by the MHLW rather than requests from providers, and Chuuikyou debates these as well. A third type of changing items occurs if a decision made in the previous review causes problems when put into practice, in which case the item will be modified in a cost-neutral way.

Because the total amount is already set, spending on new items must come at the expense of existing items and so will incur some resistance. Since evidence about costs and efficacy will be ambiguous, the price must be based on analogous items in Japan or experience abroad. The HIB's strategy is usually to set the fee as low as possible until more experience is gained.

The Art of Balance—"Baransu"

Most of the controversy in Chuuikyou deliberations is not about individual items, but rather price changes in groups of items that work to the advantage or detriment of particular categories of providers because of who uses them. The main such categories are inpatients vs. outpatients; acute vs. chronic care; hospitals vs. clinics (solo private practitioners); big urban hospitals vs. smaller and regional hospitals; and the various clinical specialties. Maintaining *baransu* or avoiding "unevenness" (*dekoboko*) is the initial assumption. A classic example is that when the birthrate and thus the number of young children declined, the prices of various procedures that were mostly carried out by pediatricians were raised to maintain physician income relative to other specialties. The guiding principle is to avoid one or another group feeling deprived—a way to maintain political consent for the fee schedule system. But the process is hardly automatic.

One effect of *baransu* is that the pattern of spending and therefore relative incomes tends to be quite stable across even long periods. The biggest example is that clinic physicians were advantaged long ago, in a simpler era, when they dominated health care provision in Japan. That advantage was maintained partly by this *baransu* norm as well as by the strength of the JMA, which disproportionally represents solo-practice clinical physicians. As we saw above, the JMA was an influential participant in the macro-level fee schedule revision process, but its biggest weight came in determining allocations across categories, where its dominating role in Chuuikyou was the key. The JMA and the HIB— Chuuikyou's staff—were perpetually in conflict: the HIB argued for a broader view including more resources for hospitals. Because the JMA's influence within Chuuikyou was backed up by its close ties to the majority party, its views most often prevailed.

Recently, the BB has increasingly played a role in these allocation decisions.[25] Earlier, it had only become involved in specific reforms aimed at constraining costs, such as conversations with the JMA when the government was trying to deal with the problem of long lengths of stay in hospitals. This role grew in the Koizumi era: with "minus revisions" the BB could not be content only to talk about macro issues, it had to get involved in showing how quality could be preserved, and to some extent new policy initiatives be supported, despite declining resources. The BB and the HIB generally agreed but because the BB was an outsider it could be more aggressive in debating with the JMA and its allied politicians. That became more important when the *iryou houkai* campaign against austerity gathered steam after 2007. BB officials felt they could not appear to be ignoring such criticism, so they argued that problems like shortages of pediatricians and obstetricians in the provinces were matters of distribution, not cuts in total spending. The solution would then lie in shifting resources from clinics to acute hospitals.

Some Rebalancing toward Acute Hospitals

This shift really took hold in the 2010 revision, the biggest change to allocation patterns since at least the early 1980s. The accounts of a "crisis in health care" that peaked in 2008–09[26] were partly in reaction to the Koizumi government's overall austerity policy in health care spending, but were primarily focused on shortages in hospital care. Many hospitals were operating in the red and particular departments or entire hospitals were closing, especially in the provinces. In contrast, clinic physicians appeared to be doing reasonably well despite the poor economy. The 2008 revisions under LDP rule made some small steps toward redressing this imbalance. The fee for outpatient revisits in hospitals was raised by ¥30 (though the level was still much lower than for clinics—tenacious JMA opposition prevented that from being lowered). The increase in revenue to the hospital sector was about ¥150 billion.[27]

The takeover of government by the DPJ in 2009 led to a much bigger shift toward hospitals, with the increase devoted only to improving acute inpatient care estimated at about ¥400 billion.[28] The MHLW political leadership promoted this cause, an explicit promise in the DPJ's election manifesto. They cited the results of the June 2009 Medical Economics Survey that the average hospital was running about ¥200 million in the red and that the number of surgeons had dropped by 8 percent (obstetricians by 11 percent) since 1996. MHLW Minister Nagatsuma visited Tokyo Women's Medical University in early December to highlight a shortage of doctors specialized in newborn babies and proclaimed that "lives are being lost that shouldn't be; the fee schedule must be properly tailored."[29] Now that the LDP had lost an election, and much of the providers' weight on Chuuikyou had shifted to the hospital side, the JMA was not in a position to offer much opposition.

This shift of resources toward hospitals continued in a less drastic way in the 2012 revision, when the DPJ's priorities were about the same as in 2010: support for medical care in provincial areas (especially pediatrics and obstetrics), acute care hospitals, better working conditions for hospital doctors, in-home care for older people with chronic conditions, and high-tech treatments as for cancer.

A Little Daylight Penetrates

The micro-level fee schedule revision process, which used to take place in a small, closed arena, was opened up in the 2000s. On the one hand, the BB increasingly intervened to assert its economizing policies, and even to support increased financing in priority areas so long as it could be accomplished by savings elsewhere. The "elsewhere" inevitably meant reductions for the items that supported the high incomes of solo-practice clinic physicians, whom the JMA was dedicated to protecting. The sudden plunge of JMA influence when the LDP lost power in 2009, along with the victorious DPJ's determination to implement its election promise to improve hospital care, led to a major shift in micro-level allocation patterns.

Insights

The details of how the biennial process of fee schedule revision works are "Made in Japan," but the underlying logic nevertheless has broader ramifications. It is likely that in any nation the basic conflict between payers and providers will come to the fore whenever the issue of health care spending is on the agenda. Elected politicians at the leadership and rank-and-file levels will be drawn in. Where, how often, and in what manner negotiations take place will vary widely, but the process will probably be quite different depending on whether macro- or micro-level spending is in question. Finally, most variations in outcomes will be caused by three sets of changes: economic, policy, and political—the shifts in the balance of power among participants.

Universal Health Coverage for Inclusive and Sustainable Development
http://dx.doi.org/10.1596/978-1-4648-0408-3

How did these three factors affect outcomes in Japan? First, economic: shifts in the overall economy and the fiscal situation and in the supply, demand, and costs of various items, fed pretty directly into price decisions. In figure 6.1, we observed that prices grew more slowly in the second half of the period after 1990, a trend partially caused by tougher constraints on expenditures overall due to the economy and stringent fiscal policies.

Second, policy: the preferences of the main actors in the "normal" process are too stable to account for much change in spending patterns, but when the political leadership wants change and is willing to push for it, as with Prime Minister Koizumi for less spending in general and the DPJ administration for more outlays (particularly on hospitals), they can have a big impact at macro level. At micro level, there is always a lot of back and forth on policy issues, as for example when the government decided it wanted to increase home visits, or improve acute inpatient care.

Third, politics: fee scale revision is a conflictual negotiation process where power matters. Changes in power relationships can bring change in price decisions, as when the JMA lost influence (at least for a time) in 2010, and when the government changes hands (it remains to be seen what the return of the LDP to power will mean for the fee schedule). However, the biggest impact of politics has been to prevent rather than cause change. The careful attention to "balance" in the income going to various sorts of providers avoids a sense of relative deprivation that could lead to protest. Careful adjustment to preserve the status quo is the norm. It takes exceptional effort to disturb the equilibrium, though, as seen in 1998, 2002, and 2010, it can happen.

A key is the routine. Every two years all the main participants in health care financing and delivery are drawn into a highly structured review process. Current problems are identified via formal surveys and informal assessments. Priorities emerge from long negotiations; firm deadlines force compromises. At the end of each cycle, there is a new fee schedule that strikes a balance in the many long-standing conflicts of interest that pervade health care. The changes are not very great, so that the system remains relatively stable, but in the aggregate and over time new problems have been managed and shifts in policy priorities accomplished. No doubt results are far from optimal, but then the process starts again two years later and the problems can be addressed once more.

Are there lessons for other nations? Obviously, the system as a whole cannot just be transplanted: health care is too embedded in broader society and past experience for that. But three aspects of the Japanese approach are worthy of attention. First, controlling prices can be an important key to controlling how the overall health care system works. Second is the usefulness of a regular review cycle that can realign all the moving parts incrementally without turning the system upside down. The third is that a structured and iterative process for negotiations among the key participants should be developed—or, more likely, allowed to emerge.

Universal Health Coverage for Inclusive and Sustainable Development
http://dx.doi.org/10.1596/978-1-4648-0408-3

Interviews Conducted for the Chapter

Endo, Hisao, Gakushuin University (former chairman of the Central Social Insurance Medical Council), January 8, 2013 (Takagi).

Inoguchi, Yuuji, Vice-Chair, All Japan Hospital Association (former member of the Central Social Insurance Medical Council), January 11, 2013 (Takagi).

Konno, Kouichi, Budget Bureau, Ministry of Finance, February. 6, 2013 (Campbell).

Nakagawa, Makoto, Advisor to the Vice President for Concessional Finance and Global Partnerships, World Bank (former Budget Examiner for Social Security, Ministry of Finance), August 15, 2012 and March 5 2013 (Campbell).

Nakamura, Shuuichi, Special Advisor to the Cabinet, The Cabinet Office (former Director, Health Insurance Bureau, MHLW), August 24, 2012 (Takagi).

Shinkawa, Hirotsugu, Budget Examiner, Budget Bureau, Ministry of Finance, February. 5, 2013 (Campbell).

Suzuki, Kunihiko, Standing Director, Japan Medical Association, February. 1, 2013 (Takagi).

Suzuki, Yasuhiro, Ministry of Defense (former senior official, MHLW), December. 18, 2012 (Takagi).

Tanaka, Shigeru, Professor, Graduate School of Business Administration, Keio University, and Chair, Management Committee, Kyoukai Kenpo, August 21, 2012 (Campbell).

Yamada, Takashi, President, Taito Hospital and key person, the Japan Association for Development of Community Medicine, September 4, 2012 (Takagi).

Notes

1. This chapter is based on prior research (reported in Campbell and Ikegami 1998); newspaper accounts, primarily from the *Asahi Shimbun*; and published and unpublished documents of the MHLW, Ministry of Finance, Liberal Democratic Party, and Democratic Party of Japan. Interviews were conducted with past and present government officials and other health policy leaders (see "Interviews" at the end of the chapter).

2. Discussed in detail in chapter 5.

3. That would be a mandatory "global budget," which means a limit or a target for total expenditures by a nation, a state, a medical care system, or even a hospital.

4. The changes in fees for dental services and dispensing medications are also calculated and reported (medical devices are included in pharmaceuticals), but these do not matter much for the overall rise and fall and are not contentious at the macro level.

5. That is quite different from the budget process, where the BB and other ministries are front-line adversaries (Campbell 1977).

6. It thus was always in a delicate financial position compared with the program for big-firm employees. This program can be called Association Health Insurance (Kyoukai Kenpo), although its official English name is "Japan Health Insurance Association-managed Health Insurance." Until it was semi-privatized in 2008, this program was called Government Managed Health Insurance (Seikan).

7. He was prime minister for two and a half years in the 1990s. In a sense health-care politics ended his career—he withdrew from politics in 2004 after disclosure of a ¥100 million political contribution (around US$1 million) from the Japan Dental Association.

8. See chapter 5 for details.

9. Nakagawa, second interview.

10. This was in the coalition cabinet led by Socialist Tomiichi Murayama. He resigned in January 1996 and Hashimoto became prime minster.

11. Note that the unusual rise in pharmaceutical prices for 1997 was technical: an extra review was required to adjust to a hike in the consumption tax rate from 3 percent to 5 percent, which affected the prices of medications directly.

12. See chapter 5; Nakagawa second interview.

13. *Asahi Shimbun*, September 22, 2001.

14. Pharmaceutical manufacturers were now in a weaker position because the government had largely succeeded in separating prescribing from dispensing; most doctors and hospitals no longer depended on profits from selling drugs and so had no reason to join the manufacturers in contesting price cuts.

15. *Asahi Shimbun*, December 6, 2001.

16. Shinkawa interview.

17. This account relies mainly on coverage by the *Asahi Shimbun*.

18. For the manifesto, see http://www.dpj.or.jp/english/manifesto/manifesto2009.pdf.

19. Official translation.
http://www.kantei.go.jp/foreign/hatoyama/statement/200910/26syosin_e.html.

20. The issue of improving hospital care is treated below.

21. Due partly to his leadership in the Diet in exposing a scandal about mishandled pension records.

22. *Asahi Shimbun*, December 24, 2010, p. 4.

23. For more details on the micro process, see Campbell and Ikegami 1998. How this works for pharmaceuticals is described in chapter 5; here we concentrate on allocations in medical services. This account is based partly on interviews with Yasuhiro Suzuki, Kunihiko Suzuki, and Yuuji Inoguchi.

24. In recent years, two subcouncils—for medical care and for health insurance—of the MHLW's multifunction Social Security Deliberation Council are said to play an increasingly important role in setting the general framework, but they still do not have the intimate link to the fee schedule process that Chuuikyou has.

25. Shinkawa interview and second Nakagawa interview.

26. The number of articles per year mentioning *iryou houkai* in *Asahi Shimbun* from 2005 to 2012 were: 2, 7, 35, 121, 112, 82, 24, 19.

27. *Asahi Shimbun*, October 31, 2009, p. 3.

28. *Asahi Shimbun*, December 26, 2009, p. 6.

29. *Asahi Shimbun*, December 11, 2009, p. 3.

References

Asahi Shimbun, from the digital archive Kikuzo II.

Campbell, John Creighton. 1977. *Contemporary Japanese Budget Politics.* Berkeley: University of California Press.

Campbell, John Creighton, and Naoki Ikegami. 1998. *The Art of Balance in Health Policy: Maintaining Japan's Low-Cost, Egalitarian System.* New York: Cambridge University Press.

Ministry of Health, Labour and Welfare (MHLW). 2012 "Central Social Insurance Medical Council." http://www.mhlw.go.jp/stf/shingi/2r98520000008ffd.html (accessed March 2014).

———. 2013. "National Medical Expenditures." http://www.mhlw.go.jp/toukei/list/37-21.html (accessed March 2014).

CHAPTER 7

Factors Determining the Allocation of Physicians in Japan

Naoki Ikegami

Abstract

Decisions made by the Japanese government around 1880 to concentrate resources at university level and to establish vocational medical schools were crucial in setting the path to today's health care system. One legacy is a two-tier structure: the premier medical schools that include almost all the relatively large, high-tech (and predominantly public) hospitals; and the less prestigious medical schools whose graduates tend more to have their own private practices.

The forces encouraging physicians to practice as specialists in big-city medical centers have, however, been mitigated by the higher incomes both of private-practice physicians focusing on primary care and of physicians in rural hospitals.

The Japanese experience suggests that by providing dual entry levels and offering multiple career paths for physicians, limiting the development of high-tech hospitals, and balancing monetary and nonmonetary rewards, physicians can be better allocated than otherwise. These successes owe much to the government's control of the payment system, which has contained costs and out-of-pocket payments, and set higher fees for primary care than specialty services.

Objectives and Historical Context

The objectives of this chapter are to present Japan's experience in physician allocation, as it may offer lessons for countries attempting to make service delivery more balanced and thus meet universal health coverage goals.

Physicians are at the core of health care, and along with factors like physician numbers and quality of training, allocation is key to successful health outcomes. Appropriate allocation in the ratios between physicians working in hospitals and in private practice, between general practitioners and specialists and among the various specialties, and between those practicing in urban and in rural areas is hard to achieve because policy makers must contend both with the demands of professional autonomy and the need to adhere to global standards of medical education. These forces—as suggested by experience in advanced and middle-income countries alike—tend on their own to concentrate power and resources among specialists and big-city hospitals at the expense of primary care and rural facilities. In Japan, countervailing dynamics have mitigated these trends.

The historical context for the development of physicians and hospitals in Japan goes back to the middle of the eighteenth century. Even at that date, the country had many well-established private practitioners of traditional medicine. This system, and the principle of freedom to open their own practice, remained essentially intact even after the government embarked on rapid modernization throughout society from 1868 (Fuse 1979), mainly because the transition to Western medicine was gradual. Thus the policy decisions that were made over a century ago have continued to influence the health care system to this day (Campbell and Ikegami 1998).

In 1882, practitioners of traditional medicine (plus their sons if at least 25 years old) were formally given licenses by the government to continue practicing. This assured the livelihood of existing practitioners, continued access to service for the general population, and left intact the basic structure of the delivery system. However, from the following year, new licenses required passing an examination exclusively focused on Western medicine. This move effectively closed the door to any future for traditional medicine, despite vigorous lobbying by its leaders, so that a dual system of Western and traditional medicine (as in contemporary China and Korea) never developed.

Japan's limited resources were concentrated on establishing the Tokyo University Medical School in 1877. Most of the faculty were recruited from Germany at great expense. Hiring at least three of its graduates as faculty was made a condition for establishing university-level medical schools. This cascade process led to a pyramid structure of the medical profession, with Tokyo University graduates at the apex. Moreover, the strength of these academic-based vertical relationships impeded the development of specialist organizations based on horizontal peer relationships.

In addition to university-level training, vocational medical schools were permitted. Many were initially established by the private sector or by local governments and at first accreditation standards were not high (although, unlike university medical schools, their graduates had to pass a licensing examination). The government later raised standards, restricting enrollment to five-year middle-school graduates and requiring a structured four-year course.[1] As a result, most private sector schools had to close. Soon most local government schools were also forced out of business by an austerity campaign prohibiting subsidies. By 1915 most of the remaining vocational medical schools were run by the national government, and these operated until 1952 when vocational schools were abolished by the American occupation as part of an effort to upgrade and reform medical care.

Japan was well served by the dual structure of medical education (university and vocational) from the 1880s into the immediate post–World War II period, when its modern health care system was being developed: world-class standards in physician training were set as the norm, and despite limited resources, an adequate supply of physicians was trained. An important principle was that instead of explicitly classifying vocational school graduates as "second-class" physicians, the government set appropriate accreditation standards for the schools, and allowed graduates to sit for a licensing examination that gave them the same status as university graduates. This practice facilitated their integration into the profession, helped enforce quality standards, offered an alternate career path for less academically qualified students, and became a valuable source of physicians for primary care.

The way hospitals developed has also had lasting impact. Hospitals, or even public or religious institutions that could serve as nuclei for hospitals, had not existed before Westernization, when they were set up to serve three main purposes: *teaching and research*—because Western medicine could not be taught without studying patients, hospitals had to be built along with medical schools;[2] *military needs*—the rebellions and wars of the Meiji era created a pressing need for hospitals to treat combat-related diseases and injuries;[3] and *quarantine anxieties*—concerns about communicable diseases brought local governments to build specialized hospitals. At the same time, without any explicit policy direction, many successful private practitioners added beds to their offices and then expanded them into hospitals, which soon became the most numerous type.

The lack of well-equipped hospitals, coupled with a shortage of well-qualified, university-educated physicians, led to the establishment of "closed networks" between hospitals and university clinical departments. The practice has persisted to this day: virtually all staff physicians in major hospitals have been trained in and dispatched from one university. This network extended to smaller hospitals, which included those located in rural areas that had forged links with university clinical departments through personal relationships between departmental chiefs and hospital owners. As there were too few senior positions in the major hospitals for all graduates even from prestigious universities, some graduates went to these hospitals.

The hierarchical structure of university clinical departments was not restricted to the university hospital, but extended to most hospitals in Japan. Thus heads of university clinical departments, beyond overseeing research and clinical practice at their own hospital, saw their authority and responsibility extend to specialists in their affiliated hospitals. With the university as its focal point, a close-knit body of physicians grew, which proved to be more effective than that of government or professional organizations. Private-practice physicians and some private hospitals were left outside.

A two-tier structure in health care has thus emerged.[4] The upper tier is composed of the premier medical schools that include almost all the relatively large, high-tech (and predominantly public) hospitals. The lower tier consists of the less prestigious medical schools whose graduates tend more to have their own private practices. However, this division is not altogether rigid because, while very few physicians have become university professors, they can pursue the following career options:

Universal Health Coverage for Inclusive and Sustainable Development
http://dx.doi.org/10.1596/978-1-4648-0408-3

- Becoming departmental chief of a major affiliated hospital with the further possibility of being named hospital director
- Developing the clinical department to which they have been dispatched, and, by becoming the hospital director, upgrade the hospital to a regional center
- Opting out of the hierarchical system by going into private practice, opening an office and focusing on primary care
- Expanding their offices to hospitals. Several private medical schools originated from solo practices.

Physicians in the last two groups may have less prestige among their peers, but generally have higher incomes. They form the backbone of the Japan Medical Association (JMA), the most powerful professional body in Japan. Ambitious physicians can aspire to becoming president and chief executive officer of its prefectural and local chapters, if not of the JMA itself.

Another key point about Japan is that, apart from the JMA, specialist medical organizations remain weak compared with those in other countries: the vertical relationship (of physicians within the university clinical department) is stronger than the horizontal peer relationship (within specialist organizations). Aside from a few exceptions such as anesthesiology, it was only from the 1980s that specialist organizations started to develop formal accreditation programs, because there was little need to obtain formal accreditation in either part of the two-tier structure. Those within hierarchical university clinical departments focus on academic research for their advancement, not clinical skills. Those opting out of that system seek maximum freedom to open their own practice, including the right to proclaim any specialty. Although the great majority of younger physicians have gone through the formal process of specialist accreditation, even in the early years of this century about half the accredited specialists had been "grandfathered in" (Ikegami 2003), and specialist societies have less influence than in the West.

Aside from setting the structure of medical education (see next paragraph) and limiting development of public hospitals, the government has rarely attempted to directly control the activities and income of doctors and medical facilities. In the upper tier the university clinical departments retain substantial autonomous power over their hierarchies. In the lower tier, strong political influence via the JMA has prevented any limitations on the expansion of private-sector providers. Indeed, their opportunities for expansion were increased when low-interest loans became available when the Medical Finance Corporation was set up in 1960, and again in 1964 when restrictions were imposed on expansion of public-sector hospitals. The advent of regional health planning in 1985 extended the control of hospital beds to private hospitals, but there are still no restrictions on purchasing equipment or expanding services.

The government has exercised direct control in setting the number of medical schools and students entering them, which are legally the purview of the Ministry of Education, Culture, Science and Technology (MEXT).[5] Over the years, policy has gone back and forth: restrictions served the dual purpose of containing costs and assuring quality, but there were also expansions when physician shortages became a political issue. In 1948, the cap on student enrollment was reduced to 2,840 in 47 medical schools, down from the prewar level of 3,030.[6] Later, as health care use increased with the expansion of health insurance coverage, enrollment was gradually increased, reaching 4,040 in 1969. In the 1970s, when local physician shortages were criticized, 33 new medical schools were opened and enrollment doubled to 8,260 under the slogan of "one prefecture, one medical school." However, with the economy in recession and a surplus of physicians projected, the cap on new enrollment was lowered to 7,710 in 1995. Renewed concern about physician shortages in the media then led to another reversal, with a gradual increase to –9,041 new enrollees in 2013 (MEXT 2012).

Status of Physicians and Hospitals

The number of physicians in Japan, at 2.2 per 1,000 population in 2010, is below the average for the Organisation for Economic Co-operation and Development (OECD), but the number of hospital beds is the highest in the world at 13.4 per 1,000 population in 2011. This high bed number is partly because Japan has many psychiatric hospitals and chronic-care hospitals that function much as nursing homes. However, even without those, the country has 8.0 curative care beds (which encompasses acute and post-acute care in Japan) per 1,000 population in 2011, which is still very high (OECD 2013).[7]

The discrepancy between numbers of physicians and hospital beds suggests that inpatients in Japanese hospitals are underserved. Moreover, the one-third of all physicians in private practice generally do not have access to hospitals, and almost all hospitals maintain large outpatient departments staffed by their own physicians. The result is an extreme shortage of time to treat inpatients.

Another distinctive characteristic of Japanese physicians is that virtually all profess to belong to a specialty—not only internal medicine or surgery, but also ophthalmology, orthopedics, and so forth—because they have continued to identify themselves with their medical school departments. That is true not only in hospitals, but also in physicians' offices. Even though most private practitioners perform mainly primary care and often treat most problems their patients present, they profess to be specialists (a claim they are not required to justify).

This combination of shortages of physicians treating inpatients plus specialization in their training and self-identity can have unfortunate outcomes. For example, Japanese hospitals are often criticized for refusing to admit patients through the emergency room. The ambulance service often has to call several before gaining admission, sometimes leading to delays of several hours, and incidences of patients dying. A simple lack of an available physician is the commonest excuse, but another factor is that Japanese physicians may lack the confidence to treat a new serious case outside their specialty. Very few have

Universal Health Coverage for Inclusive and Sustainable Development
http://dx.doi.org/10.1596/978-1-4648-0408-3

specialized in general practice or family medicine that spans specializations, and only a few in emergency medicine.

The Ministry of Health and Welfare produced a report with a proposal to establish general practice or family medicine as part of the medical school curriculum and to recognize it as a specialty in 1987. This proposal was opposed by the JMA because it could have restricted its professional autonomy.[8] Moreover, medical schools and the Ministry of Education—in charge of undergraduate medical education—did not support it because they continued to focus more on biomedical research and on subspecialties. Although the first department of general practice was established at Saga Medical School in 1978 and the majority of medical schools now have such a department, the formal recognition of general practice as a specialty will only start in 2015.[9]

The Ministry of Health, Labour and Welfare (MHLW)[10] introduced one measure with a significant impact on postgraduate education of physicians—its 2004 initiative to make the two-year residency program not only mandatory (earlier it was just recommended), but also to require it to be a rotating residency that included the major specialties and emergency medicine. Final-year students apply for the residency programs through a matching system. Its introduction effectively closed the door to the long-established practice of newly licensed physicians directly entering university clinical departments of the medical school from which they had graduated to be trained as specialists.

However, before the impact of this new program could be fully evaluated, the length of mandatory rotating period was shortened to one year in 2010 because of opposition from medical school faculty, who claimed that the new program had resulted in their graduates obtaining residency positions in large urban hospitals and not remaining in the university where they had graduated. This tendency was particularly serious in medical schools in provincial cities. To fill the shortage, they had to withdraw physicians from their affiliated hospitals, which in turn led to serious shortages there.

This case illustrates the difficulty of attempting piecemeal reforms of physician training. Before taking action the government should have considered some significant advantages of the existing system. First, partly because the process of credentialing specialists has not fully developed in Japan, physicians are more willing than their counterparts in other countries to enter areas where they have not had much formal training—in particular, physicians leaving hospitals for private practice provide mainly primary care, despite professing to be specialists. Thus the recently graduated physicians' wish to become a specialist is fulfilled but, since the number of hospital positions for the specialty is limited, the great majority have to broaden their scope of practice to provide more generalized primary care services. This approach differs from that in other countries that restrict entry into specialties by limiting the number of residency positions in each specialty rather than at the point of final employment.[11] The second advantage was that the control of physician appointments by the university clinical departments was more effective than the new approach in meeting rural health care needs, because once a hospital had become affiliated it was assured of having physicians dispatched to it.

Variations in Physician Incomes

Although payment is basically fee for service, prices and the conditions of billing are strictly regulated by the MHLW's fee schedule, and the amount is the same for the same item whether in the public or private sector.[12] This schedule is the government's key mechanism for exercising indirect control of physician allocation. Although the impact has not necessarily been as intended because of the need to negotiate with provider organizations—particularly the JMA—the fee schedule has had a decisive impact on how much money physicians earn.

Because the JMA's main constituents are physicians providing primary care in their own offices or owners of private hospitals, the JMA has provided countervailing forces against pressures common to the practice of medicine everywhere—specialization and urbanization. The fee schedule sets the same fee for the same service regardless of specialist accreditation. Primary care on average pays more than specialized care because of the way fees are structured, and doctors in rural areas earn more than those in urban areas primarily because the same amount is paid for the same service regardless of the local cost of living (urban areas are of course more expensive). These facts are broadly understood in the field and affect physicians' decisions on where they work, although unfortunately the data do not allow more than suggestive illustrations.

Specialization versus Primary Care

The fee schedule determines not only prices but also the conditions of billing for physician and hospital services. Payment is only made to the facility, and not to individual physicians. For physicians in offices—overwhelmingly solo practices—this payment would be their income less expenses. In contrast, hospital-based physicians are paid fixed wages and do not receive any direct payment from patients (charging more than the fees set in the fee schedule by "balance billing" is strictly prohibited). These wages tend to be based on seniority and not on the physician's specialty or the amount they earn (except for the physician who owns the hospital).[13] Average wages of hospital-based physicians are relatively low in Japan—over the last couple of decades around two and half times those of the average worker (figure 7.1).[14]

Physicians in private practice do better financially, largely because fees for services in primary care are relatively high compared with fees for high-tech procedures in hospitals. When the fee schedule was established in 1927, the bulk of medical services were delivered by private practitioners. Subsequent item-by-item revisions have been incremental, thus favoring those who initially had a large share. Moreover, the JMA has played a dominant role in negotiating with the government on fee schedule revisions.

Universal Health Coverage for Inclusive and Sustainable Development
http://dx.doi.org/10.1596/978-1-4648-0408-3

Figure 7.1 Wages of Physicians in Nongovernment Hospitals Relative to the Average of All General Workers

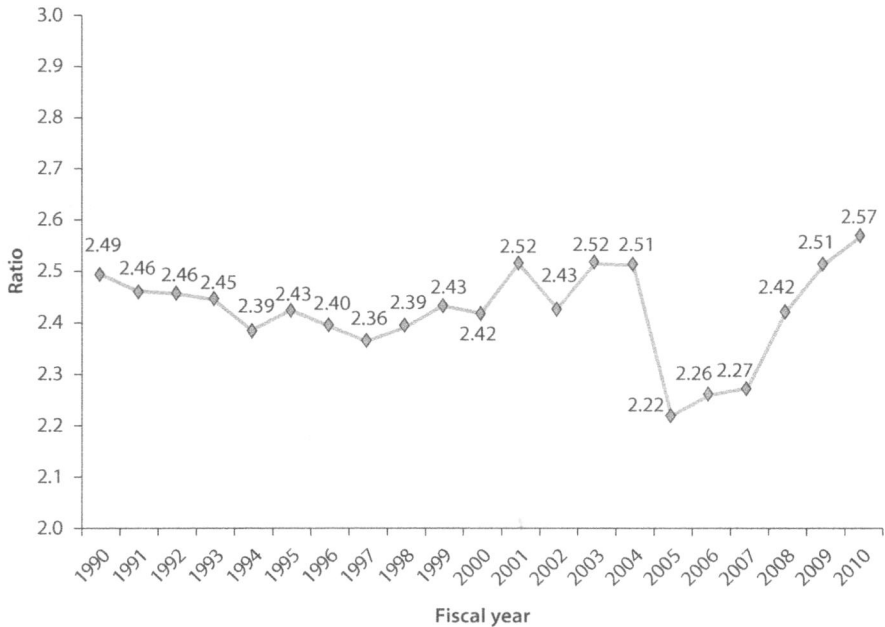

Source: Wage Census Surveys 1990–2010 (MHLW 1991–2011).
Note: Standardized to the consumer price index and age composition.

The average annual net income of physicians in private practice in 2011 was ¥21.0 million according to the *Financial State of Hospitals and Clinics,* based on a sample survey carried out by the MHLW every two years (MHLW 2011a). In contrast, the average wage of hospital-based physicians was ¥11.4 million[15] according to the MHLW's *2010 Wage Census* which includes all physicians, except for those employed in government-owned hospitals (MHLW 2011b). While there is no way to estimate wages of specialists in the upper tier hospitals directly, we know that physicians in the 46 hospitals owned by "designated" cities (those having a population of over half a million), which are definitely "upper tier," average ¥16.4 million in the same year (MIC 2012) above the average for all hospital-based physicians, but below that for all private-practice physicians.

Some caveats apply, however:

First, the wages of hospital-based physicians do not include additional income earned from part-time work, which is carried out by a significant proportion of hospital-based physicians. Part-time physicians in general hospitals accounted for 19.2 percent of the total when converted to full-time equivalents in 2010 (MHLW 2011c). However, specialist physicians employed in designated city hospitals are generally not allowed to work part time, which may be one reason why their wages were higher than the average to compensate for the restriction in the *Wage Census*. Also, some of these part-time physicians, especially if female or old, do not have a full-time position. Thus the income of all hospital-based physicians would not, in fact, increase by a fifth.

Second, the recent average age of hospital-based physicians is 40, compared with 58 in private clinics. The wage paid to nongovernment hospital physicians in the 55–59 age range was ¥18.5 million because of the seniority-based wage structure. However, because 20 percent of clinic physicians are 70 years and over (MHLW 2011c) and may not be working full time, comparisons by average age are not valid.

Third, physicians in private practice must take the same risk as other small business owners.

Urban versus Rural Areas

The fee schedule, as seen, pays the same amount for the same service to all providers throughout Japan, regardless of local living costs or wages, enabling rural hospitals to pay higher wages than rural hospitals to their physicians as they pay lower wages to their nurses and other staff. Key are differences in preferences: physicians tend to be more mobile and more attracted to cities, while nurses and other staff are less mobile, with stronger ties to their home community. This wage pattern came about not by government design so as to pay higher wages for physicians in rural areas, but by each hospital setting wage scales in tune with local labor market conditions.[16]

We tried to analyze the extent of this urban–rural difference in practice, although here too we came up against a lack of comprehensive data. We could not delineate "urban" and "rural" from the data because the *Wage Census* only shows the national aggregate. We therefore focused on wages in public hospitals owned by municipalities and compared the 41 hospitals owned by designated cities with the 178 hospitals owned by towns and villages.[17]

Physicians in designated city hospitals earned ¥16,376,100 and those in town and village hospitals earned ¥19,742,500 in 2010 (MIC 2012); in contrast, wages for registered nurses were ¥5,955,300 in urban areas and ¥5,418,500 in rural locations in 2010 (MHLW 2011b). After adjusting for differences in age structure,[18] physicians in hospitals owned by towns and villages earned 1.2 times that of their peers in designated city hospitals, registered nurses 0.88 times, and licensed practical nurses 0.77 times. (These differences narrowed in the two decades after 1990 from 1.43 for physicians, but widened from 0.79 for registered nurses and 0.75 for licensed practical nurses in 1990. This could stem from the fact that the number of hospitals owned by towns and villages has decreased due to merging into cities. Also, although data are unavailable, the difference in wages between physicians and nurses is likely to be greater in private-sector hospitals because their nurses' wages are less seniority based than those in the public sector.)

Universal Health Coverage for Inclusive and Sustainable Development
http://dx.doi.org/10.1596/978-1-4648-0408-3

Providing Services in Rural Hamlets

That hospital physicians tend to have lower incomes in urban areas mitigates the scarcity of physicians in rural areas, but scarcely solves the problem. Although it is hard to break down data into urban and rural areas in Japan, some areas have had difficulties in attracting physicians.[19] Responsibility for providing rural access to medical services has generally been left to local governments, Citizens' Health Insurance programs, agricultural cooperatives, and the private sector, via setting up and running hospitals and physicians' offices.[20] The national government's role has generally been less direct: for example, a need for more rural physicians was one motive in decisions to increase the number of medical schools and enrolled students in the 1970s and again after the Democratic Party of Japan's election victory in 2009. More targeted initiatives have also been tried, with varying effect.

The most sustained financial support to provide services for rural hamlets came as part of the subsidies from the national government to the prefectures for remote areas. "Areas without a physician," defined as 50 or more inhabitants living within a radius of 4 kilometers which had difficulty in accessing a health care facility, were targeted under the rolling Health and Medical Plans for Sparsely Populated Areas that first started from 1957. These plans have usually spanned five years, with the most recent being the 11th plan starting from 2011. However, the effects of these subsidies have not been systematically evaluated and thus it is hard to know how successful they have been. It is true that the number of designated areas without a physician fell from 2,920 (population 1.19 million) in 1966 to 705 (population 140,000) in 2009 (MHLW 2010a), but there is no way of knowing how much of the reduction came from providing services and how much from continued migration from these rural areas to cities.

However, one program under the Special Promotion Act starting from 1975 has been recognized as effective. This was the designation of "regional core hospitals," and to date there are 263 of them in 30 of Japan's 47 prefectures. Their responsibility is to dispatch and rotate physicians to staff clinics in rural hamlets. These physicians typically serve a three-year term, after which they return to the hospital. In a sense, this system replicates the pattern long established by university clinical departments and hospitals in their hierarchies. The skills for practicing in a rural clinic may differ from those required in the hub hospital, but the transition is similar to the common practice of hospital specialists moving to primary-care-focused physicians' offices. Indeed, rotation often broadens physicians' knowledge and perspectives wherever they practice.

The most distinctive element of Japan's efforts to improve rural health care is the Jichi Medical School, founded in 1973 specifically to educate physicians for service in rural communities. Although technically classified as private, it is funded and jointly operated by the prefectures (hence its name in Japanese is "local government" medical school). Each prefecture has a quota of two or three students for enrollment, but the selection of students is left to the university and is made primarily on their academic qualifications. Students are given loans to cover a monthly stipend as well as tuition fees. Graduates are obligated to spend nine years working at health care facilities designated by the prefecture, at least half in a rural setting. If they meet these obligations (97 percent of the graduates do: Matsumoto, Inoue, and Kajii 2008a), their loan is waived.

The original idea for this school came not from the Ministry of Health and Welfare, but from the Ministry of Home Affairs, in charge of local governments. Ministry officials were concerned about the shortage of physicians in rural areas. They first proposed reincarnating the old vocational medical schools (with entry being open to graduates of junior high school), but this notion was strongly opposed by the Ministry of Health and Welfare and the medical profession. Hence the Jichi Medical School was founded as a political compromise that left unresolved many structural issues such as the huge population differences among prefectures—13 million in Tokyo to 600,000 in Tottori, or more than 20 times— and variation in the number of people living in "rural" areas. Naturally, the commitment of both the prefectural governments and the students varied. The proportion continuing to practice in a rural area after their nine years of obligatory service was 29.5 percent overall (MHLW 2010b), but was higher (69.8 percent) for students coming from the more rural prefectures (Matsumoto, Inoue, and Kajii 2008b, 2010).

Another model is for medical schools to preferentially admit students from local high schools and offer better residency programs. For example in 2005, when Hirosaki University Medical School in Aomori Prefecture (northern Japan) was faced with an acute decrease in enrollment in its residency program, it started a quota system for preferentially admitting students from local high schools. As with the Jichi Medical School, loans for tuition and stipends are forgiven if the graduates work in designated facilities for nine years. It is too early for a full evaluation of this program, but the number of students entering from local high schools doubled from 23 in 2004 to 46 in 2010. Efforts made by the medical school faculty have also increased the number of students who took their two-year residencies within the prefecture from 56 in 2004 to 70 in 2011 (Fujimoto 2012).

Insights

Japan's medical schools have focused on research and training of subspecialists because the number of hospitals equipped to provide specialized care is limited, but the majority of physicians have broadened their scope to meet the needs of their patients or have expanded their facilities to reflect their professional aspirations. At the same time, the fee schedule has not only managed to contain expenditures and thus physicians' incomes, but also to provide physicians in offices and in rural hospitals with higher incomes than specialists in big-city hospitals.

And implications for other countries? It would be hard to transfer Japan's approach—reflecting a mixture of responses to specific needs at given times in the country's history rather than a conceptual framework—elsewhere. Still, the country's experience suggests the following.

First, it may be possible to take a more flexible approach toward educating physicians. In countries that have vocational schools in parallel with university schooling, their graduates should not treated as inferior.

Second, specialists can be induced to expand their scope to meet population needs if they get the freedom and right incentives in mid-career.

Third, allocation would be better if specialists in big-city hospitals were paid less as they may well be compensated by higher professional status and the advantages of city living, such as more opportunities for continuing medical education and better amenities for their families.

Fourth, university clinical departments or regional hospitals could serve as a base for dispatching and rotating physicians to serve in rural facilities.

Fifth, partial solutions, such as mandatory rotation of two-year residency, may actually exacerbate geographic maldistribution of physicians.

The Japanese system may not be in line with orthodox views on how physicians should be educated and allocated. However, for this very reason, it may offer an alternative perspective for low- and middle-income countries.

Notes

1. University-level medical schools required an additional three years of higher education before entry and their graduates were waived from taking the licensure examination.
2. To this day, medical schools must own a hospital with at least 600 beds to be accredited.
3. Following the disbanding of the army and navy after World War II, their hospitals were transferred to the Ministry of Health and Welfare (see the chapter 9).
4. The distinction overlaps but is not identical with public/private ownership. Unlike other countries, in Japan the "public sector" includes not only facilities owned by the national and local governments, but also by quasi-public organizations such as the Red Cross, farmers' cooperatives, and social health insurance programs. Almost all of the "private sector" is made up of proprietary hospitals owned by physicians. Investor-owned hospitals that issue dividends are prohibited from entry (although proprietors are allowed to make capital gains).
5. Called so since the merger of the Ministry of Education and Culture with the Agency of Science and Technology in 2001.
6. To meet war-time demand, all university-level medical schools had established vocational schools and increased their enrollment, which led to a tripling of the number entering to 10,533 in 1945.
7. Chronic-care beds were differentiated from "acute and post-acute beds" (*ippan byoushou*) in 2003, which is why trends cannot be compared. Even within the category of acute and post-acute beds, there are many long-stay patients.
8. The JMA's motive was that it would lead to payment by capitation and replace fee for service. If paid by capitation, physicians would no longer have the freedom to open a

practice as they would become unable to start earning income from the day they opened one.

9. The Accreditation of Specialists Organization finally decided to recognize general practice as a specialty from 2015 and the implementation of formal postgraduate training from 2017.

10. The Ministry of Health and Welfare merged with the Ministry of Labour to become the MHLW in 2001.

11. While restricting entry into specialties may serve to maintain quality when accompanied by appropriate regulation, these boundaries could also introduce rigidities in the health labor structure that make it harder to restructure services to meet changing demands and needs.

12. See chapter 5.

13. One reason is that it would violate Japanese societal norms to differentiate the pay of physicians who had graduated in the same year, particularly from the same department.

14. Registered nurses make average wages, about half that of hospital physicians. "Private sector" here includes all hospitals except those owned by national and local governments. The sampling method was revised in 2005, which might account for the dip.

15. Roughly US$193,000 vs. US$103,000 at purchasing power parity. The difference was greater in the past—2.5 times in 2005, for example—but it is hard to compare trends because both surveys are based on sample data and not panel data.

16. In the National Hospital Organization, where the public sector wage rules apply to most physicians and to all other staff, wages reflect the local cost of living and so are higher in big cities. However, for all other nongovernment hospitals, the magnitude of difference in the physicians' wages would also hold for their total income because the same mechanism would apply, and the opportunities for part-time work would be essentially the same in urban and rural settings.

17. There are fewer private sector hospitals in rural areas and it is not possible to obtain their data. Wage data are from MIC (2012). Of the 19 designated cities, 16 owned hospitals. Towns and villages are municipalities that have a population below 20,000. Of the total of 941 towns and villages, 178 entities owned hospitals.

18. The average age of physicians and registered nurses in designated city hospitals was three to four years younger than in towns' and villages' hospitals: physicians 44 vs. 47; registered nurses 37 vs. 41. For licensed practical nurses, the difference was reversed: 53 and 49.

19. The per capita number of physicians varies twofold between the prefecture with the highest and lowest density. However, the prefecture with the lowest is adjacent to Tokyo and has a relatively young population. This difference has declined from 2.24 in 1990. It is difficult to split municipalities into urban and rural, based on whether they are "cities" or "towns and villages," especially after 2003 when many municipalities merged so that "cities" would include sparsely populated areas.

20. Even aside the political responsibility of the mayor, municipal governments tend to be more focused on health care because they administer the Citizens' Health Insurance programs, which may also own hospitals and clinics. In contrast, prefectural governments' concerns tend to be limited to managing the hospitals they own.

Universal Health Coverage for Inclusive and Sustainable Development
http://dx.doi.org/10.1596/978-1-4648-0408-3

Bibliography

Campbell, J. C., and N. Ikegami. 1998. *The Art of Balance in Health Policy: Maintaining Japan's Low-Cost, Egalitarian System.* New York: Cambridge University Press.

Fujimoto, Y. 2012. "Challenge of Aomori Prefecture." *Byoin* 71 (2): 107–10.

Fuse, S. 1979. *History of Physicians—Japanese Characteristics.* Chuo-ku, Tokyo: Chuou Kouronsha.

Hashimoto, K. 2008. *Policy Process of Specialist Education.* Bunkyo-ku, Tokyo: Gakujutsu Shuppankai.

Ikegami, N. 2003. "The Role of Specialists in the Japanese Health Care System." *Sougou Rinshou* 52 (12): 3125–30.

Matsumoto, M., K. Inoue, and E. Kajii. 2008a. "A Contract-Based Training System for Rural Physicians: Follow-up of Jichi Medical University Graduates (1978–2006)." *Journal of Rural Health* 24 (4): 360–68.

———. 2008b. "Long-Term Effect of the Home Prefecture Recruiting Scheme of Jichi Medical University, Japan." *Rural Remote Health* 8 (3): 930.

———. 2010. "Definition of 'Rural' Determines the Placement Outcomes of a Rural Medical Education Program: Analysis of Jichi Medical University Graduates." *Journal of Rural Health* 26 (3): 234–39.

MEXT (Ministry of Education, Culture, Sports, Science and Technology of Japan). 2012. "FY2013 Student Quotas for Medical Departments." http://www.mext.go.jp/b_menu/houdou/24/12/1328793.htm (accessed October 2013).

MIC (Ministry of Internal Affairs and Communication of Japan). 2012. "2010 Annual Report on Local Government Enterprises." http://www.soumu.go.jp/main_sosiki/c-zaisei/kouei22/html/mokuji.html (accessed October 2013).

MHLW (Ministry of Health, Labour and Welfare). 1987. "Report of Family Doctor Roundtable." Daiichi Houki Shuppan, Minato-ku, Tokyo.

———. 2010a. "2009 Survey on Medically Underserved Areas." http://www.mhlw.go.jp/stf/houdou/2r9852000000ulrk.html (accessed October 2013).

———. 2010b. "2009 Report of The Eleventh Committee on Rural Health." http://www.mhlw.go.jp/shingi/2010/04/s0401-4.html (accessed October 2013).

———. 2011a. "2011 Financial State of Hospitals and Clinics." http://www.mhlw.go.jp/topics/2011/10/tp1019-1.html (accessed October 2013).

———. 2011b. "2010 Wage Census." http://www.mhlw.go.jp/toukei/list/chingin_zenkoku.html, detailed data on http://www.e-stat.go.jp/SG1/estat/List.do?bid=000001028607&cycode=0 (accessed October 2013).

———. 2011c. "2010 Survey on Physicians, Dentists and Pharmasists." http://www.mhlw.go.jp/toukei/saikin/hw/ishi/10/index.html (accessed October 2013).

———. 2011–13. "Specialist System Committee 2011–2013 Reports." http://www.mhlw.go.jp/stf/shingi/2r985200000300ju.html (accessed October 2013).

OECD. "OECD Health Data 2013." http://www.oecd.org/health/health-systems/oecd-healthdata.htm (accessed October 2013)

CHAPTER 8

Licensed Practical Nurses: One Option for Expanding the Nursing Workforce in Japan

Naoki Ikegami and James Buchan

Abstract

In common with many other high-income countries, Japan has two levels of nurse: a licensed practical nurse (LPN) and a registered nurse (RN). The number of LPN school entrants exceeded that of RNs from the mid-1950s to the 1970s, and for a decade when hospitals were expanding rapidly (1968–77) LPNs actually outnumbered RNs, although declined after that. More recently, a weak labor market and expanding needs of Japan's aging society have generated a resurgence of those wanting to enter LPN schools. And so, although the proportion of LPN has declined, LPNs remain a significant part of the workforce providing nursing care and are one option for employers looking at the best staffing mix, as they present alternative career entry points. Countries that wish to develop their nursing and broader workforce need to weigh up the time required to scale up different staff types, and consider their staffing options and costs, for achieving the optimum staffing level and mix within their labor and resources pool.

Objectives and Context

The objectives of this chapter are to examine the role of LPNs in Japan with a focus on identifying key aspects of their education, regulation, and employment. It assesses trends over time in the size, profile, and characteristics of the LPN workforce there, and sets out the broader human resources for health (HRH) implications of LPN employment and deployment. The key aims are to identify the aspects of the LPN role in Japan that are context specific and that have been determined by the political economy of the country, and to draw out any wider HRH policy lessons of relevance to other countries.

There are a range of possible roles within the broader nursing workforce. One key distinction is if there are one or two main levels of qualified nurse. Some high-income countries, such as the United Kingdom and Ireland, do not have a "second-level" nurse (known under different titles such as "enrolled nurse," "licensed vocational nurse," or "licensed practical nurse"). The United Kingdom ended enrolled nurse training in the 1980s, and offered bridging training for many enrolled nurses to achieve "first-level," or registered, nurse level (Seccombe, Smith, and Buchan 1997).

Many other countries, including Japan, as well as Australia, Belgium, Canada, Finland, the Netherlands, Sweden, and the United States, employ a "second level" nurse (in some countries termed a LPN, in others an enrolled nurse role) (National Nursing Research Unit 2007). One country, New Zealand, ended training of enrolled nurses in the 1990s but subsequently reintroduced training for the role 10 years later (Gerritsen 2002). In addition, another country context issue which must be considered when examining effective skill mix options is that there will also be varying levels and mix of other health professions and midlevel workers in the workforce in different countries and systems. For example. some countries employ a different category of worker who is trained and regulated as a midwife (for example in Japan, nurses take additional education and training to become qualified as midwives) while in others there is no separate category of midwife. (As such, this chapter does not examine the role of midwives.)

This brief description of the situation with second-level nurses in different countries serves to highlight the marked variation in use and role, and changes over time, and highlights that caution must be exercised if attempting to translate one country experience into another country situation. To explore more clearly the experience in Japan, this section now describes in more detail the evolution of the LPN role and its current situation.

In Japan, as in any country, the requirements for health professional education and qualifications can be difficult to reconfigure because of system rigidities, funding-mechanism inflexibilities, and vested interests, as well as for legitimate reasons of quality assurance, regulatory oversight and cost effective use of resources and skills.

While the proportion of LPNs in Japan have declined in the last three decades, they continue to play an important role in providing nursing care, and are one option among several for employers looking at determining staffing mix, with a good balance between overhead costs and quality of care. Part of this overall process must be to ensure that the training (content and delivery) that nurses receive, and their licensing and regulation system, make them "fit to practice," irrespective of LPN or RN status. More broadly, in Japan as in all countries there is need to ensure that recruitment and career progression in the health workforce is supported by developing flexible career pathways and ensuring that requirements for entry to training are appropriate. As noted above, this is an issue not just about first- and second-level nurses but also for other health professions and mid-level workers. In different countries the actual training content and role of second-level nurses vary, but the focus is on practical and vocational/technical training and a direct caregiving role, often supervised by first-level nurses.

In Japan, a rapid increase in training capacity in the middle decades of the last century, plus widespread employment of LPNs (*junkangoshi*), sometimes called "assistant nurse," contributed to a rapid increase in nurse staffing levels. The LPN license, which requires only two years of training and a prefectural exam, compared with at least three years of training and a national exam for registered nurses (RNs, *kangoshi*)[1] provides a faster route to a nursing qualification, and can also be used as a springboard for career transition to RN (LPNs can subsequently advance to an RN license by taking a two-year course and passing the same national exam to become RN).

A license for nurses was first issued in Japan at prefectural level by the Tokyo Metropolitan Government in 1899 (Kameyama 1983). The first national licenses were issued by the Ministry of Interior in 1915, drawing from prefectural examples (Hirao 2001). The nursing license (*kangofu*) could be obtained by either passing an exam or graduating from a school with one or more years of training. In the same year a license for "licensed practical nurses" (LPNs, *junkangofu*) was also established, with the authority delegated to prefectural governors (Kameyama 1983). As such, prefectural governments were the issuing authority for LPN licenses, while for RN it was the central government.

This two-track system essentially continued until the end of World War II, after which the occupation forces tried to improve the quality of hospital care, that of nursing in particular. The practice had been for families to provide care, food, and bedding for inpatients, with the nurse's role primarily focused on assisting physicians. The Act for Public Health Nurses, Midwives and Nurses of 1948 formally defined the nurses' role as caring for patients as well as assisting physicians. The act stipulated that LPNs officially were not allowed to provide care for patients in critical conditions, although in practice this restriction was difficult to enforce (JNA 2009b).

This restriction was revised by the amendment of the Act for Public health Nurses, midwives and nurses reinstated in 1952, with a two-year course requirement in schools accredited by the prefectural government; the license was recognized nationally but the licensing exam was held at prefectural level.[2] Entry to LPN school required completing only nine years of compulsory education. While the level and content of training were different between RNs and LPNs, the only legal distinction in the tasks performed by the two levels was that LPNs were supervised by RN's and MD's.[3]

After LPN reinstatement in 1952, the proportion of young women in Japan advancing to senior high school—a prerequisite for entering RN school— increased rapidly, from 42 percent in 1951 to 68 percent in 1964 (MEXT 2012). This provided a much larger pool of recruits into RN education and was a contributing factor in the subsequent relatively fast growth of the RN workforce.

Universal Health Coverage for Inclusive and Sustainable Development
http://dx.doi.org/10.1596/978-1-4648-0408-3

During this period, the Japanese Nursing Association (JNA) continued to oppose the use of LPNs, on grounds that they were detrimental to the quality of nursing care and demeaning to the nursing profession, and even to women in general (JNA 1995). This pressure was one factor in a 1959 revision of payments to cover hospitalization that resulted in hospitals with a majority of RNs on their nursing staff being paid higher fees by the government. (Eligibility for this staffing ratio–based payment was moved up to 70 percent of total nursing staff being RNs in 1995, which solidified the dominance of RNs.)

In 1964 the JNA formally proposed that the LPN system be abolished through a revision in the Law for Public Health Nurses, Midwives and Nurses (JNA 1995). The JNA stance was strongly opposed by the Japan Medical Association (JMA). A key reason for the JMA stance was that doctors feared they could not staff inpatient units without LPNs (Tamura 2009), at a time when the number of hospital beds was growing quickly (from 275,804 in 1950 to 873,652 in 1965) (MHW 1956, 1966).

Nearly all LPN schools were established by local medical associations and hospitals. Physicians in private practice and owners of hospitals had long favored training and hiring LPNs because they felt them to be easier to recruit as student employees, and as noted, could obtain their license in two years. Tuition was usually provided free at the schools and a monthly stipend was provided by their employers. Some courses were at night so that students could work as nurse assistants during the day. After receiving a license, graduates were obligated to work at a prescribed hospitals or clinics at low wages.[4] A related issue was that the relatively lower education level for many girls in the 1950's had been a constraint on supply of entrants directly to RN education.

There were thus divergent views between the JNA, which supported "professionalizing" the nurse workforce through the use of RNs and the JMA, which represented its member interests in trying to maintain supply of LPNs.

We now turn to three aspects of the training and deployment of LPNs in Japan, before looking at some insights primarily for low- and middle-income countries.

Education

In examining the education/training system and the subsequent "pipelines" from education to employment, it should be noted that while there are different entry routes into education and training for both LPN and RN, there is also sufficient flexibility in the system in Japan to enable subsequent transition from LPN to RN. This is an important message for policy makers to consider when looking at supporting effective "bridges" between education and employment- that there should be multiple entry points and flexible career paths so that there is scope for effective recruitment, retention and also "return" (attracting back and supporting professionals who have been out of practice).

Numbers of LPNs trained saw rapid growth in 1950–70, but then an equally rapid decline. The number of LPN schools more than doubled from 344 in 1952, when their licensing was reinstated, to 776 in 1970 (figure 8.1), but then dropped back to 251 by 2011. In addition, from 1964 special vocational high schools were established, allowing students to obtain enough LPN credits during their three years' of high school to take the LPN exam on graduation. The number of these schools had grown to 136 by 1978, but fell to only 17 by 2012 because 72 of them became five-year programs leading to the RN exam, and most of the rest became two-year schools for LPNs to become RNs.

The sharp decrease in the number of LPN schools was caused in part by a government directive in 2002 to increase the minimum required number of full-time faculty in a school from two to five, which was financially unsustainable for many schools. The government set a transition period for this requirement to be implemented, and then lowered the requirement for full time faculty to three, in order to minimize negative effects.

In contrast to the rapid rise and decline in LPN school numbers, the number of RN schools increased steadily from the 1950s. This is reflected in the overall trends in the composition of RNs and LPNs in the workforce (figure 8.2). The

Figure 8.1 Number of LPN and RN Schools, 1950–2011

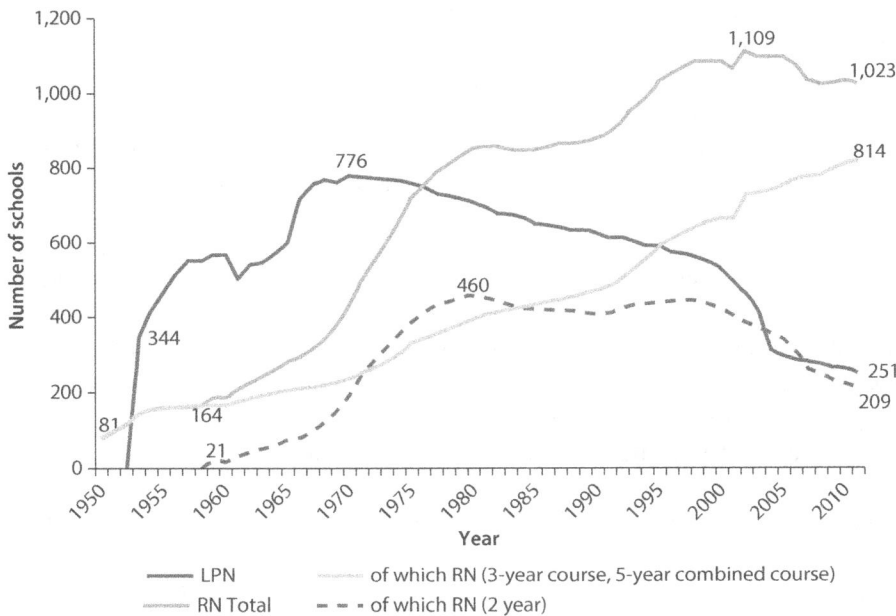

Source: JNA 2009a, MHLW 2012a.
Note: RN = registered nurse; LPN = licensed practical nurse.

Figure 8.2 Total Number of Licensed Nurses and Share of LPNs, 1952–2010

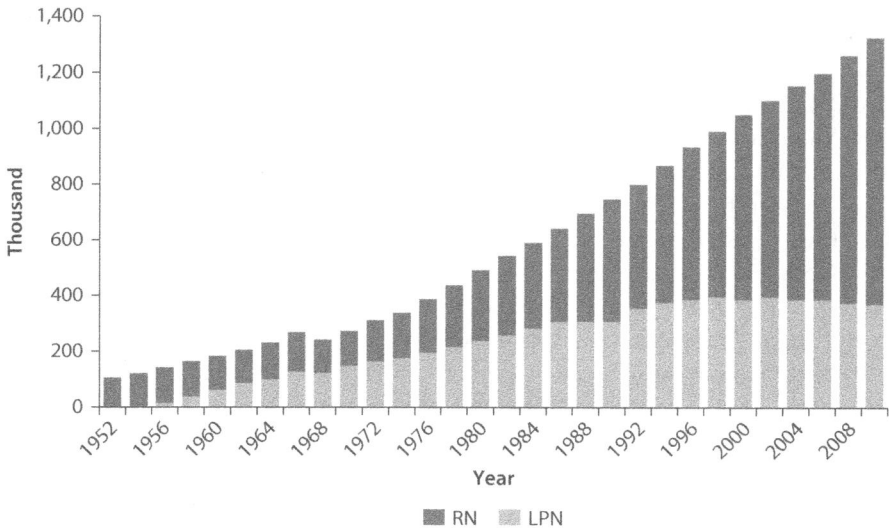

Source: MHLW, "Health Administrative Reports 1953–2011."
Note: RN = registered nurse; LPN = licensed practical nurse.

number of LPNs exceeded that of RNs from 1967 to 1978, but after that the proportion of LPNs to RNs gradually decreased to a third (33.7 percent) in 2004, and then a quarter (27.9 percent) in 2010.

In recent years, some 85 percent of LPN school enrollees have graduated within the prescribed two years. There is also a distance learning course, introduced in 2004, for LPN's that have been practicing for more than 10 years in order to qualify to undertake the RN examination.

Passing the LPN licensing exam is relatively easy because they can sit for the exam in any prefecture. Because five regions have set different dates for the exam, LPN candidates could theoretically sit in all of them during the same year. Among LPN school graduates, 65.9 percent start working immediately, while 27.2 percent enroll in the two-year program to become an RN (as of 2011). Despite the long-term trend reduction in LPN training, the number of LPN school applicants has recently increased from 26,000 in 2009 to 35,000 in 2012 (MHLW 2012a). The LPN license has become more attractive because of the stagnant economy and the weak job market in Japan for women in their late twenties and early thirties. Among LPN school enrollees in 2012, only 10.3 percent were junior high school graduates; 71.3 percent senior high school graduates; and 17.8 percent university or junior college graduates (MHLW 2011).

The age profiles of LPNs and RNs vary markedly. The LPN workforce is much older on average, as a result of the reductions in training numbers since the 1970s, and relative growth in RN training intakes and employment (figure 8.3). This will have implications for policy makers as proportionately more LPNs will retire over the next 10 years.

Figure 8.3 Age Distribution of Licensed Practical Nurses and Registered Nurses, 2010

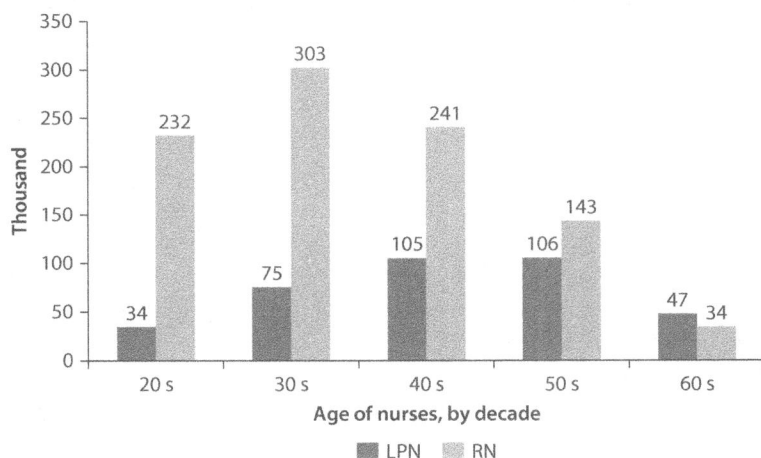

Source: MHLW 2011.
Note: LPN = licensed practical nurse; RN = registered nurse.

Regulation

One policy challenge in any health system is to develop an approach to regulation, quality assurance and standard setting of health worker education and deployment that achieves clear delineation between the roles of different types of workers. This is particularly the case for health professionals, and is needed both for cost effectiveness in the use of resources, and to ensure quality of care and patient safety. In Japan, as in all countries, there continues to be a need to assess risks and attempt to reach clarity on role delineation. Specifically there continues to be some lack of clarity in the roles and functions of LPN, which while not unique to Japan (for example, see also Spetz 2014) do highlight the need for caution when considering the boundaries of safe and effective deployment of any particular category of health worker.

Each country has developed its own approach to certification, accreditation, and regulation of the nursing profession, to guarantee standards and patient safety. Many have developed a system based on professional self-regulation via an autonomous nursing council, while others have vested this responsibility in one or more government departments. In Japan, the model in use relies primarily on legal statutes and licensing control by departments in government Ministries. There is no autonomous professional council or "standalone" body responsible for standards.

The first nursing professional qualifications in Japan were established by the Midwives Rules of 1899, followed by the Nurses Rules of 1915 and the Public Health Nurses Rules of 1941. The National Healthcare Act passed in 1942 regulated public health nurses, midwives, and nurses as health care professionals along with medical doctors and dentists (JNA 1995). A "nurse" in Japan is a person who engages in providing care to a person with injury or illness (or both), or to postpartum women, or in assisting in medical treatment under the license of the Minister of Health, Labour and Welfare (Article 5 of the Act on Public Health Nurses, Midwives and Nurses). She or he must complete a required curriculum at a recognized educational institution, pass a national exam that can be taken once a year, and obtain a license granted by the Minister of Health, Labour and Welfare. The basic academic background is 12 years school, and at least three years' basic nursing education is required. The education contents required to be eligible to take the national exam are prescribed jointly by the Ministry of Health, Labour and Welfare (MHLW) and by the Ministry of Education, Culture, Sports, Science and Technology (MEXT). Foreign nursing personnel who want to work in Japan have to pass the Japanese national nursing exam—overseas nursing licenses are not accepted (JNA 2011).

Once licensed, there is no requirement for any periodic relicensing of either RN's or LPN's as they are licensed for life; although "making efforts" for continuing education is required after having obtained the license. Some regulation responsibilities related to accreditation of nursing schools are held by MEXT, whilst some related to licensure of RN's, and training content are held by MHLW.

The certification of post-basic qualifications and specialized nurses is not specified by law, but certification is offered by a range of organizations. For example, the JNA certificates nurse specialists and nurse administrators. The government-led review meeting to establish "advanced practice nurses" decided instead to organize specific courses upon completion of which nurses would be able to perform certain procedures under the comprehensive orders of physicians (MHLW 2013).

At the time of writing this chapter, two new bills have just been approved by the Lower House MHLW committee. One is for revisions of the health and long term care provision, and the second is to strengthen recruitment of long term care givers. While these bills are not specifically about regulation of nurses, both will place an emphasis on a more comprehensive approach to harmonizing the roles of health and long term care workers.

Employment

As well as different trends in numbers of LPNs and RNs in recent decades (see figure 8.2), their distributions too have varied. Newly licensed RNs tend to work in the public sector because it is more prestigious and because their lifetime earnings will be higher (Tsunoda 2012). Public-sector hospitals can afford to hire them on these terms because of the subsidies received from local governments allowed hospitals to employ more RNs than would be compensated by the fee schedule. In addition, the labor cost differential between hiring a RN and a LPN in public-sector hospitals narrows and becomes marginal after 10 years of employment owing to the seniority-based wage structure.[5] As a result, 95 percent of public-sector hospital nurses were RNs in 2010, and just 5 percent were LPNs. In other areas, the proportion of

RNs is much lower because the available number of RNs has been concentrated in the public sector. The proportions of RNs are 72 percent in private sector hospitals, 53 percent in clinics, and 57 percent in long-term care facilities (MHLW 2013).

What are the pros and cons of becoming an LPN rather than an RN? Despite the lack of clarity in role differentiation with RNs, the LPN license clearly has lower status than the RN license, and this is reflected in the wage difference. The wages of LPNs are well below those of RNs, with the difference widening from 21.0 percent in 1990 to 24.5 percent in 2010 (figure 8.4). These overall trends are similar relative to all workers (figure 8.5): LPNs earned 74–79 percent of the average wage of general workers, RNs 89–100 percent over the same period.

This raises the question: Why enroll in an LPN training school when you can become an RN by undergoing one additional year of education? One reason is to become licensed and start work more quickly. In addition, the possibility of night study for LPN licensing means students can continue to work and earn during the day. Tuition fees are also much lower in LPN schools. The average for the first year of enrollment is ¥551,142 for an LPN but ¥840,418 at a vocational RN school; ¥1,563,346 at an RN three-year junior college; and ¥1,731,315 at a four-year college (Takahashi 2011). The societal cost for educating an LPN is also

Figure 8.4 Income of Nurses in Nongovernment Hospitals Standardized to the Consumer Price Index and Age Composition, 1990–2010

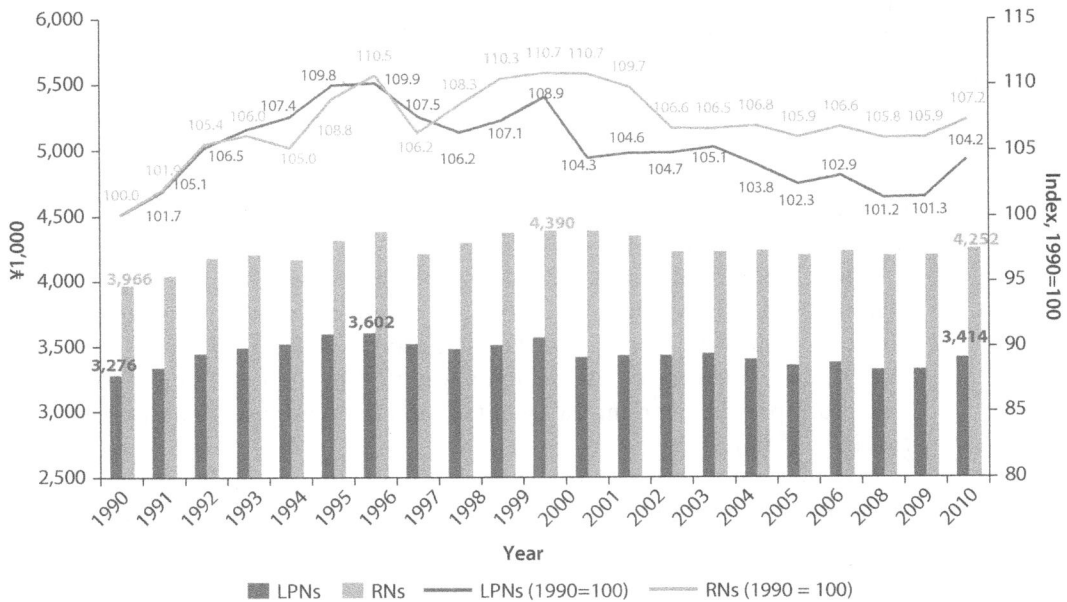

Source: MHLW, "Wage Census Surveys 1991–2011."
Note: LPN = licensed practical nurse; RN = registered nurse.

Universal Health Coverage for Inclusive and Sustainable Development
http://dx.doi.org/10.1596/978-1-4648-0408-3

Figure 8.5 Income of Nurses in Nongovernment Hospitals Relative to the Average of All General Workers

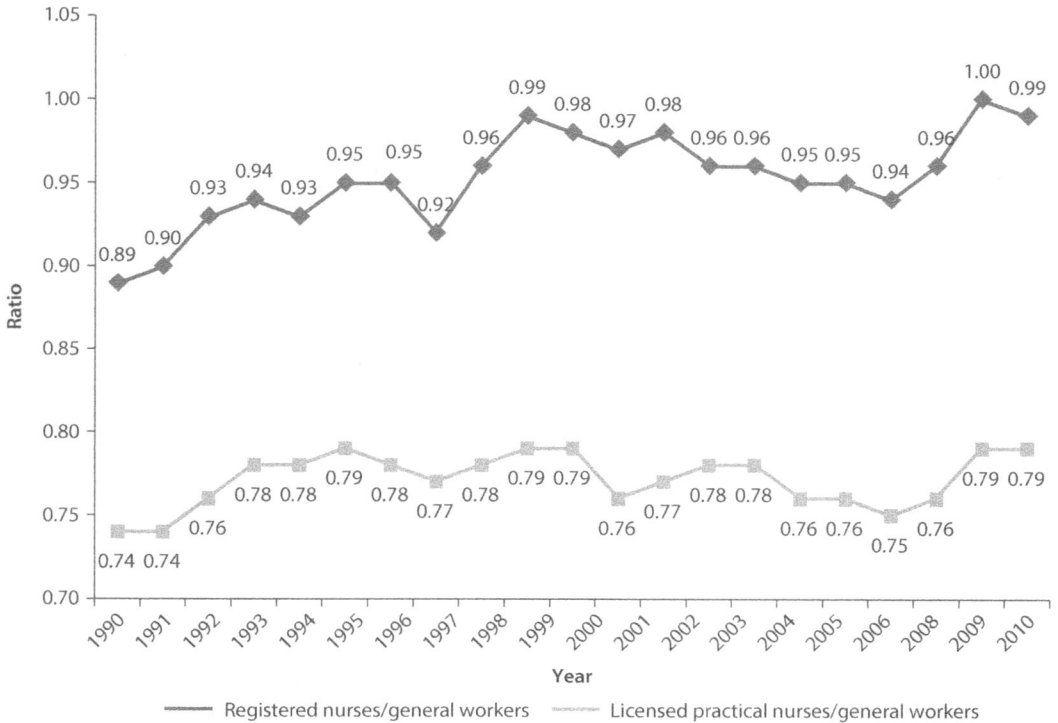

Source: MHLW, "1990–2010 Wage Census Surveys."
Note: Standardized to the consumer price index and age composition.

lower. Comparing schools run by local medical associations, most LPN schools receive subsidies of ¥8 million–10 million per school, while most RN schools receive ¥150 million–200 million (both have the same average annual enrollment of 50) (JMA 2011).

There are some differences in the employment patterns of LPNs and RNs. Data for 2012 shows that, for LPN's, 20.3 percent worked in long-term care facilities, while 42.5 percent worked in hospitals and 35.5 percent worked in clinics. The comparative data for RN's was 10.0 percent working in long term care, 70.9 percent working in hospitals, and 15.8 percent working in clinics (MHLW 2013).

The long-term care sector also employs many care workers paid through the public Long-Term Care Insurance system. There is a certification program for home-based care workers, who must complete a minimum of 130 hours of training, but some analysis has argued there are chronic shortages of both unlicensed and vocationally qualified long-term care workers remain, partly because there are few prospects for career development (Ishibashi and Ikegami 2012).

Insights

There has been a general trend for nurses to achieve higher levels of profession-alization and recognition in Japan (as in many other nations). The RNs dominate the nursing staff of hospitals, particularly large hospitals, and this is in part pro-moted by the fee schedule offering higher reimbursement rates to hospitals with higher RN staffing ratios. However, LPNs continue to have significant employ-ment shares in a range of care settings, such as clinics, private hospitals, and long-term care institutions. After a long decline, but the student enrollment in LPN training programs slightly increased briefly in 2008 and 2009.

The government subsidy for RN employment in hospitals, the regulatory approach (based on prefectural or national government licensing), the multiple career entry and career progression points (including scope for a direct flow from LPN to RN training), the segmented, if overlapping labor markets for LPN and RN in employment, and the lack of complete role clarity between RN and LPN are some key characteristics of the Japanese context of LPNs. Similarly, LPNs have a much older age profile—a policy consideration for Japan. With these context-specific factors in mind, what lessons does the situation in Japan offer for low- and middle-income countries?

First, it must be noted that different countries have different regulation systems that will determine and differentiate scope of practice, education con-tent, and standards of training and practice. The government-led approach in Japan may not therefore be directly replicable in countries that have profes-sional self-regulation, but any system should make a clear differentiation between scopes of practice of different categories of nurse, and also more broadly between other different professions and mid-level workers, to avoid the inefficiencies of role confusion and unnecessary role overlap, and to ensure safe care provision.

Second, countries that wish to scale up their workforce, including the nursing component, need to weigh up the time to develop different staff types, and their staffing options, costs and quality implications, in terms of achieving the opti-mum staffing level and mix within their available pool of labor and resources.

In order to make evidence-informed decisions on the most effective staff mix, policy makers will require information on the relative costs of employing differ-ent types of staff, as well as the effect on care quality and outcomes of different types of staff. There is some limited published research examining the regulatory enablers, utilization, costs and outcome impact of different mixes of first- and second-level nurses, mainly in North America (for example, McGillis Hall 2003; Needleman 2006; Chapman et al., 2006; Spetz 2014); there is also some research on implications of RN staffing levels and education on care outcomes in European countries (Aiken et al., 2014). Policy makers must also give consideration to broader-based analysis of the scope and benefits of advanced practice nurses, and of different types of alternative "mid-level practitioners" (for example Lassi et al. 2013). However, overall there is limited published research and evidence drawn from low- and middle-income countries on skill mix implementation and impact.

As such, caution must be used when interpreting the findings from high-income country contexts, and assuming they have a similar relevance in other care contexts.

Third, policy makers must heed issues of access to, and availability of, health services, which in part are determined by the availability of suitably skilled and qualified workers at the right time and place. Achieving effective geographic distribution of the workforce to meet population health demands, including enough staff in rural and remote areas, is a necessary component of effective scaling up.

Table 8.1 summarizes the nursing workforce staff options that may be available in a country, notes where Japan fits in, and highlights key points for policy makers considering scaling up. The key point is that different countries have

Table 8.1 Different Nursing Workforce Staff Categories: An International Overview

Nursing workforce category	Does Japan employ this role?	Issues to consider in scaling up
Unlicensed nursing assistant	YES. Mainly employed in hospitals and long-term care facilities	Relatively quick and inexpensive to train and employ. Requires supervision, will make a limited contribution, and with relatively little scope to develop
Unlicensed, certified/ vocationally qualified care assistant	YES. Exclusively employed as helpers in long-term facilities and home care, but shortages exist	Relatively quick and inexpensive to train, but requires some form of standardized training and certification/qualification. May have portable qualifications across health and social care. Requires supervision, but can have some autonomy; scope to develop through structured training and career developments
Licensed second-level nurse (LPN)	YES. Approximately 80% of the workforce is in hospitals, and clinics, and 20% in LTC. Limited, and reducing, numbers employed in public-sector hospitals	2 years' training, but with different options, including evening study. Faster and less expensive than RN to train. Practical/technical focus of role. Limited career progression opportunities but can upgrade to RN with additional training
Licensed/registered first-level nurse (RN)	YES. Growing workforce; nearly all of the nurse staffing in public-sector hospitals	More than 3 years of education. More expensive to train, and to employ (differential between LPN and RN varies in different countries) but can be deployed across all care environments, can provide supervision to other staff, and can be trained further to specialize, and progress to advanced roles
Advanced practice nurses (APN)—nurse practitioner, clinical nurse specialist	YES (small numbers but growing)	Will require additional training, perhaps additional license, but can practice at a high level; with prescriptive authority may act as an independent practitioner

Source: World Bank.

different current levels and mixes of the different staff categories. The relative risks and opportunities of focusing on these different categories must be given full consideration

Another factor that differentiates the options available among countries is the extent to which midwifery is a distinct and separate profession from nursing, with its own training, skills, standards, career paths, and employment patterns— or is combined with nursing. As noted in the introduction, Japan and some other countries have "direct entry" training, and midwifery is therefore a separate profession, while in other countries midwifery is a post basic qualification for nurses, or is part of a combined nurse-midwifery basic training (UNFPA 2011, 2).

Scaling up the workforce will require consideration of the current workforce profile, the training capacity and the availability of new recruits into the workforce as well as capacity to "train up" those already in the workforce. Scaling up should not be considered only in terms of additional staff and the introduction of new roles, but also in the provision of additional training to current staff so as to increase their skills level and contribution. It must also take into consideration the costs and quality issues. If the quality of education is not assured, a higher level of training may not be in itself a guarantee of higher quality of care, and policy attention must also focus on regulation.

The overall regulatory system, the standards set for accrediting schools, the caliber of the faculty, the exam process, and the process of recertification (if any) will all be factors contributing to high-quality nursing care. Without an appropriate process of accreditation of nursing schools by government or an independent agency, there is a risk that curriculum content quality can be compromised, and schools can become "paper mills." It is also important to have in place mechanisms that can align the interests of educational institutions providers with that of health sector employers, in order to achieve and sustain effective and relevant quality of education. This will often require an effective dialogue between government ministries representing education and health.

For high-income countries that face increased demand for long-term care, declining numbers of high-school graduates and increasing opportunities for women (who usually comprise the majority of the nursing workforce) to pursue other careers, scaling-up options will have to include mechanisms to broaden the recruitment pool, and examine the scope for flexible or "nontraditional" routes into the workforce in nursing and also in nursing and in midlevel practitioner categories, and as career progression within the workforce. Examples include the United Kingdom's National Vocational Qualification approach, which has led to the development of vocationally qualified health care assistants, the role of *Altenphlegehelfer in* Germany (Tsuchida 2012), and Finland's *lahi hoitaja* (practical nurse).

The key lesson for policy makers from the case study of the situation of LPN's in Japan is that there is a need to have role clarity, effective regulation, and multiple/flexible career entry points and paths if a country is to maximize its opportunities to make best use of its health workforce, and its education pipelines to the workforce. This includes looking at the options to scale up through increased numerical use of a current role, introducing a new role, or developing and advanced practice version of a current role, and taking a whole of workforce perspective rather than examining one category of worker in isolation. Often the reality is that there is an absence of role clarity, and an inadequate evidence base on which to make scaling up decisions. In these circumstances policy makers must give full attention to balancing risk and opportunity, and exercise appropriate caution when considering the health workforce lessons that can be learned, and perhaps applied, from one country to another.

Notes

1. These terms were changed from *kangofu* and *junkangofu* in 2002 because the suffix *fu* is used only for women.

2. The prefectural committee for the LPN exam included members of the local medical association and hospitals. It was in their interests to set the pass level low in order to have more nurses qualified. The only requirement set by the national government was for 60 percent of the questions to be answered correctly. Exams came to be integrated from the prefecture level to eight regional blocks in 2003.

3. There is no legal statement that differentiates the functions of LPNs from the RNs, except that LPNs must follow orders of physicians and RNs. Studies that demonstrate how their capabilities differ could not be found, although one article (Yamada et al. 2007) showed some differences in intrinsic intuition between the two among those who had 10 or more years of experience. However, this study was based on a sample of 135 RNs and 52 LPNs in three hospitals using a self-written questionnaire.

4. This practice of providing stipends in exchange for requiring nurses to work at prescribed facilities after receiving the license was prohibited in 1997 as being an indentured service.

5. While the starting wage would be of the same level, their lifetime earnings would be higher because of the seniority-based wage scale. A nurse about to retire would earn about 1.7 times that of a newly licensed nurse in the public sector, compared to 1.1 times in the private sector.

Bibliography

Aiken, L., D. Sloan, L. Bruyneel, K. Heede, P. Griffiths, R. Busse, M. Diomidous, J. Kinnunen, M. Kózka, E. Lesaffre, M. D. McHugh, M. T. Moreno-Casbas, A. M. Rafferty, R. Schwendimann, P. A. Scott, C. Tishelman, T. van Achterberg, and W. Sermeus. 2014. "Nurse Staffing and Education and Hospital Mortality in Nine European Countries: A Retrospective Observational Study." *Lancet*, Early Online Publication, February 26, 2014. doi:10.1016/S0140-6736(13)62631-8.

Chapman, S., W. Dyer, J. Seago, and J. Spetz. 2006. "Can the Use of LPN's Alleviate the Nursing Shortage?" *American Journal of Nursing* 106 (7): 40–49.

Gerritsen, J. 2002. "Enrolled Nurses' Training Scheduled to Start in July." *New Zealand Nursing Review* 2 (10): 1–2.

Hirao, M. 2001. "A Study on the Process and Significance of the Establishment of the Nurse Regulations in 1915." *Nihon Ishigaku Zasshi* 47 (4): 796.

Ishibashi, T., and N. Ikegami. 2012. *Kaigojinzai wo doukakuhosuruka—Nipponban career path no kensho* (How to Obtain Care Workers—Examining Japanese Career Paths). *Hospitals* 71 (9): 708–12.

JMA (Japanese Medical Association). 2011. *Heisei 23 Nen Ishikairitsu Josanshi Kangoshi Junkangoshi* Gakko Yoseijo Chosa (*2011 Survey on the Midwife, RN, and LPN Schools by the Local Medical Associations*). http://dl.med.or.jp/dl-med/teireikaiken/20120328_8.pdf (accessed October 2013).

JNA (Japanese Nursing Association). 1995. *Dai 4 Pan. Kindai Nihon Kango Sounenpyo* (*Comprehensive Chronology of Nurses in Modern Japan*, 4th Edition). Shibuya-ku, Tokyo.

———. 2009a. "Hojokanpou no Hensen to Kango Gyosei no Topics (Changes in the Act for Public Health Nurses, Midwives and Nurses and Topics in Nursing Administration)." *Hokenshi Jyosanshi Kangoshihou 60 Nenshi (60 Years History of the Act for Public Health Nurses, Midwives and Nurses)*, 78–151.

———. 2009b. "Hojokanpou no Hensen to Kango Gyosei no Topics (Changes in the Act for Public Health Nurses, Midwives and Nurses and Topics in Nursing Administration)." *Hokenshi Jyosanshi Kangoshihou 60 Nenshi (60 Years History of the Act for Public Health Nurses, Midwives and Nurses)*, 270–71

———. 2011. "Nursing in Japan." Tokyo. http://www.nurse.or.jp/jna/english/pdf/nursing-in-japan2011.pdf (accessed October 2013).

———. 2012. *Kangokankei Shiryoshu* (Nurse Related Data Compilation). Shibuya-ku, Tokyo.

Kameyama, M. 1983. *Kindai Nihon Kangoshi 1, Nihon Sekijujisha to Kangofu* (Nursing History *of* Modern Japan I, The Japan Red Cross and Nurses). Shibuya-ku, Tokyo: Domesu.

Lassi, Z., G. Cometto, L. Huicho, and Z. Bhutta. 2013. "Quality of Care Provided by Mid-level Health Workers: Systematic Review and Meta-analysis." *Bulletin of the World Health Organization* 91: 824–833I.

MEXT (Ministry of Education, Culture, Sports and Technology). 2012. Heisei 24 Nendo Gakkou Kihon Chosa (Schooling Survey 2012), http://www.e-stat.go.jp/SG1/estat/NewList.do?tid=000001011528 (accessed October 2013).

MHW (Ministry of Health and Welfare). 1956. *Shouwa 31 Nendoban Kousei Hakusho* (1956 White Paper on Health and Welfare), 113. Chuo-ku, Tokyo: Touyou Keizai Shinpousha.

———. 1966. *Shouwa 40 Nendo Kousei Hakusho* (1965 White Paper on Health and Welfare), 418–19. Chiyoda-ku, Tokyo: Ministry of Finance Printing Office.

MHLW (Ministry of Health, Labour and Welfare). 1991–2011. 1990–2010 Wage Census Surveys.

———. 2011. "Heisei 23 Nen Eisei Gyosei Hokoku" (2010 Health Administrative Reports). https://www.e-stat.go.jp/SG1/estat/GL08020103.do?_toGL08020103_&listID=000001083541&requestSender=dsearch (accessed October 2013).

———. 2012a. "Heisei 23 Kangoshitou Gakkou Youseijo Nyugakujyoukyo oyobi Sotsugyousei Jyoukyou Chosa" (2011 Survey on Nursing School Entrants and Graduates). http://www.e-stat.go.jp/SG1/estat/NewList.do?tid=000001022606 (accessed October 2013).

———. 2012b. "Heisei 22 Nen Byoin Hokoku" (2010 Hospital Report). http://www.mhlw.go.jp/toukei/saikin/hw/iryosd/10/ (accessed October 2013).

————. 2013. *Kango Kankei Toukei Shiryousho* (Statistical Data on Nursing Services in Japan 2013), 8–11. Chiyoda-ku. Tokyo: Ministry of Finance Printing Office.

————. 2013. "Tiimu Iryo Sushin Kaigi Houkokusho" (Report of the Team Care Promoting Council). http://www.mhlw.go.jp/stf/houdou/2r9852000002yq50.html.

McGillis Hall, L. 2003. "Nursing Staff Mix Models and Outcomes." *Journal of Advanced Nursing* 44 (2): 217–26.

National Nursing Research Unit, Kings College London. 2007. "Points of Entry and Specialization in Nurse Education: International Perspectives." Policy Plus, Issue no 5. London: Kings College London. http://www.kcl.ac.uk/nursing/research/nnru/policy/Policy-Plus-Issues-by-Theme/nurseeducationtraining/PolicyIssue5.pdf (accessed October 2013).

Needleman, J. 2006. "Nurse Staffing in Hospital: Is There a Business Case for Quality?" *Health Affairs* 25 (1): 204–11.

Seccombe, I., G. Smith, and J. Buchan. 1997. "Enrolled Nurses: A Study for the UKCC." Report 344, Institute for Employment Studies, December, IES, Brighton. http://www.employment-studies.co.uk/summary/summary.php?id=344.

Spetz, J. 2014. "How Do Scope of Practice Regulations Affect Demand for LPN's?" University of California, San Francisco, March.

Takahashi, M. 2011. *Kango Gakko Juken Zen-gaido ('13 Nenban) (2011 The Guides of RN School Entrance)*. Shinjuku-ku, Tokyo: Narumi -do.

Tamura, Y. 2009. "*Junkango seido wo meguru torikumi*" ("Actions Taken Towards LPNs"). In Japan Nurse Association (2009): *Hokenshi Josanshi Kangoshi-ho 60 Nenshi (60-year history of Act on Public Health Nurses, Midwives and Nurses*, 270–76. Shibuya-ku, Tokyo: The Japan Nurse Association Publishing Company.

Tsunoda, Y. 2012. *Kangoshoku no chingin no genjyo—Kanmin kakusa no shiten karano bunseki* (Current state of wages among nursing staff- From the perspective of public-private disparity). *Hospitals* 71 (5): 356–61.

Tsuchida, T. 2012. "Training of Altenphlegehelfer in Germany." *Shakai Jigyou Kenkyu* 51: 101–07.

Tsutsui. 2012. "Kaigojinzai niokeru jissenn career-up seido kouchikunotameno kihon-tekina kangaekata (Developing a System of Career Advancement for Care Personnel)." http://www.kantei.go.jp/jp/singi/kinkyukoyou/suisinteam/TF/kaigo_dai2/siryou2.pdf (accessed February 2, 2013).

UNFPA (United Nations Population Fund). 2011. *The State of World's Midwifery 2011: Delivering Health, Saving Lives.* New York. http://www.unfpa.org/sowmy/resources/docs/main_report/en_SOWMR_Full.pdf (accessed October 2013).

Yamada, R., K. Izumi, T. Hiramatsu, M. Kayo, and M. Shogenji. 2007. "Investigation of Clinical Nurses' Intuition Relationships between Hospital, Years of Experience and Nurses' License." *Journal of the Japan Academy of Nursing Administration and Policies* 10 (2): 40–47.

CHAPTER 9

National Hospital Reform in Japan: Results and Challenges

Yohei Tagawa, Yusuke Tsugawa, and Naoki Ikegami

Abstract

Following two earlier waves of reforms, all 154 national hospitals and sanatoriums (apart from eight national center hospitals for specific diseases and 13 sanatoriums for Hansen's disease) were transferred from the national government to operate under the independent, nonprofit National Hospital Organization (NHO) on April 1, 2004. Before reform, the national government gave each hospital a budget and received all earnings made by the hospitals. In the first fiscal year of the transfer, close to half the hospitals were operating at a deficit. After the reform, the number of hospitals with a deficit fell, profits rose, and local needs were better met.

Reform was achieved through recruitment of strong top executives who had robust political support; increased autonomy of hospital directors; evaluation of hospitals' financial performance and greater accountability; introduction of healthy competition among hospitals; and a tighter investment process. It was carried out within the payment regulations of the fee schedule—conditions that may be required for public hospital reform elsewhere to succeed without undermining equity.

Objectives and Context

The objectives of this chapter are to evaluate the issues that the national hospitals in Japan were facing at the time of reform, the political challenges associated with it, the design of the reform and how organizations were restructured, and the impact of the reform on financial status of national hospitals and the government budget.

Medical Service Provision

Most—80 percent—of hospitals in Japan are private. The remaining 20 percent are public hospitals, affiliated with national or local governments, or with quasi-public organizations such as the Japanese Red Cross Society (MHLW 2012a).

Public and private institutions receive the same payments under the fee schedule,[1] but many public hospitals (other than the NHO's) are compensated for disparities between income and expenditures through budget allocations from national or local governments. The justification is to deliver policy-driven health care services such as medical treatment in remote areas or to provide services for those with specific disabilities and diseases. However, critics have argued that because deficits are covered by subsidies, hospitals have little incentive to improve their management.

Three Waves of Reform

Most of Japan's national hospitals were originally military hospitals, which were transferred to the Ministry of Health and Welfare (MHW)[2] after World War II. There were two types: "national hospitals" to provide acute medical care, and "national sanatoriums" to provide convalescent care mainly for tuberculosis, mental disorders, intractable neurological diseases, and so forth. Most national sanatoriums were in remote areas with limited access, reflecting the public's concern of becoming infected with tuberculosis. These facilities were owned and operated by the MHW.

Until 2004, each hospital was given a budget and all earnings made through the fee schedule and reimbursed by health insurance plans went to the MHW. Some national hospitals lacked the motivation to provide care to meet local residents' health needs because they had to provide policy-driven health care services such as tuberculosis treatment. This isolation from local needs became the main reason—and excuse—for the national hospitals to keep running a deficit.

In 2004, national hospitals were transferred from the Ministry of Health, Labour and Welfare (MHLW) and converted into an Independent Administrative Agency (IAA) (*Dokuritsu gyosei houjin*)—the NHO. This transfer can be regarded as the third wave of national hospital reform.

The first wave was in the early 1950s. National hospitals were incurring huge deficits, which had to be made up by subsidies from general tax revenue. In 1952, the Ministry of Finance unofficially suggested that the MHW transfer some national hospitals to prefectural governments (Japan has 47 prefectures). The prefectures strongly opposed the plan, arguing that they did not have the resources to invest in improving the dilapidated hospital buildings and run the money-losing organizations. As a result, only 10 facilities were transferred to prefectural governments (JNHWU 1968).

The second wave began in 1985, when the MHW formulated the "Basic Guidelines for Restructuring and Streamlining National Hospitals and Sanatoriums" (*Kokuritsu byoin ryouyou-jo no saihensei gourika no kihon houshin*). This plan was part of a major administrative reform effort launched by Prime Minister Zenkou Suzuki in 1981, seeking to restructure public finance without tax increases through privatizing public agencies (*Zouzei naki zaisei saiken*). This effort saw three major national public companies (railroads, tobacco, and telecommunications) privatized in the mid-1980s. The hospital reform plan—only partly implemented—proposed that basic health care services should be delivered by private providers, local government-owned facilities, and other (nongovernment) health care providers.

National hospitals were to focus on policy-promoted medical services, including highly advanced medical treatment, treatment of specific diseases (such as tuberculosis and progressive muscular dystrophy, which may be neglected by private facilities), clinical research for designing health policies, and the education and training of health workers. In 1986, the MHW presented a master plan for restructuring national hospitals, including the merger and transfer of many facilities, and to reduce the total number of national hospitals and sanatoriums from 252 to 165 over the following 10 years.

However, opposition from powerful interest groups stalled the reform. By 1996 the number had been cut to only 239. The proposal was again challenged by prefectural governments that continued to argue they could not afford to run the deficit-incurring institutions. In addition, because the reorganization would have led to sizable decreases in personnel, there was fierce resistance from labor unions. The labor union for health workers at national hospitals (the Japan National Hospital Workers' Union) formed a coalition with the labor unions for civil servants (the Japan Federation of National Service Employees) and for health care workers in general (the Japan Federation of Medical Worker's Unions), and with patient groups. They launched a signature campaign, and protested the MHW's restructuring plan. The national government continued to slowly cut the number of national institutions and number of beds, with the number of facilities declining to 220 in 1999 and the total number of beds to around 78,000.

The third reform wave began in 1996, when Prime Minister Ryutaro Hashimoto appointed an Administrative Reform Council, which in its final report proposed to reduce the number of national government employees and to convert many government organizations to nongovernment ones. It stated that national hospitals and sanatoriums should undergo "systematic consolidation and streamlining ... with the aim of establishing an independent administrative agency." The MHW regarded transferring the NHO hospitals to an IAA as an ideal way to meet the across-the-board cuts in personnel imposed on all ministries. Some national hospital directors also welcomed it because they would no longer be bound by the comprehensive cap on the number of employees and other regulations. The Ministry of Finance approved the plan because this restructuring were expected to improve management and cut subsidies. It took several years to develop the reform plan, before its launch in 2004 radically changed financial flows (figure 9.1). Instead of each hospital being given a budget and all its revenues taken by the MHLW, national hospitals are largely now in the same financial position as all other hospitals.

Figure 9.1 Financial Flows to National Hospitals before and after the 2004 Reform

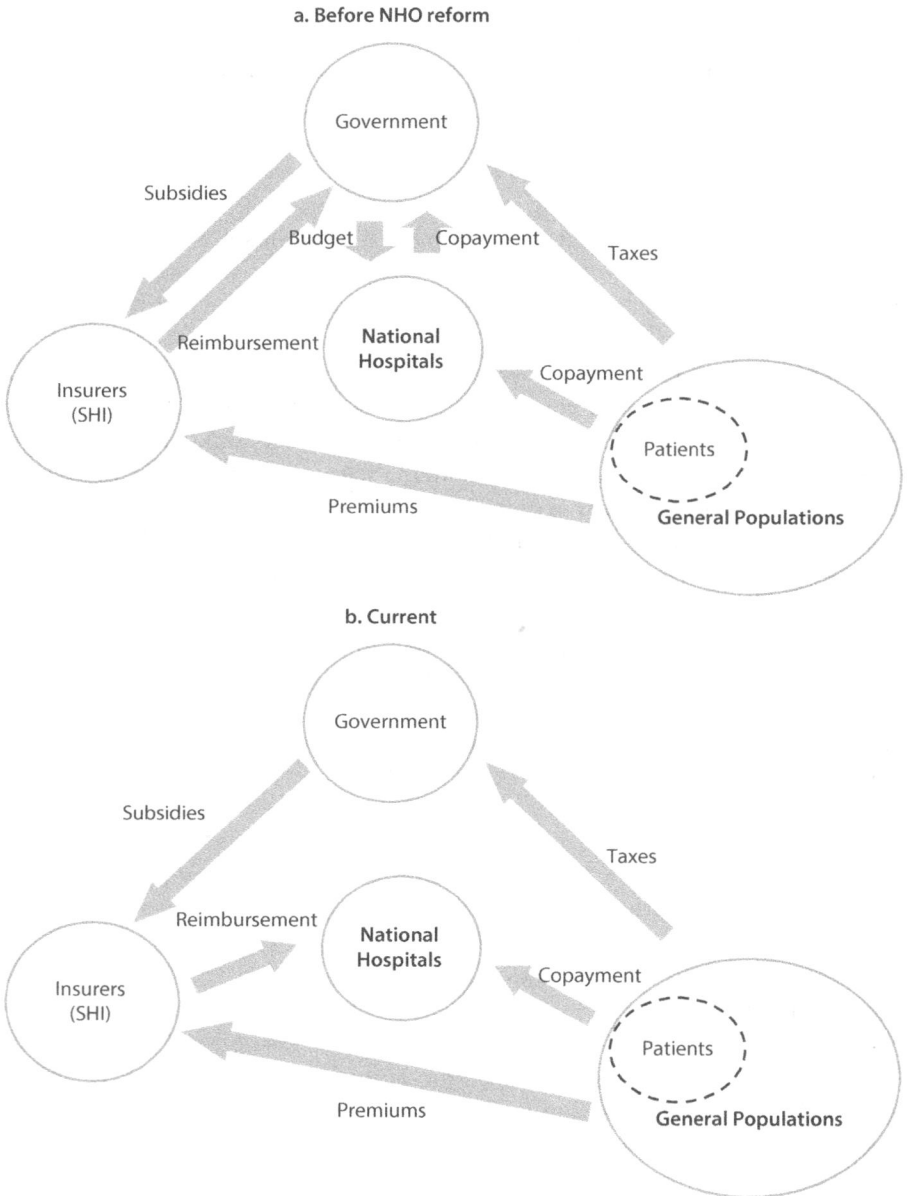

a. Before NHO reform

b. Current

Source: World Bank.

Management Reforms

Organizational Framework and Leadership

Although some had called for an IAA for each hospital, the MHLW organized all the national hospitals and sanatoriums into a single IAA, the NHO. Outstanding leaders were appointed. Leadership was a contributing factor in the reform's success and the leaders were given a high level of discretion by the government to do the difficult work of hospital reform, for example, flattening salaries for senior employees. The first chief executive officer, Dr. Yoshio Yazaki, was regarded as the authority in both academia and the health sector, being a former professor of internal medicine and dean of the University of Tokyo School of Medicine, and the former director of the National Center for Global Health and Medicine. He introduced new strategies such as enhancing service provision to meet national needs, expanding use of second-opinion services and of clinical pathways, and strengthening clinical research and clinical trials. He also encouraged each hospital director to exercise strong leadership and to enhance the hospital's autonomy (which entailed high accountability and healthy competition).[3]

Dr. Yazaki was chief executive officer (CEO) until March 2012, when he was succeeded by Dr. Takaaki Kirino, former professor of neurosurgery and former vice-president of the University of Tokyo. Dr. Yazaki was supported by the vice-chief executive officer, Mr. Hiroumi Kawamura, who had been a career MHLW bureaucrat long committed to the reform of national hospitals. Mr. Kawamura had worked on the national hospital reform for a total of 11 years. He was succeeded by Mr. Michio Shimizu in September 2011, who had headed the planning office for national hospitals within the ministry before coming to the NHO. These managers with deep understanding in national hospital reform seamlessly supported the managerial restructuring.

The Reforms

The principal reforms are in table 9.1; additional details are provided in the following paragraphs.

Establishment of the NHO Board: The board was given full responsibility and authority for managing the NHO. It is composed of the CEO, vice-CEO of the NHO, a few executive directors and nine part-time directors (six are chiefs of regional blocks and the three others are the vice director and director of nursing of the NHO Tokyo Medical Center Hospital, a private hospital director and a medical journalist; as of 2013). All NHO hospitals contribute to the financing of the administrative costs of the NHO headquarters and the regional blocks.

"Regional blocks": To facilitate the reform and to provide support to hospitals facing serious problems, six regional blocks were formed (figure 9.2). Although their geographic areas more or less corresponded to the regional offices of the MHLW,[4] instead of a senior MHLW bureaucrat, the hospital director from one of the leading hospitals in each block was named chief. Under his or her authority, nurses, allied health staff and administrative staff of hospitals in each block are recruited.

Authority of hospital directors: The responsibilities and authority of the hospitals were clarified based on personnel and financial rules drawn up by the NHO's head office. The discretionary authority of hospital directors was expanded. The remuneration of senior physicians was linked to performance based on hospital evaluations, to give them incentives to improve management.

Table 9.1 Main Reforms Stemming from IAA Conversion

	Item	Before IAA conversion	After IAA conversion
Personnel	Employee status	Regular national government officials	Personnel remain national government officials, but salaries, working hours, etc. may be set independently
	Wage system	Seniority-based wage system of national government officials. • Personnel cost ratio was higher than private hospitals • Top management's (for example hospital directors, vice-directors) salary was lower than in private hospitals • Salary for nurses was higher than in private hospitals, a trend increasing with their age	Introduction of performance-based rating system • Performance-based bonus for senior physician holding management positions • Flattening of salary curve for ordinary registered nurses of mid- to advanced age • If the annual account shows a profit and meets prescribed financial conditions, then bonuses reflecting the profit generated by the hospitals and the wage level of the employee are given to all employees of the hospital
	Personnel appointments	Increasing personnel was not easy due to staff quotas, in the framework of the Act on Limitation on Number of Personnel of Administrative Organs	Increase in personnel is allowed if it meets certain criteria (for example, increase in revenue)
	Physicians taking outside jobs	Permission of the Ministry required	At discretion of the hospital director and based on defined conditions
Accounting	Accounting system	"Government accounting" on an annual basis (not carried over to the next accounting year)	Introduction of corporate accounting with a mid- to long-term focus for each hospital and for the NHO
	Income and expenditures	Difficult to ascertain profit or loss at each hospital	Accounts for each hospital and for the NHO
	Disposition of deficits	Single-year disposition (not carried over)	Deficits increase cumulatively on the balance sheet of each hospital
Management	Business plan	Investment based on government health-policy objectives and the need to secure physicians. The Ministry decides investment and hikes in personnel. Soft projections to secure budgets	Investment decisions based on economic rationality • Investment and personnel increases are possible in the judgment of each hospital within a framework • External assessment by a review board
	Primary entity with authority	Non-physician head of administration in each hospital. who confers directly with the Ministry	NHO Board composed of four full-time and nine part-time members. Physician director at each hospital
	Performance assessments	No true assessments	Performance assessments of all hospitals through hospital evaluations
Investment	Investment rules	Not applicable	Investment rules newly established. Formulation of the Hospital Construction Investment Standard Specifications in 2005 set overall reconstruction the costs about 50% of the amount before conversion

Sources: MHLW 2012b; NHO documents; interviews with executives at the NHO.

Note: IAA = Independent Administrative Agency; NHO = National Hospital Organization.

Figure 9.2 Decision-Making Processes before and after NHO Reform

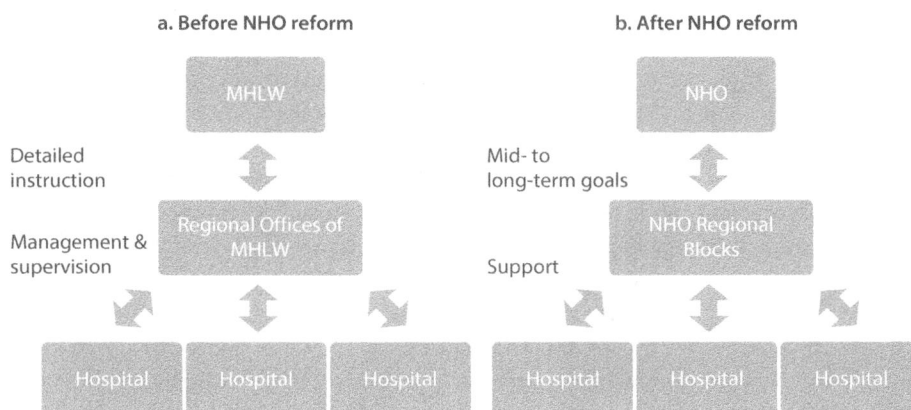

| a. Before NHO reform | b. After NHO reform |

Source: World Bank.

Number of nurses: Following the removal of the cap on the number of personnel by the Act on Limitation on Number of Personnel of Administrative Organizations, it became possible to hire more people; accordingly the nurse–patient ratio rose, allowing hospitals to bill higher daily hospital fees and thereby raising revenues. It also led to increases in patient acuity because the higher fee was conditional on having the hospital's average length of stay shorter than the prescribed number of days (under the fee schedule).

Investment process: After conversion, the NHO controlled construction investments through setting a unified guideline on buildings. Investment in medical equipment was now determined on the basis of each hospital's depreciation expense and the previous year's operating income and expenditure. This allowed the hospital more discretion in investment decisions (in principle, no approval was needed if under ¥50 million).

Limitations: The NHO is still subject to the same government oversight that is extended to the other IAAs. The NHO does not have the authority to fully retain its internal reserves above the amount that the government would permit. This has made investment decisions more difficult. Other limitations include strict rules on procurement by tender that delay decisions and inability to increase the number of administrative staff.

Recovery plans: Hospitals with significant financial problems were required to prepare recovery plans that specified targets and the processes to achieve them. The NHO head office found that 58 hospitals had difficulty in repaying construction debts (incurred before the transfer) with earnings from their own facilities. Each was ordered to draw up a three-year recovery plan, with FY2010 as the final year. They were assisted by the head office and their block office.

Before the NHO was set up, the MHLW and its regional offices had provided management guidance, but this tended to be shortsighted advice that focused on single-year income and expenditures. The recovery plans, though, were based on a mid- to long-term perspective, and goals were set to achieve the financial self-sustainability of each hospital (that is, their depreciation plus operating income exceeded annual debt repayment plus interest). Thirty of the 58 hospitals achieved their goals and recovered their investments (table 9.2). Hospitals were paid under fee for service according to the fee schedule,[5] which sets uniform prices for health care prices to all hospitals across Japan (the revenue per services were same for the NHO hospitals as for any other hospitals in Japan); therefore, such "recovery" was made possible by increasing volume, shifting to higher-priced services (such as higher fees with higher nurse–patient ratios), and reducing relative costs (tendering in capital investment, bending the seniority curve for wages), but not by increasing patients' out-of-pocket costs.

Restart plans: The 25 hospitals that did not achieve the goals of the recovery plans were asked to prepare restart plans to begin in 2012. These targeted hospitals' problems were typically related to their rural location, including difficulty in securing physicians.

These material and human resources reforms built on strengths that had existed in national hospitals, such as exemption from property and other taxes and the generally high caliber of physicians, while rectifying weaknesses, such as lack of management accountability (table 9.3).

Table 9.2 Recovery Plans for Poorly Performing Hospitals and Sanatoriums

		Number of hospitals, 2007	Number of hospitals, 2010
Final goal (accomplishing self-sustainability)	Depreciation (hospital building, medical equipment) plus operating income exceeded annual debt repayment plus interest	–	22
Target level 1	Depreciation (medical equipment) plus operating income exceeded annual debt repayment plus interest	4	12
Target level 2	Operating income exceeded annual debt repayment plus interest	9	2
Target level 3	Operating income exceeded annual debt interest payment	31	13
Minimum target level	Operating income does not exceed annual debt interest payment but able to cover operating costs (for example personnel expenses, material costs)	3	5
Less than minimum target level	Operating income is insufficient to cover operating costs	11	4
Target hospitals, number		58	58

Source: NHO internal documents.

Table 9.3 Effects of the Reform

		Legacy	Reforms
Material	Strengths	• Occupied national government land and buildings so was exempted property tax	• Discretion for investment broadened and investments made based on management accountability, allowing effective utilization of assets
	Weaknesses	• Construction costs for facilities did not come from government budget, and interest-bearing debts incurred for construction were transferred to the NHO account • Repayment of construction costs and associated interest rates were burden on national hospitals • Construction unit costs were high, which increased depreciation costs	• Uniform standards for construction unit costs. Per area unit costs halved and the burden of depreciation expenses alleviated
Human	Strengths	• Outstanding physicians attracted by their generally high reputation • Environment where research can be performed	• Bonuses of the director and senior physicians determined by objective assessment standards with hospital evaluations • The new business environment (higher autonomy and accountability, healthy competition) allows staff to demonstrate their abilities
	Weaknesses	• Public-sector seniority system • Employees with low motivation in increasing profits	• Flattened salary curve checked salary hikes for older nurses • Employees with low motivation retired on their own accord • Average age of employees fell from 42.2 years (2004) to 39.0 (2011)

Sources: MHLW 2012b; NHO documents; interviews with executives at the NHO.
Note: NHO = National Hospital Organization.

The number of hospitals decreased, following the plan that was drawn prior to the transfer to the NHO. When the NHO was established on April 1, 2004, the NHO included 154 facilities (56 national hospitals and 98 national sanatoriums).[6] Over time nine hospitals were merged with neighboring hospitals and one sanatorium was closed. The total thus dropped to 144 as of 2010, and was scheduled to reach 143 in 2013 with another merger.

Performance Evaluations

The process of carrying out hospital evaluations improved the quality of management, measured and visualized financial performance of each hospital, increased accountability, and stimulated healthy competition. For performance assessments

Universal Health Coverage for Inclusive and Sustainable Development
http://dx.doi.org/10.1596/978-1-4648-0408-3

of the entire NHO, criteria were developed based on a Mid-Term Plan approved by the National Hospital Committee, an independent administrative institution review board under the Ministry. From these criteria, hospital evaluation indices were prepared for each hospital. "Managerial aspects" (50 points) are drawn from the assessment criteria, and include "ratio of revenue to expenditure" (12 points), "ratio of personnel and contracted-out costs to revenue" (5 points), and so on. "Medical service aspects" (50 points) cover performance and quality of "medical care", "clinical research", and "education and training". These evaluation items are revised annually, based on requests from each hospital and on actual operating conditions.

The "managerial aspects" of the Mid-Term Plan define the tasks of the NHO within the framework of the fee schedule. The fee schedule provides higher daily fees if the hospital has a higher nurse–patient ratio and the average length of stay is below the threshold. Some of the points for "medical service aspects" are also tied to the fee schedule's incentive payment. For example, the hospital will receive an additional ¥10,000 for the first day of hospitalization if it is designated a Community Health care Supporting Hospital by meeting the thresholds in the share of outpatients referred from outside facilities. (Forty hospitals in the NHO are so designated.) The medical service aspects have taken the criteria for designation and then fine-tuned the referral standards so that the hospitals could earn from 2 to 6 points. In general if each hospital sets targets and improves performance as indicated by the hospital evaluation, its ranking in the NHO improves and its revenues increase.

Financial Improvements

Profit and Loss

When the NHO was established in 2004, 74 of its hospitals ran a deficit.[7] The initial goal was to curtail unnecessary expenditures. For investments, it was decided immediately that, in principle, no investments would be made except in unavoidable cases. In the following year, a set of Standard Specifications for Hospital Construction Investment was prepared. Construction unit costs were reduced to about half of what they had been under national government management, reducing depreciation expenses.

After becoming an IAA, the NHO's earnings rose steadily, a result of a higher contribution to meet local needs (including emergency care) and provision of better nursing care, reflecting the higher nurse–patient ratios. The number of hospitals with a deficit fell to 25 in 2011. By reducing facility and construction investments and such like, the growth rate of revenues exceeded that of expenditures, resulting in a shift to a profitable structure: recurrent profits climbed from ¥190 million in FY2004, the first year after IAA conversion, to ¥58.3 billion in FY2010 (figure 9.3).[8]

Figure 9.3 Trends in Earnings and Expenditures of NHOs

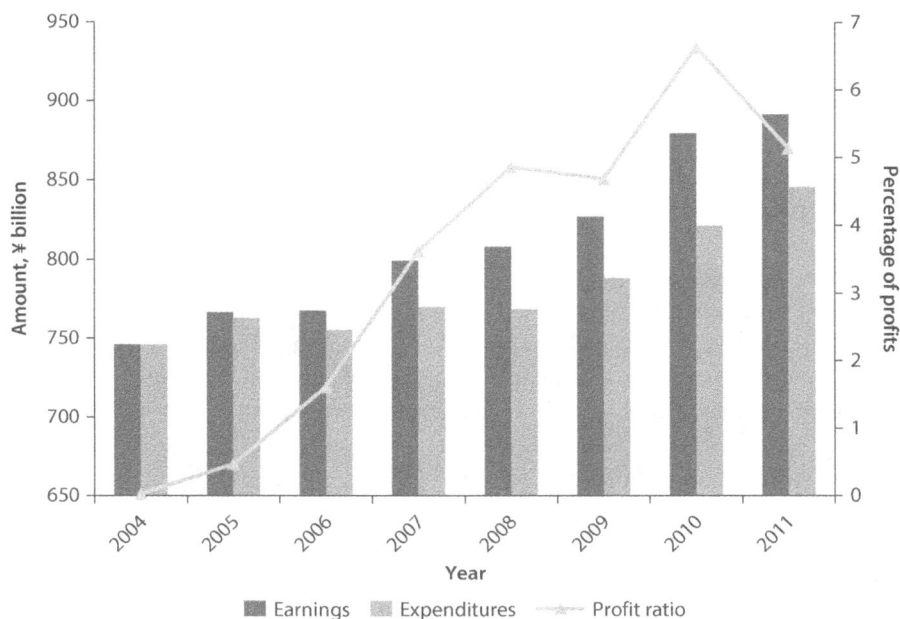

Source: NHO annual financial statements.

Although financial transfers from the MHLW to the NHO have continued in the form of "Management Expense Grants," these grants have been made to fund the employees' retirement reserve to cover for the period prior to the transfer, for the proportion of pension benefits that were funded from the old Civil Servant Pension scheme, and for project-based subsidies for defined clinical activities. These grants declined from 7.8 percent of total operating income in 2004 to 4.7 percent in 2011. By 2012, none had been allocated in the form of project-based subsidies. Still, the NHO continues to make transfers to the government's National Pension Fund in the form of partial payment of the employees' basic pension contributions that would have been covered by the government in private organizations, and payment from the reserves that have been evaluated as being excessive by the government.[9]

Inpatient Profitability

By upgrading inpatient medical services, the fees for inpatient medical procedures have been raised, thereby improving profitability. An influx of new inpatients arose from new community medical service cooperation offices, which lifted rates of referral and reverse referral (the fee paid to the hospital for referring back the patient). In 2007, the increase in revenues due to the increased work intensity (increased number of operations, etc.) and higher nurse–patient ratio exceeded the accompanying increase in personnel costs, also boosting

profitability. In 2011, profitability[10] was 27 percent higher than in 2007 for former national hospitals (350–499 beds) and former sanatoriums with general
beds.

Long-Term Borrowing

Management improvements have reduced long-term borrowing. It was ¥747.1
billion in FY2004, but dropped to ¥475 billion in FY2011 through regular
annual repayments.

Examples of Particular Hospitals

Here are four examples of how the reforms affected particular hospitals:

Okayama Medical Center (Okayama City, Okayama Prefecture; 609 beds). It
significantly shortened the average number of days of hospitalization. It is
steadily repaying the ¥34 billion long-term debt held at the time of IAA conversion.

Yonago Medical Center (Yonago City, Tottori Prefecture; 250 beds). It moved out
of its chronic deficit and restored profitability through the recovery plan. It
specializes in specific cancer treatments—previously lacking in its community—and has set up a clinical department of hematology.

Nagasaki Medical Center (Omura City, Nagasaki Prefecture; 643 beds). It improved earnings and simultaneously developed a system for dispatching registered nurses to improve medical services in remote islands.

*Nagasaki Kawatana Medical Center (Kawatana-cho, Nagasaki Prefecture; 285
beds, of which 60 are for muscular dystrophy patients).* It continues to provide
medical services for intractable neurological diseases, and is establishing community medical services as a new pillar of its operations.

Insights

The 2004 reorganization helped create an environment where national hospitals
can work autonomously with expanded authority and responsibility. Key success
factors were the transformation of management that changed the motivation and
mindset of the entire staffs.

Japan's reform of national hospitals involved a complex package of multiple
organizational reforms: creating a single independent, nonprofit agency; appoint-
ing high-quality leadership; expanding the authority of the hospital's physician
director accompanied by higher accountability; changing the investment process;
introducing comprehensive evaluations; changing accounting practices to allow a
hospital-by-hospital assessment of financial performance (healthy competition);
and requiring the preparation of recovery plans for hospitals operating at a deficit. In retrospect, the decision to transfer all hospitals to one NHO, and not to
make each hospital an IAA, allowed management resources to be concentrated

and facilitated healthy competition and cooperation among hospitals, within regional blocks and throughout the NHO. These reforms may be relevant for low- and middle-income countries—if payment regulations to protect equity can be enforced.

Notes

1. See the chapters 5 and 6.
2. Restructured into the MHLW in 2001.
3. We know that autonomy without accountability and regulatory oversight has led to major problems in public hospital reform in some countries.
4. The MHLW's Regional Offices of Hokkaido and Tohoku were combined into one regional block. The rest are the same.
5. More precisely, case-mix payment—diagnostic procedure combination/per diem payment system (DPC/PDPS)—was introduced in Japan in April 2003. The DPC/PDPS initially enrolled 82 academic hospitals (80 university hospitals and two national centers), rapidly expanding to other acute care hospitals that joined the system voluntarily.
6. The number of national facilities in the NHO was reduced from 175 in 2003 to 154 in 2004 by keeping 21 national facilities under the MHLW, including 6 national advanced medical centers for patients requiring highly specialized care for certain diseases (such as cancer) plus all sanatoriums for patients with Hansen's disease (leprosy).
7. The proportion of hospitals running deficit was around 52 percent in FY2004, 51 percent in FY2005, 43 percent in FY2006, 32 percent in FY2007, 27 percent in FY2008, 22 percent in FY2009, and 14 percent in FY2010 (out of 143 hospitals not merged in 2010) (MHLW 2012).
8. Financial data cannot be compared before and after IAA conversion because hospital budgets did not use corporate accounting.
9. In June, 2009, after audits of the past five year plan had been completed, the NHO paid ¥3.2 billion from its accumulated reserves of ¥50.7 billion.
10. Profit per patient per day.

Bibliography

JNHWU (Japan National Hospital Workers' Union). 1968. "Twenty-year History of JNHWU/Zen-iro" (in Japanese), JNHWU, pp. 17–20.

Matsuda, S., K. B. Ishikawa, K. Kuwabara, K. Fujimori, K. Fushimi, and H. Hashimoto. 2008. "Development and Use of the Japanese Case-mix System." *Eurohealth* 14: 25.

MHLW (Ministry of Health, Labour and Welfare). 2004. "The First Mid-term Goals." MHLW, Chiyoda-ku, Tokyo.

———. 2009. "The Second Mid-term Goals." NHLW, Chiyoda-ku, Tokyo.

———. 2012a. "Survey of Medical Institution." http://www.mhlw.go.jp/toukei/saikin/hw/iryosd/12/dl/1-1.pdf (accessed November 2013).

———. 2012b. "Review Commission for National Hospital Reform." http://www.mhlw. go.jp/stf/shingi/2r9852000002jmtj.html (accessed November 2013).

NHO (National Hospital Organization). 2004. "Comparison of Wage Curves of the National Hospital Organization and the Private Sector." NHO internal document, Tokyo.

———. 2004a. "The First Mid-term Plans." NHO, Meguro-ku, Tokyo.

———. 2004b. "The Rules of Wages of the National Hospital Organization." April 1, 2004, NHO internal document, Tokyo.

———. 2004–2011. "Business Reports." NHO, Meguro-ku, Tokyo.

———. 2004–2012. "Annual Financial Statements." NHO, Meguro-ku, Tokyo.

———. 2004–2012. "Annual Plans." NHO, Meguro-ku, Tokyo.

———. 2005a. "Regarding Wages of the Vice President and Others." No. 0304001, March 4, Revised on December 1, 2010, NHO internal document, Tokyo.

———. 2005b. "The Guidelines for Maintaining National Hospital Organization Buildings." NHO internal document, Tokyo.

———. 2009. "The Second Mid-term Plans." NHO, Meguro-ku, Tokyo.

———. 2012. "The Rules of Wages of the National Hospital Organization." May 1, 2012, NHO internal document, Tokyo.

CHAPTER 10

Improving Population Health through Public Health Centers in Japan

Yusuke Tsugawa, Naoki Ikegami, Naoko Miake, and Michael R. Reich

Abstract

Japan has hugely improved the health status of its population over the last 60 years, and now has one of the highest life expectancies in the world. Effective public health interventions targeted at reducing prevalence of major preventable diseases, such as tuberculosis and stroke, were important for these gains. Such interventions were also essential for the country to achieve and maintain universal health coverage (UHC) by complementing medical services covered under national health insurance plans.

The government has played a major part in developing and implementing public health services. After World War II, public health centers were redesigned under the leadership of the General Headquarters of the Allied Forces (GHQ) and were key to improving maternal and child health outcomes, controlling tuberculosis, and containing stroke attributable to high blood pressure.

Low- and middle-income countries can learn from Japan's experience of improving population health through government-provided preventive medicine services—crucial for progressing toward UHC—by providing public health services that may not be covered by health insurance plans but may help contain health expenditures.

Context

Japan has improved its population's health status in the last several decades. In 1947, life expectancy for men was 50 years and for women 54 years; by 2012, it had improved to 79.9 years for men and 86.4 years for women, giving the country one of the highest life expectancies in the world. The infant mortality rate and neonatal mortality rate decreased from 76.7 and 31.4 per 1,000 live births in 1947 to 2.3 and 1.1 in 2011 (MHLW 2011). The country achieved UHC in 1961, and the entire population has access to health care through a social health insurance system developed from the German (Bismarckian) model (Ikegami et al. 2011).

What is unique about the history of public health in Japan is that the good health of its population was attributed at least partially to the public health centers (PUBHCs), or *Hoken-jo*, organized by central and local governments, with public health nurses (PHNs) or *Hoken-shi*[1] playing an important role. Together they have been crucial in the nation's UHC system by complementing the medical services covered under health insurance plans. The majority of preventive medicine services, such as vaccinations and cancer screenings, are not listed in the uniform fee schedule and are thus not covered by these plans in Japan. Such services are municipal government responsibilities.[2]

History

The evolution of Japan's public health services can be broadly divided into two phases. First, the concept of hygiene (*Eisei*) was introduced from Germany in the mid-1870s; second, "public health" (*Koshu-eisei*) came in under the occupation of the General Headquarters of the Allied Forces (GHQ) in 1945–52.

Japan's approach to hygiene originated in the concept of "social defense" against infectious diseases after 1868, and expanded largely through government involvement. When Japan ended 250 years of national isolation that year, foreign trade and greater mobility of people brought infectious diseases such as cholera and smallpox into the country, which caused frequent epidemics. To cope, the government introduced the concept of hygiene and strengthened public health administration with a focus on hygiene and sanitation. The police were responsible for the frontline quarantine of patients, under the strong governance of central government.

In the late nineteenth and early twentieth century, several elite military doctors[3] studied in countries such as Germany (and the United Kingdom less so), which had advanced knowledge about public health. On their return, they played a major role in designing public health (hygiene) policies with the primary aim of maintaining the health conditions of soldiers. Until the end of World War II, the police department remained accountable for the environmental hygiene of the population (JICA 2005).

The history of PUBHCs dates back to 1914 when the Infant Health Consultation Center (*Nyuyoji Kenko Sodan Jigyosho*) was developed by the Japanese Red Cross. The government recommended large cities to host Children's Health Centers (*Shouni Hokensho*) in 1926, and their number rose to 458 by 1928. With a greater need for healthy soldiers and productive manufacturing workers as the war in China intensified, the Public Health Center Law (*Hokenjo hou*) was enacted in 1937. The following year, the Ministry of Health and Welfare was established, and the Institute of Public Health[4] was created with financial support from the Rockefeller Foundation. The Institute functioned as the focal education and research institution for public health. Based on various types of health centers already in operation, about 40 official PUBHCs were built nationwide to provide care for tuberculosis control, maternal and child health, and nutrition. The Citizens' Health Insurance Law (*Kokumin Kenko Hoken Hou*) was enacted in 1938, which included the provision to place public health nurses (PHNs, *Kokuho Hoken-fu*) nationwide. The PUBHCs were run by local governments and other bodies, and their number grew to more than 700 by 1944 (JICA 2005; Katsuda et al. 2011).

The role of PUBHCs changed post war under the occupation of GHQ. At that time, people were suffering from severe food shortages and frequent epidemics of acute infectious diseases. During the occupation, General McArthur, Supreme Commander of the Allied Forces, began by setting up 14 "sections," each designed to supervise the functions of an existing Japanese ministry. The Public Health and Welfare Section was responsible for designing the public health provision system (Nishimura 2009). Colonel Sams, chief of this section, defined its mission as disease prevention, medical care, welfare, and social security (Sams 1952). They exerted strong leadership in redesigning and implementing new public health systems (Nishimura 2009).

In May 1946, GHQ ordered the Ministry of Health and Welfare to reform its structure and establish sanitation departments in each prefecture nationwide. The right to live a healthy life (*Seizon ken*) had been included as a basic human right in the new constitution in 1947, which stipulated that the nation was responsible for promoting public health. In April 1947, GHQ submitted a "memorandum about expansion and reinforcement of public health centers," based on which major changes were made to the Public Health Center Law (*Hokenjo hou*) in September that year, and the functions of the PUBHCs were expanded and strengthened (Marui 1990a). The new law explicitly defined the role of PUBHCs to cover medical and pharmaceutical issues, food sanitation, and environmental health. The PUBHCs were placed under the control of the prefectures or designated municipalities, and with strong support from GHQ, gained higher authority as the first-line public health service providers in broad areas of public health issues.

Although the post-occupation government in 1952 overturned several measures that GHQ had introduced, the PUBHCs' structure remained intact, probably because the government acknowledged it to be effective and beneficial (Marui 1990b). Between 1950 and 1960, life expectancy improved from 58.0 years to 65.3 years for men and 61.5 years to 70.2 years for women. During this period, per capita GDP also increased from US$3,415 to US$6,249 (2005 international dollars) (JICA 2005; Ikeda et al. 2011).

Japan had moved forward with public health policies without public health schools: medical schools had only small departments of public health. These departments were established at medical schools under the occupation, based on a recommendation of the United States education mission to Japan after the war. The first such department was created at the University of Tokyo School of Medicine in December 1948. Public health was taught either as one of the fields of medicine at medical school or at the National Institute of Public Health. The first school of public health as a professional school (independent of a university's faculty of medicine) was built in 2000 (Kyoto University School of Public Health), and even now the country has only six schools of public health.

Universal Health Coverage for Inclusive and Sustainable Development
http://dx.doi.org/10.1596/978-1-4648-0408-3

To support operations of PUBHCs, the central government established the PUBHC operation subsidy fund (*Hokenjo uneihi hojokin*). Set up in 1964, it amounted to about ¥34 billion 1986, although central government subsidies had decreased incrementally over this period, and were eventually incorporated into the general revenues–funded budget by 1994. In 2005/06, the government budget for PUBHCs was transferred to local governments (MHLW 2010).[5]

In response to the change in the social structures and the diversified needs of communities for PUBHCs, the Public Health Center Law was incorporated into the Community Health Law (*Chiiki Hoken Hou*) in 1994, which came into effect in 1997. The law clearly specified the responsibilities of the prefectural governments and local governments for community health. The law designated municipal health centers (Local Health Center or *Shichoson hoken center*) as the subsidiary organizations of PUBHCs. The directors of PUBHCs were still medical doctors, and PUBHCs were legally authorized to undertake the supervision, auditing, licensing, and suspension of medical facilities, restaurants, and other facilities. On the other hand, maternal and child health and health services for the elderly were the main focuses of Local Health Centers, which were run mainly by PHNs (box 10.1)—no medical qualification was required to be a director. The law stated that each prefectural PUBHC was expected to cover a population of around 300,000, and cities with more than that were recommended to set up their own PUBHC. Since 1997, prefectural PUBHCs with a small population have been integrated into neighboring PUBHCs, or transferred to a municipal government with a population over 300,000.

Box 10.1 Role of Public Health Nurses (*Hoken-shi*)

Since the war, PHNs have played a key role in providing public health services, attributable to the importance given to this function by GHQ during postwar reconstruction. PHNs existed as early as the 1930s, but their role was limited and not well defined until the late 1940s.

The role of PHNs increased during the postwar democratization of community-based public health administration, and expanded markedly when a new Public Health Center Law (*Hokenjo hou*) was enacted in 1947. In 1949, the guideline defining duties of PHNs were issued, when they were designated leading players in community-based public health services.

PHNs' responsibilities ranged from local government functions, support to medical practitioners, provision of parasite-control programs, maternal and child health checkups, family planning, and health education. In 1997, many tasks of the PUBHCs were delegated to Local Health Centers, and where there were no medical doctors the public health programs were managed mainly by PHNs. In 2008, there were 7,737 PHNs working at 517 PUBHCs, and 16,525 PHNs working at 2,726 Local Health Centers (JICA 2005; MHLW 2010; Katsuda et al. 2011).

The number of PUBHCs had been stable at around 850 in 1966–96, but after the law was passed if fell to 494 by 2010. The number of medical doctors working at PUBHCs declined from 1,170 in 1999 to 819 in 2008 (JICA 2005; MHLW 2010; Katsuda et al. 2011).

The Contributions of PUBHCs in Achieving Good Health

The rise in the longevity of the population over the past 60 years came mainly during the period of rapid health improvements in 1950–65 (Ikeda et al. 2011), which straddled the year when Japan achieved UHC (1961). In 1947, the infant mortality rate was 76.7 per 1,000 live births, tuberculosis was the major cause of death (187.2 deaths per 100,000 people), and life expectancy at birth was 50 for men and 54 for women. These indicators improved sharply, and by 2011 infant mortality had fallen to 2.3, the incidence of tuberculosis was 20 cases per 100,000 people[6] (1.7 deaths per 100,000 population)[7] and life expectancy at birth had grown to 79.9 years for men and 86.4 years for women (JICA 2005; Ikeda et al. 2011; MHLW 2012).

There are many accomplishments of PUBHCs in Japan, including gains in maternal and child health, containment of tuberculosis infections, and the reduction in deaths due to stroke through control of salt intake.

Gains in Maternal and Child Health

Even during the war, maternal and child health was of interest to the public health administrators. In 1942, the *Pregnant Mother's Handbook* (later changed to the *Maternal and Child Handbook* in 1947, and to the *Maternal and Child Health Handbook* in 1966) was developed, based on the German *Mutterpass*, and distributed. Under this program, pregnant women were required to register their pregnancy at their local municipality; were advised to take at least three medical examinations during pregnancy; and at each visit, the information about the progress of pregnancy was recorded in their handbooks. When Japan was short of food during the war, pregnant women carrying the handbook were provided with sanitary napkins, gauze, soap (necessary at the time of delivery), and eggs.

When the war ended in 1945, PUBHCs became the hub for outreach activities by PHNs, including consultancy and home visits to pregnant women and mothers. Creation of Maternal Health Centers (*Boshi Kenko Center*) and the attainment of UHC supported the rapid increase in the share of births attended by skilled staff and the sharp drop in home-based deliveries (from 95.4 percent in 1950 to 4 percent in 1970, MHLW 2005).

Containment of Tuberculosis Infections

PUBHCs were involved in collecting vital statistics (box 10.2); improving nutrition, food hygiene, water supplies, and sanitation; and detecting and quarantining tuberculosis cases. These collective efforts—along with economic growth, improved nutrition, and better access to health care due to UHC—cut deaths from tuberculosis rapidly between 1945 and 1955 (figure 10.1).

Universal Health Coverage for Inclusive and Sustainable Development
http://dx.doi.org/10.1596/978-1-4648-0408-3

Box 10.2 Institutional Capacity to Collect Statistics for Health Policies

The government has collected health-related statistics and developed public health policies using these data for over a century. Mortality statistics have been collected since 1876, and population statistics since 1899. National surveys have been conducted to estimate the number of cases for specific (mainly infectious) diseases.

In 1916, the Ministry of Home Affairs created the Health and Sanitation Research Council, designed to conduct research on, for example, child health, tuberculosis, sexually transmitted diseases, leprosy, mental illnesses, food, housing, and sanitation. Laws were passed drawing on these statistics, including the Tuberculosis Prevention Law, Leprosy Prevention Law, and Parasitic Disease Prevention Law. The first national census using modern methods was conducted in 1920.

These statistics were vital for the government to identify and tackle public health issues in a timely manner (JICA 2005), but as their collection requires a certain level of institutional capacity, it may be difficult to apply Japan's experience to many low-income countries without such capacities. However, as countries develop, they will eventually need these statistics for public health planning and services, so as to design and properly implement targeted health policies.

Figure 10.1 Trends in Causes of Death

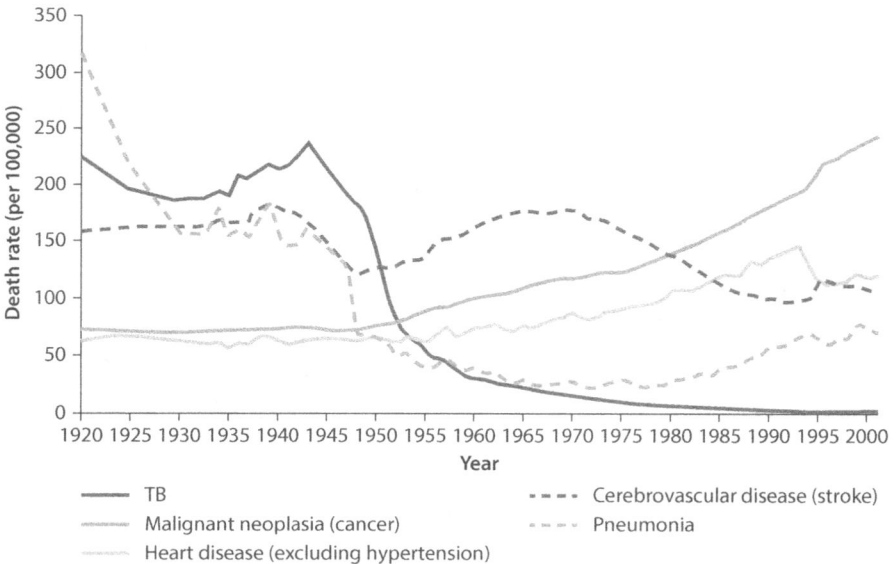

Source: JICA 2005, 12.
Note: Data for 1944–46 are based on estimates because of the devastation due to World War II.

The country had dedicated sufficient financial resources to control tuberculosis at national level, provided mass screening for tuberculosis at PUBHCs, and succeeded in controlling tuberculosis in a relatively short time. Between 1910 and 1950 tuberculosis killed almost 4 million people,[8] out of a population of 50 million in 1910 and 83 million in 1950 (Johnston 1995). In 1954, the share of total medical expenditures allocated to diagnosing and treating tuberculosis was 27.7 percent, indicating a high national priority and a large share of the national budget for controlling the disease (Shimao 1988).

A national tuberculosis program, which comprised BCG vaccination, case-finding (through mass screening) and treatment complex, and isolation of infectious cases, had been launched in 1951 (Shimao 1989). The diagnosis of tuberculosis cases was mainly conducted at PUBHCs across the country, and treatment (entailing isolation of identified cases) was the responsibility of tuberculosis sanatoriums. The program identified contagious cases and controlled the burden of tuberculosis; mortality due to tuberculosis declined by nearly one-third between 1950 and 1955 (Shimao 1989). The share of health expenditures for the disease also went down, to 1.1 percent by 1985 (Shimao 1988).[9]

Reduction in Stroke Deaths through Control of Salt Intake

In 1952, stroke took the place of tuberculosis to become the leading cause of death in Japan. The number of deaths due to stroke had been gradually rising after 1950, then began to fall more rapidly in the early 1970s (figure 10.1). The incidence of stroke was higher in northeast Japan, and the data indicated that it was associated with the amount of salt consumed and with high blood pressure (Sasaki 1964, 1980). The extremely high salt intakes in this region reflected a diet of miso soup and salted pickles, and the use of soy sauce as the primary seasoning (Sasaki 1964). Public health campaigns to lower sodium intake were introduced in the 1960s, and high salt intakes reported in the 1950s and early 1960s began to decline from the mid-1970s to the mid-1980s (Brown et al. 2009). National salt intake came down from an average of 13.5 to 12.1 grams per day, while in the northeast, salt intake fell from 18 to 14 grams per day. As the salt intake decreased, the population exhibited a concurrent fall in average blood pressure and a significant reduction in stroke-related mortality (figures 10.1 and 10.2) (Ueshima et al. 1987; Okayama et al. 1993; MHLW 2004; He and MacGregor 2010). It may be inappropriate to assume causality between reduced salt intake and lower stroke-related mortality in Japan, since the stroke-related mortality did not increase after salt intake returned to its former level in mid-1990s, but it might have been one of the contributing factors among other life-style improvements introduced at that time. Moreover, while it was in a nonlinear manner, overall salt intake did decrease nationally as the government intended.

Figure 10.2 Time Trend of National Salt Intake

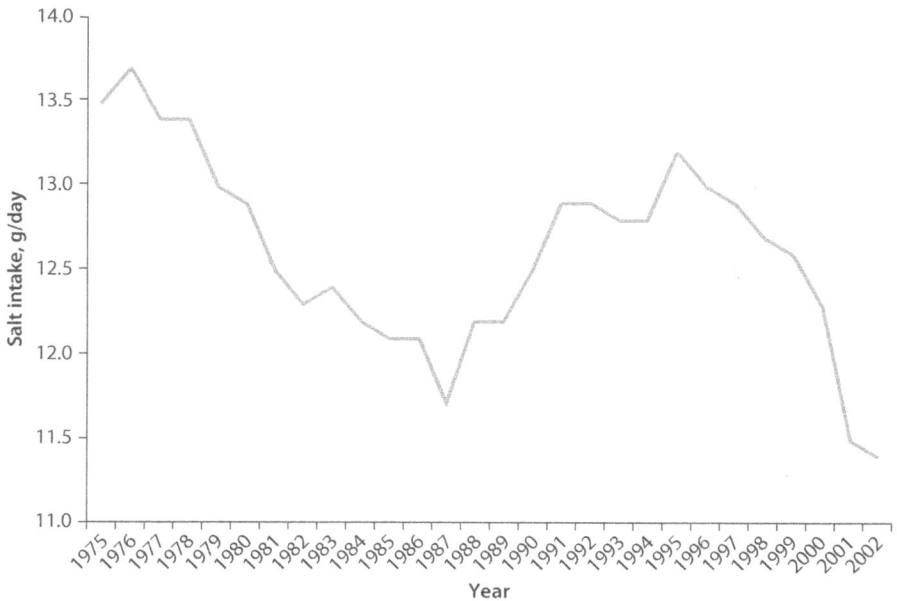

Source: MHLW 2004.

The Changing Role of PUBHCs

The role of PUBHCs has been changing in recent years, as seen above and summarized in the timeline in figure 10.3. In 1994, the roles of PUBHCs and Local Health Centers were redesigned: the government promoted decentralization, and maternal and child health and nutritional counseling were transferred from PUBHCs to Local Health Centers, and the PUBHCs were made responsible for training and providing technical advice to municipality workers (table 10.1). In 2008, health insurance programs became responsible for providing health checkups and education targeted at metabolic syndrome for beneficiaries and their families. However, associated with these changes in the expected role of PUBHCs, the provision of public health services may be fragmented. For instance, it is unclear which organizations are responsible for cancer screening, and although Local Health Centers are responsible for vaccinating children, they lack enforcement mechanisms (discussed further in the next section).

Emerging PUBHC-Related Public Health Issues

The government has for many decades provided broad public health services through PUBHCs, but Japan now faces several emerging public health issues, such as high incidence of vaccine-preventable diseases and low cancer screening rates. In many countries, primary care doctors are responsible for preventive

Figure 10.3 Changing Role of PUBHCs in Japan

1937
- Enactment of **Public Health Center Law** (*Hokenjo hou*)
  - Establishment of PUBHC (*Hokenjo*); hygiene education; control of acute infectious diseases; maternal and child health

1947
- Major amendments in **Public Health Center Law** (*Hokenjo hou*)
  - The functions of PUBHC was formally-defined, expanded and strengthened

1994
- Public Health Center Law ᵘ **Community Health Law** (*Chiiki hoken hou*)
  - Redefined the roles of PUBHC and municipalities (Local Health Centers or *Shichoson hoken center*); promotion of decentralization; maternal and child health and nutritional counseling were transferred from PUBHC to Local Health Centers

1997
- Effectuation of **Community Health Law**

2008
- **Specific Health Checkup and Specific Health Guidance** (*Tokutei kenshin/tokutei hokenshidou*)
  - Health insurance programs became responsible for health checkups and education targeted towards metabolic syndrome for their beneficiaries and families

Source: Adapted from Okumura 1997; MHLW 2010; Marui 1990a, 1990b.

services, but in Japan they were historically provided by PUBHCs (and more recently by Local Health Centers and health insurance programs), and while PUBHCs have played an important role in improving health conditions over the last few decades, it seems that they have not been functioning well in more recent years. There are several possible reasons.

First, their structures have not been appropriately revised and tailored to match current public health issues. Second, PUBHCs and Local Health Centers are given fixed budgets for providing preventive services; there is little incentive for them to expand the coverage of public health services (they may lose money if they were to expand the coverage relative to the previous year). Third, Japan lacks an institution similar to the Centers for Disease Control and Prevention (CDC) in the United States, that is, an independent agency helping protect the nation's health via critical scientific research and provision of health information. The lack of this kind of agency may have weakened the Japanese government's capacity to design scientifically robust evidence-based health policies. We illustrate the emerging PUBHC-related issues in Japan using vaccination policies as an example.

Universal Health Coverage for Inclusive and Sustainable Development
http://dx.doi.org/10.1596/978-1-4648-0408-3

Table 10.1 Functions of PUBHCs and Local Health Centers before and after the Community Health Law

	Before 1997	After 1997
PUBHCs (*Hoken-jo*)	Direct provision of public health services	Management of public health service delivery system
	- Control of tuberculosis - Mental diseases - Maternal and child health (such as health checkups for children aged 3) - Nutritional counseling - Intractable diseases - HIV/AIDS - Environmental hygiene - Food sanitation	- Surveillance of local health issues - Training and technical advice to municipality staff - Management of infectious diseases, mental diseases, and intractable diseases - Environmental hygiene - Food sanitation supervision and intervention
Local Health Centers (*Shicho son hoken center*)	- Health checkups for children aged 1 and half years - Vaccination - Health care services for the elderly	- Maternal and child health (such as health checkups for children aged 3 and children aged 1 and half year) - Nutritional counseling - Vaccination - Health care services for the elderly

Source: Adapted from Okumura 1997.

Vaccination Policies

Japan's vaccination policies have been somewhat incoherent, especially over the last two decades. The MMR (measles-mumps-rubella) vaccine was introduced and made compulsory in 1989, but it was withdrawn in 1993 in response to the reports of aseptic meningitis associated with the mumps component of the vaccine and public concerns about such events (Terada 2003). In 1994, the vaccination policy for all vaccines was changed from mandatory to "strongly recommended," and since then there has been virtually no enforcing mechanism on vaccinations, such as the mandatory immunization requirement as a prerequisite to public school enrollment in the United States. Vaccines for chickenpox (varicella),[10] mumps, and hepatitis B, which are the recommended vaccines in many developed countries, are not included in "strongly recommended" vaccines in Japan. As a result, it is voluntary for Japanese people to pay for these vaccines themselves.[11] The government traditionally has not taken a strong position on vaccination, probably because of its political sensitivity to the perspective and concerns of the public, fears of litigation from patients suffering from side effects, and protectionist policies to promote domestic vaccine companies. This leads to problems.

In 2013, the country had a nationwide rubella outbreak, with more than 8,500 laboratory-confirmed cases (O'Connell 2013), and 18 infants with congenital rubella syndrome between October 2012 and September 2013 (National

Institute of Infectious Diseases 2013). CDC officially urged unvaccinated pregnant women to avoid travel to Japan because of the outbreak (O'Connell 2013). Based on data showing that about 15 percent of men aged 20–50 were negative for rubella antibody, health care professionals in Japan have advocated mass immunization for those in their 20s to 40s, through provision of government subsidies for adults who take vaccinations for rubella (there are government subsidies for infants, but not adults), accompanied by imports of foreign MMR vaccines if there is a shortage of domestic measles-rubella vaccines. However, the government planned to overcome the shortage of domestic vaccines by prioritizing provision to people around pregnant women or women planning to get pregnant, and decided not to provide subsidies for adults or to import foreign vaccines.

Outbreaks of measles occur from time to time. One was in 1991 with 68,980 cases and 39 deaths (Nakatani, Sano, and Iuchi 2002). Another was in 2008, with 11,007 cases. In 2005, the measles incidence was 4.7 per 100,000 population, or much higher than the average in countries in the Organisation for Economic Co-operation and Development (OECD) of 1.22 (Armesto et al. 2006; Johnson and Stoskopf 2009).

Finally, despite a recommendation from the World Health Organization to switch the poliomyelitis vaccine from oral polio vaccine (OPV) to inactivated polio vaccine (IPV) in countries where polio has been eliminated, Japan (it officially eliminated polio in 2000) continued to use OPV until recently, which could potentially cause vaccine-associated paralytic poliomyelitis (it does not occur with IPV). The government waited for a domestic IPV to be developed by Japanese companies, although IPV could be imported from other countries. Responding to the pressure from patient advocacy groups, the Ministry of Health, Labour and Welfare approved foreign IPV produced by Sanofi Pasteur, and it became available in September 2012. The domestic combination vaccine, which contains vaccines for diphtheria, pertussis, tetanus, and IPV, was subsequently developed by a domestic company, becoming available in November 2012.

Other Emerging Public Health Issues

Other issues include low cancer screening rates. The screening rate for cervical cancer was 24.5 percent in Japan compared with the OECD average of 61.1 percent in 2009; the breast cancer screening rate in Japan was 23.8 percent in 2009, much lower than the OECD average of 62.2 percent (OECD 2011).

Further exploration of the public health issues, such as the health impact of the leakage of radioactive water from the nuclear power plant in Fukushima and increases in cardiovascular events due to changes in dietary habits to Western foods, are beyond the scope of this chapter, because they are not addressed primarily through public health services provided by PUBHCs. Still, Japan needs to cope with these public health issues, by developing rigorous evidence-based health policies.

Universal Health Coverage for Inclusive and Sustainable Development
http://dx.doi.org/10.1596/978-1-4648-0408-3

Insights

PUBHCs have historically played an important role in Japan's UHC program in that they complemented the services covered under health insurance plans. Yet their role appears to have eroded in recent years, probably because their structures have not been redesigned to meet current and emerging public health issues, and the fixed-budget system has led to disincentives for PUBHCs and Local Health Centers to expand the coverage of public health services. Another issue is that the country lacks an institution like CDC.

Japan may need to revitalize its public health functions through better coordination among health insurance programs, PUBHCs, and Local Health Centers. Clarifying the entities responsible for providing each type of preventive medical care (such as vaccination and cancer screening), and monitoring their performances may improve such coordination. One possible option would be to incorporate preventive medical care into the fee schedule and deliver these services within the framework of health insurance programs, in order to incentivize the health care providers to provide these services.

Notes

1. Public health nurses used to be called *Hoken-fu*, but their name was replaced by the gender-neutral *Hoken-shi* in 2002.
2. Even though preventive medicine services, such as vaccinations, are in fact provided by pediatricians or primary care physicians in Japan, the costs are not covered by health insurance plans, but are paid using the subsidies from the municipal governments' budget or out of pocket by those who receive such services. The municipal governments are allowed to charge part of the costs to those who take vaccines, but they are not allowed to charge the poor.
3. Such as Ogai Mori and Kanehiro Takaki.
4. In 1940, the Institute of Public Health (*Koshu eisei in*) was merged with Institute of Nutrition Research and named the Institute of Health Science Research (*Kousei kagaku kenkyujo*). Between 1942 and 1946, all research institutions governed by Ministry of Health and Welfare were integrated and called the Ministry of Health and Welfare Research Institute (*Kouseisho kenkyujo*). This organization returned to the Institute of Public Health in 1946, and its name was then changed to National Institute of Public Health (*Kokuritsu koushu eisei in*) in 1949. In 2002, it was restructured as the National Institute of Public Health or *Kokuritsu Hoken Iryo Kagaku in*, integrating the former National Institute of Public Health, the National Institute of Health Services Management, and a part of the Department of Oral Science at the National Institute of Infectious Diseases.
5. The PUBHC operation subsidy (*Hokenjo uneihi hojokin*) was divided into PUBHC operation funding (*Hokenjo Uneihi koufukin*) (¥33 billion) and PUBHC service-cost subsidy *(Hokenjo gyomuhi hojokin)* (¥1.3 billion) in 1986. The PUBHC operation funding was incrementally integrated into general account budget by 1994, and the PUBHC service-cost subsidy was also gradually merged into the general account budget by 2007 (MHLW 2010).

6. The prevalence of tuberculosis at 17–20 cases per 100,000 in 2011 in Japan remains much higher than in other high-income countries: 4.3 in the United States, 4.7 in Canada, 5.5 in Australia, and 9.1 in France (all 2007) (WHO 2009; MHLW 2012).

7. The number of deaths due to tuberculosis was 2,162 in 2011 (MHLW 2012).

8. This does not include deaths in 1944–46, when devastation of World War II made collection of statistics impossible.

9. Given that other factors such as improvement in nutrition status and living conditions took place simultaneously, we cannot make a causal inference between the national tuberculosis program and the observed decline in tuberculosis cases and deaths.

10. In January 2014, the Japanese government decided to include the vaccines for chickenpox and pneumococcus into "strongly recommended" vaccines.

11. Vaccines are classified into two categories: routine vaccination (*Teiki yobou sessyu*) and voluntary vaccination (*Nin-i yobou sessyu*). Routine vaccination are those vaccines "strongly recommended" by the government and covered by government subsidies (if recipients are infants), whereas the cost of voluntary vaccinations need to be paid out of pocket.

Bibliography

Armesto, S. G., M. L. G. Lapetra, L. Wei, E. Kelley, and the Members of the HCQI Expert Group. 2006. "Health Care Quality Indicators Project 2006 Data Collection Update Report." OECD Health Working Papers No. 29, OECD, Paris.

Brown, I. J., I. Tzoulaki, V. Candeias, and P. Elliott. 2009. "Salt Intakes around the World: Implications for Public Health." *International Journal of Epidemiology* 38 (3): 791–813.

He, F. J., and G. A. MacGregor. 2010. "Reducing Population Salt Intake Worldwide: From Evidence to Implementation." *Progress in Cardiovascular Diseases* 52 (5): 363–82.

Ikeda, N., E. Saito, N. Kondo, M. Inoue, S. Ikeda, T. Satoh, K. Wada, A. Stickley, K. Katanoda, T. Mizoue, M. Noda, H. Iso, Y. Fujino, T. Sobue, S. Tsugane, M. Naghavi, M. Ezzati, and K. Shibuya. 2011. "What has Made the Population of Japan Healthy?" *Lancet* 378 (9796): 1094–105.

Ikegami, N., B.-K. Yoo, H. Hashimoto, M. Matsumoto, H. Ogata, A. Babazono, R. Watanabe, K. Shibuya, B.-M. Yang, M. R. Reich, and Y. Kobayashi. 2011. "Japanese Universal Health Coverage: Evolution, Achievements, and Challenges." *Lancet* 378 (9796): 1106–15.

JICA (Japan International Cooperation Agency). 2005. Chapter 1. "The History of Public Health and Medical Services." In *Japan's Experiences in Public Health and Medical Systems.* Institute for International Cooperation.

Johnson, J. A., and C. H. Stoskopf. 2009. *Comparative Health Systems: Global Perspectives for the 21st Century.* Sudbury, MA: Jones & Bartlett Publishers.

Johnston, W. 1995. *The Modern Epidemic: A History of Tuberculosis in Japan.* Cambridge, Ma: Harvard University Asia Center.

Katsuda, N., Y. Hinohara, K. Tomita, and N. Hamajima. 2011. "Structure and Roles of Public Health Centers (*hokenjo*) in Japan." *Nagoya Journal of Medical Science* 73 (1–2): 59–68.

Marui, E. 1990a. "Public Health in Postwar Japan. Beginning of Postwar Japan: Douglas McArthur and GHQ" (in Japanese). *Hoken no kagaku* 32 (9): 603–05.

———. 1990b. "Public Health in Postwar Japan. Public Health Centers in Postwar Japan" (in Japanese). *Hoken no kagaku* 32 (12): 824–26.

MHLW (Ministry of Health, Labour and Welfare). 2004. "Condition of the National Nutrition Status, 2004" (in Japanese). Tokyo, Daiichi Shuppan.

———. 2005. "Number of Deliveries by Location" (in Japanese). http://www.mhlw.go.jp/shingi/2005/06/s0608-11/2d.html (accessed June 19, 2014).

———. 2010. "Current Status and Challenges of Public Health Centers, City, Town, Village, and Prefectures" (in Japanese). http://www.mhlw.go.jp/stf/shingi/2r9852000000g3yx-att/2r9852000000g5sr.pdf (accessed August 1, 2013).

———. 2011. "Summary of Vital Statistics of Population, 2011" (in Japanese). http://www.mhlw.go.jp/toukei/saikin/hw/jinkou/geppo/nengai11/toukei02.html (accessed October 4, 2013).

———. 2012. "The Report about Tuberculosis Patients Registry Data in 2011" (in Japanese). Tokyo.

Nakatani, H., T. Sano, and T. Iuchi. 2002. "Development of Vaccination Policy in Japan: Current Issues and Policy Directions." *Japanese Journal of Infectious Diseases* 55 (4): 101–11.

National Institute of Infectious Diseases. 2013. "Risk Assessment about Epidemic of Rubella and Congenital Rubella Syndrome" (in Japanese). http://www.nih.go.jp/niid/ja/rubella-m-111/2145-rubella-related/3724-rube-risuku20130716.html (accessed August 19, 2013).

Nishimura, S. 2009. "Promoting Health in American-Occupied Japan Resistance to Allied Public Health Measures, 1945–1952." *American Journal of Public Health* 99 (8): 1364–75.

O'Connell, P. M. 2013. "Rubella Outbreaks in Japan, Poland Prompt CDC Travel Alerts." *AAP News.*

OECD (Organisation for Economic Co-operation and Development). 2011. *Health at a Glance 2011: OECD Indicators.* Paris.

Okayama, A., H. Ueshima, M. G. Marmot, M. Nakamura, Y. Kita, and M. Yamakawa. 1993. "Changes in Total Serum Cholesterol and Other Risk Factors for Cardiovascular Disease in Japan 1980–1989." *International Journal of Epidemiology* 22 (6): 1038–47.

Okumura, J. 1997. "The Revised Community Health Law Has Got Enforced" (in Japanese). *Bulletin of National Institute of Public Health* 46 (3): 200–08.

Sams, C. F. 1952. "American Public Health Administration Meets the Problems of the Orient in Japan." *American Journal of Public Health and the Nation's Health* 42 (5;i): 557–65.

Sasaki, N. 1964. "The Relationship of Salt Intake to Hypertension in the Japanese." *Geriatrics* 19: 735.

———. 1980. "Epidemiological Studies on Hypertension in Northeast Japan." *Epidemiology of Arterial Blood Pressure*, 367–77.

Shimao, T. 1988. "Tuberculosis Control Program." In *Medical Science and Medical Care for the 21st Century* (in Japanese), edited by T. Mori, 185–202. Nihon Hyousron Sha.

———. 1989. "Institutional Capacity for Disease Research and Control: Tuberculosis." In *International Cooperation for Health*, edited by M. R. Reich and E. Marui, 58–75. Dover, MA: Auburn House Publishing Company.

Terada, K. 2003. "Rubella and Congenital Rubella Syndrome in Japan: Epidemiological Problems." *Japanese Journal of Infectious Diseases* 56 (3): 81–87.

Ueshima, H., Tatara, K., Asakura, S., Okamoto, M. 1987. "Declining Trends in Blood Pressure Level and the Prevalence of Hypertension, and Changes in Related Factors in Japan, 1956–1980." *Journal of Chronic Diseases* 40 (2): 137–47.

WHO (World Health Organization). 2009. *Global Tuberculosis Control: Epidemiology, Strategy, Financing.* Geneva.

Environmental Benefits Statement

The World Bank is committed to reducing its environmental footprint. In support of this commitment, the Publishing and Knowledge Division leverages electronic publishing options and print-on-demand technology, which is located in regional hubs worldwide. Together, these initiatives enable print runs to be lowered and shipping distances decreased, resulting in reduced paper consumption, chemical use, greenhouse gas emissions, and waste.

The Publishing and Knowledge Division follows the recommended standards for paper use set by the Green Press Initiative. Whenever possible, books are printed on 50 percent to 100 percent postconsumer recycled paper, and at least 50 percent of the fiber in our book paper is either unbleached or bleached using Totally Chlorine Free (TCF), Processed Chlorine Free (PCF), or Enhanced Elemental Chlorine Free (EECF) processes.

More information about the Bank's environmental philosophy can be found at http://crinfo.worldbank.org/wbcrinfo/node/4.

green press INITIATIVE

www.ingramcontent.com/pod-product-compliance
Lightning Source LLC
Chambersburg PA
CBHW082355270326
41935CB00013B/1628

9 781464 804083